Dear Kitty

Thank you
you did for I
truly a success ... of you
and the rest of the team!

Blessings

Signs, Secrets

Maur

And Prophecies

Road To The Triumph

By Maureen Flynn

Signs and Wonders *for Our Times*

Co-Author Of *Thunder Of Justice*

Signs, Secrets And Prophecies – Road To The Triumph

Since the abolition of Canons 1399 and 2318 of the former Code of Canon Law by Pope Paul VI in AAS 58 (1966), p. 1186, publications about new apparitions, revelations, prophecies, miracles, etc., have been allowed to be distributed and read by the faithful without the express permission of the Church, providing that they contain nothing that contravenes faith and morals. This means no imprimatur is necessary. However it is welcome!

In Chapter II, No. 12 of the Second Vatican Council's *Lumen Gentium,* we read:

"The Holy Spirit... distributes special gifts among the faithful of every rank... Such gifts of grace, whether they are of special enlightenment or whether they are spread more simply and generally, must be accepted with gratefulness and consolation, as they are specially suited to, and useful for, the needs of the Church...Judgment as to their genuineness and their correct use lies with those who lead the Church and those whose special task is not indeed to extinguish the spirit but to examine everything and keep that which is good." (confer 1 Thess. 5: 19-21)

"That private revelations occur in all times is evident as appears from the testimony of the Sacred Scripture and tradition. To stamp these testimonies as untruths gives scandal and bears witness to impiety."

Cardinal Bona

Published by SAINT DOMINIC MEDIA

P.O. BOX 345, Herndon, Virginia 20172-0345

Phone 703-707-0799 / Fax 703-707-0557

www.sign.org   E-mail: signsorders@gmail.com

Cover design by Patty Schuster

Table Of Contents

Chapter   **Page**

FOREWORD

Most Catholics would be astonished to learn how many alleged messages from Heaven have been, and are being, received regarding the times in which we live. While no definitive numbers can be given, quite a few past and contemporary visionaries, locutionists, mystics, and other prophets have apparently been entrusted with warnings and words of encouragement and hope for those who are today striving to remain faithful to Christ in the midst of an increasingly anti-Christian world.

While not all such messages can be trusted—due to over-active imaginations on the part of some alleged "visionaries," the possibility of human misunderstanding or error, and even demonic deception—the Church has always acknowledged God's freedom to communicate or reveal Himself to His people outside the "normal channels" of Scripture and Tradition. Private revelation is never a substitute for, and can never add anything to, the Church's established doctrine—but it often has a valuable, though secondary, role to play. According to the *Catechism of the Catholic Church,*

> *Throughout the ages, there have been so-called "private" revelations,*
>
> *some of which have been recognized by the authority of the Church.*
>
> *They do not belong, however, to the deposit of faith. It is not their*
>
> *role to improve or complete Christ's definitive Revelation, but to help*
>
> *[the faithful] live more fully by it in a certain period of history. Guided*
>
> *by the magisterium of the Church, the sensus fidelium knows how to*
>
> *discern and welcome in these revelations whatever constitutes an*
>
> *authentic call of Christ or his saints to the Church (n. 67).*

Thus, messages from Heaven definitely at times serve an important purpose in the Church's life and mission—thereby in a certain sense fulfilling the Lord's promise given to His people in the Book of the Prophet Joel: "I will pour out My Spirit upon all mankind. Your sons and daughters shall prophesy, your old men shall dream dreams, your young men shall see visions" (3:1). In our own day, these prophesies and visions mainly involve alleged apparitions and messages from Our Lord and Our Lady, and sometimes from various angels (e.g., St. Michael) and saints (e.g., St. Joseph). The "predictions" they sometimes contain are usually conditional—that is, the dangers or chastisements of which they speak can be mitigated or averted by sufficient prayer and penance; for this reason, exact dates are rarely given (and, in fact, may be a reason to question their authenticity). Not every message will be equally useful or applicable (and many times private revelations truly are "private," in the sense of being intended for the recipient alone). All of them, however, play their assigned role in the unfolding of God's ongoing plan of salvation—the full scope of which we will only be able to fully comprehend and appreciate in the life to come.

Contrary to what many might assume, the vast majority of alleged messages and visions are never formally investigated or ruled upon by the Church— largely because the sheer numbers are overwhelming. In fact, very few alleged heavenly apparitions and their accompanying revelations are ever declared "worthy of belief" by the Church (e.g., La Salette, Lourdes, Fatima, and several others). This does not necessarily negate the authenticity, timeliness, and importance of all the other claimed heavenly messages, however. When these are consistent with, or at least not in any way contrary to, Scripture and Tradition, and when the alleged messenger always manifests a spirit of humility and obedience, and is free of any desire for personal fame or benefit, the supposed messages and revelations may in fact be a valid source of guidance and inspiration, and may be used cautiously for this purpose—as long as those using and promoting them always acknowledge themselves, in word and deed, as being subject to the authority and judgment of the Church.

Many books of alleged revelations have been published over the years (and my own personal library has close to three hundred such titles); these supposed visions and messages have been given to canonized saints and acknowledged mystics, along with little-known seers and ordinary persons from almost every nationality, age, and walk of life. In my own novel *After the Darkness* (which relies heavily upon past and contemporary private revelations), I imagine a future branch of the Roman Curia (the Church's administrative bureaucracy) called the "Sacred Congregation for the Interpretation of Salvation History," whose responsibility will be to collect, organize, and interpret the vast number of prophecies about the last days made by the saints and by various mystics and visionaries. Whether or not such a Congregation will ever exist, trying to "get a handle" on the huge number of these alleged revelations would be a full-time job—and for the average Catholic, this task would be overwhelming.

That's why Maureen Flynn's *Signs, Secrets and Prophecies* is so timely and useful; it serves as a well-organized and thorough presentation of many of the heavenly messages having a direct bearing on our own times. This book will surely prove to be an important resource for Catholics, and other persons of good will, seeking to obey Our Lord's injunction to understand "the signs of the times" (cf. Lk. 12:54-56) and learn "the lesson of the fig tree" (cf. Mt. 24:32-33).

Whether or not the Antichrist is now in the world, and whether or not the actual end of the world will soon be upon us, there is no doubt we're now living in one of the most challenging and significant eras of history—one which, barring widespread repentance on the part of humanity, will be marked by ever-increasing threats of war, natural disasters, technological dangers, societal upheavals, and religious persecutions. Even persons basing their lives on a solid spiritual and religious foundation might easily become frightened and confused—but as many of the messages in this book make clear, true followers of Jesus are called to live in a spirit of hope, not fear. Indeed, Our Lord tells us, "When these things begin to happen, stand erect and raise your heads because your redemption is at hand" (Lk. 21:28). Furthermore, our Heavenly Father promises us:

> You shall not fear the terror of the night, nor the arrow that flies by day;
>
> not the pestilence that roams in darkness nor the devastating plague at
>
> noon. Though a thousand fall at your side, ten thousand at your right
>
> side, near you it shall not come. Rather with your eyes you shall behold

and see the requital of the wicked, because you have the Lord for your

refuge; you have made the Most High your stronghold (Ps. 91:5-9).

Let us take these words to heart, and together bear witness to the Power, Majesty, and Mercy of Almighty God.

Rev. Joseph M. Esper

Author of several books including *Catholicism in Crisis: Satan's Assault on the Church and the Coming Triumph of the Immaculate Heart* and *Spiritual Dangers of the 21st Century.*

Signs, Secrets And Prophecies – Road To The Triumph

Our Lady of Good Success, Quito, Ecuador

Venerable Mother Mariana of Jesus Torres y Berriochoa (1563-1635), a sister of the Conceptionist Order received visions and messages from Our Lady of Good Success. Our Lady gave Venerable Mother Mariana many messages about the Church and mankind in the 20th century. This apparition has been approved by the Church.

On February 8, 1906, 271 years after her death, her virginal and incorrupt body was found.

Our Lady told Venerable Mother Mariana, "The Pope's infallibility will be declared a dogma of the Faith by the same Pope chosen to proclaim the dogma of the mystery of my Immaculate Conception."

In Quito, Ecuador, on Jan. 20, 1610, Our Lady of Good Success appeared and told Mother Mariana that at the end of the 19th Century and especially in the 20th Century that Satan would reign almost completely by means of the Masonic sect.

In her messages to Venerable Mother Mariana Our Lady of Good Success revealed that in these centuries:

- **The Sacrament of Holy Orders** will be ridiculed, oppressed and despised. The Devil will try to persecute the ministers of the Lord in every possible way. He will labor with cruel and subtle astuteness to deviate them from the spirit of their vocation and will corrupt many of them. These depraved priests, who will scandalize the Christian people, will make the hatred of bad Catholics and the enemies of the Roman Catholic and Apostolic Church fall upon all priests. This apparent triumph of Satan will bring enormous suffering to the good Pastors of the Church, the many good priests, and the Supreme Pastor and Vicar of Christ on earth, who, a prisoner in the Vatican, will shed secret and bitter tears in the presence of his God and Lord, beseeching light, sanctity, and perfection for all the clergy of the world, of whom he is King and Father.

- The secular clergy will be far removed from its ideal because the priests will become careless in their sacred duties. Lacking the divine compass, they will stray from the road traced by God for the priestly ministry and they will become attached to wealth and riches, which they will unduly strive to obtain.

- Pray insistently without tiring and weep with bitter tears in the secrecy of your heart, imploring our Celestial Father that, for the love of the Eucharistic Heart of my Most Holy Son and His Precious Blood shed with such generosity and by His cruel Passion and Death, He might take pity on His ministers and quickly bring to an end ominous times, sending to this Church the Prelate that will restore the spirit of its priests.

- The effects of secular education will increase, which will be one reason for the lack of priestly and religious vocations.

- **The Sacrament of Holy Communion**. How deeply I grieve to manifest to you the many sacrileges – both public as well as secret – that will occur from profanation of the Holy Eucharist. Often, during this epoch the enemies of Jesus Christ, instigated by the Devil, will steal consecrated Hosts from the churches so that they might profane the Eucharistic species. My Most Holy Son will see Himself cast upon the ground and trampled upon by filthy feet.

- **The Sacrament of Extreme Unction** will be little valued. Many people they will die without receiving it, being thereby deprived of innumerable graces, consolation, and strength they need to make the great leap from time to eternity.

- **The Sacrament of Matrimony**, which symbolizes the union of Christ with the Church, will be thoroughly attacked and profaned. Masonry which will then be in power, will enact iniquitous laws aimed at extinguishing this sacrament. They will make it easy for all to live in sin, thus multiplying the birth of illegitimate children without the Church's blessing.

- Woe to the children of these times. It will be difficult to receive the **Sacrament of Baptism** and also the **Sacrament of Confirmation**.

- **The Sacrament of Penance**, so forgotten and even scorned by ungrateful men, who in their foolish madness, do not realize that it is the only sure means of salvation after one has lost his baptismal innocence. What is most grievous is that even the ministers of my Most Holy Son do not give to it the value that they should, even viewing with cold indifference this valuable and precious treasure, which has been placed in their hands for the restoration of souls redeemed by the Blood of the Redeemer. There are those who consider hearing confession as a loss of time and a futile thing.

- The Masonic Sect, having permeated all the social classes, will find ways of introducing themselves into the very heart of homes to corrupt the children. The Devil will glory in dining upon the exquisite delicacy of the hearts of children.

- Innocence will almost no longer be found in children, nor modesty in women. In this supreme moment of need of the Church, those who should speak will fall silent.

- The small number of souls who will secretly safeguard the treasure of Faith and virtues will suffer a cruel, unspeakable, and long martyrdom.

- When everything seems lost and paralyzed, that will be the happy beginning of the complete restoration. "This will mark the arrival of my hour, when I, in a marvelous way, will dethrone the proud and cursed Satan, trampling him under my feet and fettering him in the infernal abyss."

To my loving husband Ted,

to my wonderful adult children

Colleen and Danny Flynn

To my beautiful daughter-in-law Meredith

Thank you to my beloved parents

Frank and Peggy

Chapter 1

The Secret of Fatima
Was It Fully Revealed?

The Vatican Release Of The Third Part
Of The Secret Of Fatima On June 26, 2000

**THE "SECRET" OF FATIMA
FIRST AND SECOND PART OF THE "SECRET"
ACCORDING TO THE VERSION
PRESENTED BY SISTER LUCIA
IN THE "THIRD MEMOIR" OF 31 AUGUST 1941
FOR THE BISHOP OF LEIRIA-FATIMA**

(Official English translation of Vatican release)
... This will entail my speaking about the secret, and thus answering the first question.

What is the secret? It seems to me that I can reveal it, since I already have permission from Heaven to do so. God's representatives on earth have authorized me to do this several times and in various letters, one of which, I believe, is in your keeping. This letter is from Father José Bernardo Gonçalves, and in it he advises me to write to the Holy Father, suggesting, among other things, that I should reveal the secret. I did say something about it. But in order not to make my letter too long, since I was told to keep it short, I confined myself to the essentials, leaving it to God to provide another more favourable opportunity.

In my second account I have already described in detail the doubt which tormented me from 13 June until 13 July, and how it disappeared completely during the Apparition on that day.

Well, the secret is made up of three distinct parts, two of which I am now going to reveal.

The first part is the vision of hell.

Our Lady showed us a great sea of fire which seemed to be under the earth. Plunged in this fire were demons and souls in human form, like transparent burning embers, all blackened or burnished bronze, floating about in the conflagration, now raised into the air by the flames that issued from within themselves together with great clouds of smoke, now falling back on every side like sparks in a huge fire, without weight or equilibrium, and amid shrieks and groans of pain and despair, which horrified us and made us tremble with fear. The demons could be distinguished by their terrifying and repulsive likeness to frightful and unknown animals, all black and transparent. This vision lasted but an instant. How can we ever be grateful enough to our kind heavenly Mother, who had already prepared us by promising, in the first Apparition, to take us to heaven. Otherwise, I think we would have died of fear and terror.

We then looked up at Our Lady, who said to us so kindly and so sadly:

"You have seen hell where the souls of poor sinners go. To save them, God wishes to establish in the world devotion to my Immaculate Heart. If what I say to you is done, many souls will be saved and there will be peace. The war is going to end: but if people do not cease offending God, a worse one will break out during the Pontificate of Pius XI. When you see a night illumined by an unknown light, know that this is the great sign given you by God that He is about to punish the world for its crimes, by means of war, famine, and persecutions of the Church and of the Holy Father. To prevent this, I shall come to ask for the consecration of Russia to my Immaculate Heart, and the Communion of reparation on the First Saturdays. If my requests are heeded, Russia will be converted, and there will be peace; if not, she will spread her errors throughout the world, causing wars and persecutions of the Church. The good will be martyred;

2

the Holy Father will have much to suffer; various nations will be annihilated. In the end, my Immaculate Heart will triumph. The Holy Father will consecrate Russia to me, and she shall be converted, and a period of peace will be granted to the world."

THIRD PART OF THE "SECRET"

"J.M.J.
The third part of the secret revealed at the Cova da Iria-Fatima, on 13 July 1917.

I write in obedience to you, my God, who command me to do so through his Excellency the Bishop of Leiria and through your Most Holy Mother and mine.

After the two parts which I have already explained, at the left of Our Lady and a little above, we saw an Angel with a flaming sword in his left hand; flashing, it gave out flames that looked as though they would set the world on fire; but they died out in contact with the splendour that Our Lady radiated towards him from her right hand: pointing to the earth with his right hand, the Angel cried out in a loud voice: 'Penance, Penance, Penance!'. And we saw in an immense light that is God: 'something similar to how people appear in a mirror when they pass in front of it' a Bishop dressed in White 'we had the impression that it was the Holy Father'. Other Bishops, Priests, men and women Religious going up a steep mountain, at the top of which there was a big Cross of rough-hewn trunks as of a cork-tree with the bark; before reaching there the Holy Father passed through a big city half in ruins and half trembling with halting step, afflicted with pain and sorrow, he prayed for the souls of the corpses he met on his way; having reached the top of the mountain, on his knees at the foot of the big Cross he was killed by a group of soldiers who fired bullets and arrows at him, and in the same way there died one after another the other Bishops, Priests, men and women Religious, and various lay people of different ranks and positions. Beneath the two arms of the Cross there were two Angels each with a crystal aspersorium in his hand, in which they gathered up the blood of the Martyrs and with it sprinkled the souls that were making their way to God.
Tuy-3-1-1944".

3

Pope Benedict XVI, as Cardinal Ratzinger, had said, "Naturally there is a margin of error" when interpreting visions, which is the reason why "the Church is not imposing an interpretation."

Was This A Complete Release Of The Third Part Of The Secret Of Fatima?

The Vatican release, after the sentence "The Holy Father will consecrate Russia to me, and she will be converted, and a period of peace will be granted to the world.", leaves off the already revealed statement which can be found on page 167 of *Fatima in Lucia's Own Words, Sister Lucia's Memoirs.* In *The Fourth Memoir,* on page 167 we find the statement: "In Portugal, the dogma of the Faith will always be preserved; etc. ... Do not tell this to anybody. Francisco, yes, you may tell him." [43]

In the "Fourth Memoir" of December 8, 1941 Sister Lucia writes: "I shall begin then my new task, and thus fulfill the commands received from Your Excellency as well as the desires of Dr. Galamba. With the exception of that part of the Secret which I am not permitted to reveal at present, I shall say everything. I shall not knowingly omit anything, though I suppose I may forget just a few small details of minor importance." [43]

In the "Fourth Memoir" Sister Lucia adds after "The Holy Father will consecrate Russia to me, and she shall be converted, and a period of peace will be granted to the world" the sentences; "**In Portugal, the dogma of the Faith will always be preserved; etc. ... Do not tell this to anybody. Francisco, yes, you may tell him.**" [43]

What is the etc.? Our Lady's message is not continued in this official release of the third part of the secret. Why did the Vatican not use the **Fourth** Memoir rather than the **Third** Memoir?

This missing section of the third part of the secret is a *statement* by Our Lady *not a vision*, since Francisco could only see Our Lady, but could not hear her. If it were the vision, Francisco would have seen it and would not need to be told.

The statement in the Vatican release is: "Sister Lucia was in full agreement with the Pope's claim that 'it was a mother's hand that guided the bullet's path and in his throes the Pope halted at the threshold of death' (**Saint Pope John Paul II**, *Meditation from the Policlinico Gemelli to the Itaian Bishops*, 13 May 1994)." **This is true, however, this statement does not mean that this was the event concerning Saint Pope John Paul II that was seen in this vision.**

The reference to this Holy Father in this released vision notes he was killed by a group of soldiers who fired bullets and arrows at him. **Ali Agca who *attempted* to kill Saint Pope John Paul II on May 13, 1981 and failed was not a soldier and there were definitely no soldiers.**

In the Vatican's release and commentary we were told that the events to which the third part of the "secret" of Fatima refers now seem part of the past. Insofar as individual events are described, they belong to the past.

In a locution to Father Gobbi, message #594, May 8, 1997 at Fatima, Our Blessed Lady revealed this third secret as both a prediction and a vision. In this Vatican release which used Lucia's *Third* Memoir and not her *Fourth* Memoir we have the vision, but not the completion of Our Lady's statement, the prediction which appears to be the completion of the statement in the *Fourth* Memoir, "In Portugal, the dogma of the Faith will always be preserved; etc. ... In this memoir Lucy was told, "Do not tell this to anybody. Francisco, yes, you may tell him."

But they were not completely fulfilled with Saint Pope John Paul II. It appears now that his successor Pope Benedict XVI, through opposition from members of the Curia and worldwide members of the college of Cardinals and many Bishops worldwide, also experienced a non-bloody martyrdom. The vision of Fatima has at the time of this writing not yet been completely fulfilled.

The text as released by the Vatican is not consistent with Saint Pope John Paul II's alleged statement at Fulda, Germany in November 1980.

In the locution given at Fulda to Father Gobbi on September 8, 1985, Message #313, The *Hour of Public Witness,* Our Blessed Mother said *that Everything that my Pope has said in this place corresponds with the truth.*[2]

Saint Pope John Paul II was in Germany from November 15 –19, 1980.

This is a 1983 report of what Saint Pope John Paul II said at Fulda, Germany. (From QUEEN Magazine, published by the Montfort Fathers – Bayshore, New York, September, 1983.)

Saint Pope John Paul II, Fulda, Germany And The Third Secret Of Fatima

The German magazine, "Stimme des Glaubens," has published the following account of Saint Pope John Paul II's interview with a small group of German Catholics on the occasion of his visit to Fulda, in November of 1980.

Question: "Holy Father, what has become of the 3rd Secret of Fatima? According to Our Lady's instructions, wasn't it supposed to be revealed in 1960? And what will happen in the Church?"

The Holy Father's Response: "Because of the seriousness of its contents, in order not to encourage the world wide power of Communism to carry out certain coups, my predecessors in the Chair of Peter have diplomatically preferred to withhold its publication.

On the other hand, **it should be sufficient for all Christians to know this much: if there is a message in which it is said that the oceans will flood entire sections of the earth; that, from one moment to the other, millions of people will perish ...** *there is no longer any point in really wanting to publish this secret* **message.**

Many want to know merely out of curiosity or because of their taste for sensationalism but they forget that 'to know' implies for them a responsibility. It is dangerous to want to satisfy one's curiosity only, if

6

one is convinced that we can do nothing against a catastrophe that has been predicted."

At this point, the Holy Father, took hold of his Rosary and said: "Here is the remedy against the evil! Pray, pray and ask for nothing else. Put everything in the hands of the Mother of God!"

Then he went on to say; **"We must be prepared to undergo great trials in the not too distant future, trials that will require us to be ready to give up even our lives and a total gift of self to Christ and for Christ. Through your prayer and mine, it is possible to alleviate this tribulation but it is no longer possible to avert it, because it is only in this way that the Church can be effectively renewed.** How many times, indeed, has the renewal of the Church been effected in blood? This time again, it will not be otherwise,

We must be strong, we must prepare ourselves, **we must entrust ourselves to Christ and to His holy Mother, and we must be attentive to the prayer of the Rosary?"**

There is a message in the third part of the secret, according to this, which was not present in the official Vatican release.

This was an unscheduled event, and thus an event undocumented by the Vatican, which occurred when about 20 German pilgrims, outside the Cathedral in Fulda, asked Saint Pope John Paul II about the third secret of Fatima.

What Do Other Apparitions, Visions, And Locutions Reveal About This Vision and Message?

What do various current apparitions, visions and locutions of the twentieth century and the prior centuries tell us which could help us understand this vision in the third part of the secret of Fatima? The Church's spokesmen in this document have ignored these in making their interpretation, since they are according to them only private revelation. When there were so many private revelations in the twentieth century and preceding centuries which could have been used to explain this important event for the Church and world history they should have been used.

The many current and recent apparitions, visions and locutions from around the world paint the picture of what has been happening and what will happen to humanity, the Church and a Pope in the near future.

The entire Church – Pope, Cardinals, Bishops, Priests, Religious and lay people, rich and poor are climbing Calvary with immense physical and spiritual suffering along the Way of the Cross. Many will be physically killed or suffer from calumny along the way and when they have reached the summit of their ascent. Saint Pope John Paul II was more and more ridiculed, mocked, isolated and abandoned when he was alive. There have been and will be many martyrs along this Way of the Cross. The 20th century had been a century of Martyrs. These events in this vision are past, present and future, and not all in the past, as we shall see when we review visions and messages from Heaven's extraordinary attempt in this current Marian Era to bring our prodigal humanity back to the Father. Details predicted, prophesied, for the future are filled in by the visions, messages and locutions given by Heaven to other visionaries and locutionists.

Why Saint Pope John XXIII Did Not Release The Third Secret In 1960

According to Fr. Malachi Martin in *The Keys of This Blood*, Saint Pope John XXIII had the opportunity with the opening of Vatican II on October 11, 1962, but didn't organize the collegial consecration of Russia to Mary.

"In 1960, Pope John XXIII held a conversation in the Vatican with Nikita Krushchev's son-in-law, Aleksei Adzhubei, editor of Izvestia. *In addition, (Pope) John accepted an agreement with Krushchev himself, by which a trade-off was made concerning the Second Vatican Council: The Council would issue none of the usual statements condemning the Soviet Union's Leninist Marxism; and in return, two prelates of the Russian Orthodox Church, Metropolitans Borovoy and Kotlrov, both with KGB status, would attend Vatican II as observers....* " [23]

This agreement offers an insight as to a possible reason why Saint Pope John XXIII did not want the third secret revealed in 1960. Reflect upon the implications with this agreement for Vatican II, if he did release the Third Secret at that time.

We had been told about the role of Russia in the events of the twentieth century when the Church released the first two parts of Lucy's three part secret...."

In the past we also had been told that Saint Pope John XXIII did not release it since he said it did not relate to his pontificate and thus archived it.

Cardinal Ratzinger (Pope Emeritus Benedict XVI) said that the reason the successive popes since the 1940's have not disclosed the secret is that it could not be fully understood until the close of the 20th century. He stated, "There was no sense in offering humanity an indecipherable image which would have created only speculation."

Our Blessed Mother Has Been Releasing This Third Part Of The Fatima Secret Through Other Visionaries And Locutionists

Our Blessed Mother, in order to get this suppressed message out to the faithful through the remainder of the 20th century, increased the frequency and urgency of her apparitions and messages. Jesus, God The Father, St. Joseph, many saints and the Archangels have frequently appeared and given urgent messages to give us the means to be used to avert or mitigate the prophesied great apostasy and great chastisement.

At the time of the Second Vatican Council Our Blessed Mother and St. Michael began appearing in Garabandal, Spain (1961 to 1965). In 1961 they began to release the third part of the secret in the visions and messages of Garabandal. Garabandal was ignored. (See Chapter 2)

Our Lady Released This Third Part Of The Secret Of Fatima At Akita, Japan

On October 13, 1973 Our Lady gave us this hidden third secret:

*"My dear daughter, listen well to what I have to say to you. You will inform your superior. As I told you, **if men do not repent and better themselves, the Father will inflict a terrible punishment on all humanity. It will be a punishment greater than the deluge, such as one will never have seen before. Fire will fall from the sky and will wipe out a great part of humanity, the good as well as the bad, sparing neither priests nor faithful. The survivors will find themselves so desolate that they will envy the dead. The only arms that will remain for you will be the rosary and Sign left by My Son.** Each day recite the prayers of the rosary. With the rosary pray for the Pope, the bishops, and the priests.*

The work of the devil will infiltrate even the Church in such a way that one will see cardinals opposing cardinals, bishops against other bishops. The priests who venerate Me scorned and opposed by their confreres ... churches and altars sacked, the Church will be full of those who accept compromises and the demon will press many priests and consecrated souls to leave the service of the Lord. The demon will be especially implacable against souls consecrated to God. The thought of the loss of so many souls is the cause of my sadness. If sins increase in number and gravity, there will be no longer pardon for them.

With courage, speak to your superior. He will know how to encourage each one of you to pray and to accomplish works of reparation." [32]

Mother Elena Patricia Leonardi

Mother Elena Patricia Leonardi, born November 4, 1910, was told by Saint Padre Pio on February 4, 1947 that the Virgin would entrust her with a great mission.

Mother Leonardi received a message on March 26, 1988 from Our

Blessed Mother about flames and fire falling from heaven and ocean waters turning into vapor and a great war breaking out sowing death and hunger, diseases of all kinds. She was told about the times of the great trial for the Church when cardinals will oppose cardinals, bishops being against bishops.[16]

On February 12, 1979 Mother Leonardi was told that communism will triumph. She was told about freemasonry in the churches, and that some cardinals and bishops will confront the Pope accusing and mistreating him.[16]

These other apparitions, visions, and messages reveal in detail the Apostasy in The Church with false ideologies, false doctrines, repudiation of Dogmas of the Faith, the rise of a False Pope and the Antichrist, the abomination of desolation mentioned by Daniel, a correction of mankind's conscience in a global warning, chastisements through weather changes and catastrophes, earthquakes, tsunamis, volcanic eruptions, wars and a great chastisement with fire falling from heaven destroying three quarters of mankind in a period of three days of darkness followed by an Era of Peace in which in Jesus' "Our Father Prayer," and His prayer in the Gospel of St. John that all may be one as He and His Father are one are fulfilled.

This is why many people today are convinced that the third secret of Fatima *has not been totally* revealed.

In this book we will present Heaven's messages that seem to strongly indicate that the third secret has not been totally revealed. In many apparitions and messages we have been given tremendous insights from Our Lord and Our Blessed Mother on what is coming to our world, *if we do not repent and change.*

Chapter 2

The Great Trial For The Church

The great trial is arriving for the Church, the Mystical Body of Christ which will experience the passion of Jesus and will apparently die. The small remnant will go underground and emerge, after the end of the great persecution of the false prophet and the antichrist, in a renewed holy, humble, poor Church.

The Church will experience its greatest apostasy, betrayal, abandonment, schism, infiltration and takeover by Freemasonry. The man of iniquity, the Antichrist, will sit upon the throne in the temple of God and bring about the abomination of desolation prophesied by Daniel which will last for three years and a half.

Cardinals will oppose cardinals, bishops will oppose bishops, priests will oppose priests in a division producing confusion among the faithful. A revolt of congregations, religious orders and among the hierarchy will bring about the exile and martyrdom of the pope.

There will come a time when two popes will reign, one true the other false. A vast majority of the faithful will follow the false pope. Among those who do not will be the small remnant that, after the great chastisement and three days of darkness, will enter the era of peace which Jesus prayed for in the Lord's Prayer, the *Our Father* prayer.

In this era of peace there will be a humble, poor, renewed Church. There will be one flock and one shepherd. God will give to the people many if not all of the preternatural gifts lost by Adam for himself and for us in *Original Sin*.

Preternatural gifts are favors granted by God above and beyond the powers or capacities of the nature that receives them but not beyond those of all created nature. Such gifts perfect nature but do not carry it beyond the limits of created nature. They include three great privileges to which human beings have no title – **infused knowledge, absence of concupiscence**, and **bodily immortality.** Adam and Eve possessed these gifts before the Fall.

These were the preternatural gifts that Adam lost:
1. Immortality – You don't die.
2. Impassibility – Don't feel pain or harm.
3. Freedom from concupiscence (sexual desire), ignorance, and sin.
4. Lordship over the earth.

The people living in this era of peace will live in the Divine Will during the Eucharistic Reign of Jesus, according to many of these prophecies.

Revolt And Division In The Church

Rome Will Lose The Faith And Become The Seat Of The Antichrist

At La Salette, on September 19, 1846, in the Leece version of the message, Melanie was told by Our Blessed Mother: "Rome will lose the faith and become the seat of the Antichrist …. The Church will be in eclipse …. Pagan Rome will disappear." [7]

Pedro Regis

Messages About Revolt, War Among The Religious, And A Great Schism

Division In The Reign

May 31, 2008. Message 3004 – from Our Lady of Peace, Anguera, Bahia, Brazil. Dear Sons and Daughters, **a rock will hit a great ship, which will break in two and there will be great suffering for My poor**

14

children.... **The day will come when a war between religious will leave many men and women withdrawn from the truth.** That which I have predicted in the past will come to pass.

June 24, 2008. Message 3014 – from Our Lady of Peace, Anguera, Bahia, Brazil. Dear Sons and Daughters, **the revolt of many consecrated persons will cause great suffering for the Church. The heart of the Church will be wounded by a great schism. The work of the devil will cause many consecrated souls to go away from the truth....**

July 8, 2008. Message 3020 – from Our Lady of Peace, Anguera, Bahia, Brazil. Dear Sons and Daughters,... **When the reign is divided, there will be great disorder among religious leaders. Many faithful men and women will wander aimlessly, full of doubts. They won't know what side to be on.** A wound will be opened in the heart of the Church.

September 11, 2008. Message 3052 – from Our Lady of Peace, Anguera, Bahia, Brazil. Dear Sons and Daughters, bend your knees in prayer for the Church. **A religious leader will arise against the authority of the Pope and will cause great division in the Church. The darkness of apostasy will fall upon the Church of My Jesus....**

The Church, The Barque, The Pope

The Smoke Of The Enemy Will Spread Out, And Great Will Be The Spiritual Confusion In The House Of God

3.757 – Message of Our Lady Queen of Peace, delivered on January 1, 2013. Dear children, I am the Queen of Peace and I came from Heaven to bring you peace. Be filled with courage and in every way be like Jesus. Give me your hands. I will walk at your side. Bend your knees in prayer. **Pray for the Church. The cross will be heavy for men and women of faith. The smoke of the enemy will spread out, and great will be the spiritual confusion in the house of God. Stay with the truth. Those who remain in the truth will never experience defeat. Do not be afraid. After the cross, victory will come. In joy or in pain, stay with Jesus.** This is the message which I bring to you today in the name of the Most Holy Trinity. Thank you for allowing me to gather you here one more time. I give you my blessing in the name of the Father, the Son, and the Holy Spirit. Amen. Peace be with you.

Difficult Days Are Coming For The Church

3.762 – Message of Our Lady Queen of Peace, on January 12, 2013. Dear children, witness by your example and your words that you belong to the Lord. Do not stand about with your arms crossed. God is in a hurry. What you have to do, do not put off until tomorrow. **You live in a time worse than the time of the Biblical flood, and my poor children walk about as blind people leading other blind people. Humanity has become unfaithful to God, and each day the number is growing of those who are being eternally lost.** I am your Sorrowful Mother. You know well how much a Mother loves her children. I came from Heaven to show you the way. Listen to me. I do not want to obligate you, but what I say must be taken seriously. Bend your knees in prayer, for only thus can you live by my appeals. I want to tell you that now is the time of grace. Open your hearts. **Difficult days are coming for the Church. The devil will cause great confusion upon the Earth and great will be the pain of my faithful ones.** I do not come from Heaven as a joke. Take my appeals to the world, and you will be generously rewarded. Courage. This is the message which I bring to you today in the name of the Most Holy Trinity. Thank you for allowing me to gather you here one more time. I give you my blessing in the name of the Father, the Son and the Holy Spirit. Amen. Peace be with you.

The Smoke Of The Enemy Will Bring Great Suffering To The Church Of My Jesus

3.763 – Message of Our Lady Queen of Peace, delivered in Maragojipe/BA, Batatan Community, on January 13, 2013. Dear children, your future depends upon what you sow today. Take care of your spiritual life, and your reward will be Paradise. Do not live in sin. You belong to the Lord. You are in the world, but you are not of the world. Flee from everything which paralyzes within you the love of God. You who are listening to me, do not be discouraged. **Difficult days will come, but I will be with you.** Have courage, faith and hope. If you should fall, call upon Jesus. He is your hope. Only in Him is your

16

Salvation. Return to Him who sees what is hidden and knows each of you by name. When everything seems lost, the great victory of God will come. Bend your knees in prayer. **Only through the power of prayer can you bear the weight of the trials which are coming. The smoke of the enemy will bring great suffering to the Church of my Jesus. The Church will be persecuted, but in the end the victory will belong to Jesus. Go forward without fear.** This is the message which I bring to you today in the name of the Most Holy Trinity. Thank you for allowing me to gather you here one more time. I give you my blessing in the name of the Father, the Son and the Holy Spirit. Amen. Peace be with you.

The Church Will Be Persecuted, Judged, And Condemned

3.775 – Message of Our Lady Queen of Peace, on February 12, 2013. Dear children, do not permit the flame of faith to be extinguished within you. My Jesus is with you. Courage. **You still have ahead of you long years of difficult trials. That which I announced in the past will come to pass. The Church will be persecuted, judged, and condemned. Men and women of faith will carry a heavy cross, but after all the pain, the Lord will dry your tears. Listen to what I tell you.** Be alert. I suffer because of what is coming for you. Bend your knees in prayer. Seek strength in the words of My Son Jesus and in the Eucharist. Pray and do penance. God will act, and His victory will also be the victory of all those who remain faithful until the end. Go forward. This is the message which I bring to you today in the name of the Most Holy Trinity. Thank you for allowing me to gather you here one more time. I give you my blessing in the name of the Father, the Son and the Holy Spirit. Amen. Peace be with you.

Now The First Steps In The Direction Of Calvary Have Been Taken

3.776 – Message of Our Lady, Queen of Peace, on February 13, 2013. Dear children, stay with Jesus. Do not be afraid. God is in control of everything. Be men and women of faith. Courageously accept the Gospel of my Jesus and do not hold back. You belong to the Lord and no evil will touch you if you remain faithful. I am your Mother and I know your needs. With your examples and your words show everyone that you are in the world but not of the world. **The time which I revealed to you in**

17

the past has now arrived. **Courage. Now the first steps in the direction of Calvary have been taken, but the way of the cross is still long. Have trust, faith and hope. After all the tribulation, your victory will come.** Do not hold back. Love the truth and defend it. Bend your knees in prayer. Return to the One who is your All and who knows you by name. This is the message which I bring to you today in the name of the Most Holy Trinity. Thank you for allowing me to gather you here one more time. I give you my blessing in the name of the Father, the Son and the Holy Spirit. Amen. Peace be with you.

The Church Will Walk In The Midst Of Great Tribulation And Will Still Have Peter

3.777 – Message of Our Lady Queen of Peace, on February 16, 2013. Dear children, follow Jesus. The road to holiness is full of obstacles, but you are not alone. Trust in Jesus. Your victory is in Him. Do not permit the flame of faith to be extinguished within you. Be men and women of courage. **Be filled with hope. My Jesus will not abandon you. In these days, intensify your prayers for the Church. The Church will walk in the midst of great tribulation. Do not be afraid. The Church will still have Peter. That which I have announced in the past will come to pass. Go forward along the path I have shown you.** Do not hold back. I know your necessities and I will plead with my Jesus for you. I am your mother and I love you. Listen to me and I will lead you by the path of goodness. What you have to do, do not put off until tomorrow. This is the message which I bring to you today in the name of the Most Holy Trinity. Thank you for allowing me to gather you here one more time. I give you my blessing in the name of the Father, the Son and the Holy Spirit. Amen. Peace be with you.

The Direction Of The Church Will Change

3.782 – Message of Our Lady Queen of Peace on February 28, 2013. Dear children, bend your knees in prayer. **You are going toward a future of great spiritual tribulation. The Boat of Peter will face great tempests and the throne will tremble. Peter will walk among thorns. The direction of the Church will change and many of the faithful will wash their hands of it. I am your Sorrowful Mother and I suffer because of what is coming for you.** Listen to me. Pray. **War will come**

18

where there should be peace. **That which I have announced to you in the past will come to pass.** Love the truth and accept the Gospel of my Jesus. **When everything seems lost, men and women of faith will witness the powerful action of the Lord. The just shall not be defeated. Courage.** This is the message which I bring to you today in the name of the Most Holy Trinity. Thank you for allowing me to gather you here once again. I give you my blessing in the name of the Father, the Son and the Holy Spirit. Amen. Peace be with you.

The Great Ship Will Face Tempests Never Seen Before Encircled By Enemies

3.783 – Message of Our Lady Queen of Peace delivered on March 2, 2013. Dear children, return to Jesus. He is your All and only in Him is your Salvation. Trust in Him who sees what is hidden and knows each one of you by name. When you feel the weight of the cross, call upon Jesus. Face your needs with courage and you will be victorious. Difficult days are coming for humanity. Now is a time of great and painful tribulations. Pray. Do not stop praying. **The great ship (the Church) will face tempests never seen before. She will be encircled by enemies and many will leave her. The net will be cast, but it will break, letting many important fish escape. Jesus is your Way, Truth and Life. Believe firmly in His power and everything will end well.** Do not hold back. Go forward without fear. This is the message which I bring to you today in the name of the Most Holy Trinity. Thank you for allowing me to gather you here once again. I give you my blessing in the name of the Father, the Son and the Holy Spirit. Amen. Peace be with you.

The Agreement Will Cause Great Confusion

3.786 – Message of Our Lady Queen of Peace, on March 9, 2013. Dear children, I am your Sorrowful Mother and I suffer because of what is coming for you. **You are going toward a future of great spiritual confusion. Trust in Jesus.** He is your All and only in Him is your victory. Do not be afraid. **Listen to what I say to you. My Jesus is in control of everything. The agreement will cause great confusion. Where there is no fidelity, there is no truth. Do not permit anything to separate you from the truth. Whatever happens remain on the path I have shown you over the years.** Courage. I am at your side even though you do not see me. Bend your knees in prayer on behalf of the Church. This is the message which I bring to you today in the name of the Most Holy Trinity. Thank you for allowing me to gather you here once again. I give you my blessing in the name of the Father, the Son and the Holy Spirit. Amen. Peace be with you.

The Church Will Be Persecuted And Humiliated And Face A Painful Storm

3.787 – Message of Our Lady, delivered in Rio de Janeiro, delivered in the afternoon on March 11, 2013. Dear children, I love you as you are. I ask you to keep alight the flame of your faith and to be like Jesus in every way. You are not alone. Walk with the certainty that Jesus is very near to you. Do not hold back. Give Angüera the best of yourself to the mission which the Lord has entrusted to you. There is no victory without the cross. **The Church will carry a heavy cross. It will be persecuted and humiliated. It will face a painful storm, but it will not sink. Be alert. You still have long years of hard trials ahead.** Courage. I will plead with my Jesus for you. Rejoice, for your names are already written in Heaven. This is the message which I bring to you today in the name of the Most Holy Trinity. Thank you for allowing me to gather you here once again. I give you my blessing in the name of the Father, the Son and the Holy Spirit. Amen. Peace be with you.

Jesus Will Calm The Storm Affecting The Great Barque. It Will Arrive At A Safe Port

3.788 – Message of Our Lady, delivered in Rio de Janeiro, delivered at night on March 11, 2013. Dear children, trust in Jesus. He will calm the storm which will affect the great barque. There will be conflicts, but in the end the barque will arrive at a safe port. The victory will belong to Jesus. You who are listening to me, do not be discouraged. I came from Heaven to help you. Do not be afraid. I am your Mother and I know what is coming for you. Bend your knees in prayer. Only through the power of prayer can you reach victory. Love the truth and defend it. Accept the Gospel and witness everywhere to your faith. You are in the world, but you are not of the world. Open your hearts and follow me. I want to lead you to the One who is your Way, Truth and Life. I know your needs, and I will plead with my Jesus for you. Go forward without fear. This is the message which I bring to you today in the name of the Most Holy Trinity. Thank you for allowing me to gather you here once again. I give you my blessing in the name of the Father, the Son and the Holy Spirit. Amen. Peace be with you.

The King (The Pope) Will Suffer Because Of His Subjects. The Road Will Be Short For The King

3.790 – Message of Our Lady, delivered on March 16, 2013. Dear children, **St. Peter will direct his barque amidst great tempests. Pray. The successor of Peter is going to need your prayers. He will experience his Calvary. He will be loved and hated because of his positions. Now is the time of suffering. The poison is in the tree, not in the fruit. The Church of my Jesus is going toward a future of great trials, but as I have already told you, Jesus is in charge of everything. Peter in the land of Peter. What I am telling you, you may not comprehend now, but calm your hearts, for Jesus walks with you. The king will suffer because of his subjects. Do not be afraid. I am your Mother and I will plead with my Jesus for you. The road will be short for the king, similar to the crossing of the famous plaza.** Bend your knees in prayer. **In the end, the victory will belong to the Lord. Love the truth and remain with the Church.** The lessons of the past should not be forgotten. Go forward without fear. This is the message which I bring to you today in the name of the Most Holy Trinity. Thank you for allowing me to gather you here once again. I give you my blessing in the name of the Father, the Son and the Holy Spirit. Amen. Peace be with you.

The Barque Of St. Peter Will Be Surrounded By Enemies And Peter Will Suffer Much

3.791 – Message of Our Lady, delivered at Foz do Iguacu/PR, on March 17, 2013. Dear children, be filled with trust, faith and hope. Even though you are facing difficulties, do not be discouraged, do not hold back. Whoever is with Jesus will never experience the weight of defeat. Trust completely in the power of the Lord. Do not live separated from His grace. He is calling you. Say yes with courage and joy. Humanity is moving toward the abyss of destruction which men have prepared with their own hands. Pray. **Only through the power of prayer can you**

21

withstand the weight of the trials that are on the way. I am your Mother and I am at your side. I ask you to intensify your prayers on behalf of the Church. There will be great confusion, but the victory will belong to Jesus. Do not be afraid. The victory will occur. The barque of St. Peter will be surrounded by enemies and Peter will suffer much. Pray, pray, pray. I am your Mother and I will plead with my Jesus for you. Courage. This is the message which I bring to you today in the name of the Most Holy Trinity. Thank you for allowing me to gather you here once again. I give you my blessing in the name of the Father, the Son and the Holy Spirit. Amen. Peace be with you.

Death Will Be Present In The House Of God
The Enemies Will Arrive By The Apian Way

3.792 – Message of Our Lady, delivered in Paranoa/DF, on March 18, 2013. Dear children, give your best to the mission which the Lord has entrusted to you. By your example and your words, show everyone that you belong to the Lord. You are in the world, but you are not of the world. Remain steadfast upon the way I have shown you. When you happen to fall, call upon Jesus. In Him is your strength and only through Him will you achieve victory. Do not live in sin. Return to the Lord who loves you and awaits you with the immense love of a Father. I am your Mother and I came from Heaven to take you to Heaven. Open your hearts and I will lead you to my Son Jesus. **You are going toward a future of painful trials. This is a time of great spiritual confusion. Seek strength in the words of my Jesus and in the Eucharist. Pray for the Church. Its enemies will act with great fury. Death will be present in the house of God. The enemies will arrive by the Apian Way. I suffer because of what is coming for you.** Pray. Pay attention to what I tell you. Be alert. What you have to do, do not put off until tomorrow. This is the message which I bring to you today in the name of the Most Holy Trinity. Thank you for allowing me to gather you here once again. I give you my blessing in the name of the Father, the Son and the Holy Spirit. Amen. Peace be with you.

A Great Event Will Occur In The Church:
Thousands Left, Thousands Will Return

3.793 – Message of Our Lady, Aguas Lindas de Goias/GO, on March

19, 2013. Dear children, **a great event will occur in the Church: thousands left, thousands will return. Intensify your prayers for the Church.** I am your Mother and I want to help you. Do not stand about with your arms crossed. Make an effort and return to my Jesus. He awaits you with open arms. Be courageous and do not hold back. Accept the Gospel and be reconciled with God. Do not live in sin. This is the opportune time for your return to the Lord. Open your hearts and listen to the voice of God. **You live in a time of great tribulation. Bend your knees in prayer and everything will end well for you. Courage. My Jesus is at your side.** This is the message which I bring to you today in the name of the Most Holy Trinity. Thank you for allowing me to gather you here once again. I give you my blessing in the name of the Father, the Son and the Holy Spirit. Amen. Peace be with you.

Cardinals, Bishops, Priests, Religious

Cardinals Will Oppose Cardinals
Bishops Will Oppose Bishops
Satan Will Walk Among Them

At Garabandal, 1961-1965, St. Michael the Archangel gave to Conchita, one of the visionaries, **the message from Our Blessed Mother on October 18, 1961:** "Before the cup was filling up, now it is flowing over. **Many cardinals, many bishops, and many priests are on the path of perdition and taking many souls with them. Less and less importance is being given to the Eucharist.** You should turn the wrath of God away from yourself by your efforts...." [19]

At Garabandal on June 18, 1965, St. Michael the Archangel appeared and delivered a **message from Our Lady, "Because the message of October 18, hasn't been fulfilled, and the world doesn't know about it, I tell you that this is the last one. I said before the cup was filling up. Now it is overflowing. Many priests, bishops, cardinals are on the road to perdition and are taking many souls with them. Each day we give the Eucharist less and less importance.** We should use all our efforts to avoid God's wrath. If you ask sincerely for pardon, He will forgive you. Your Mother, through the mediation of Saint Michael, the angel, asks you to correct your ways. You are now receiving the last warnings. Think of the passion of Jesus." [19]

At Akita on October 13, 1973 regarding the Apostasy we were told: "Each day recite the prayers of the Rosary. With the Rosary pray for the bishops and priests. **The work of the devil will infiltrate even into the Church. One will see cardinals opposing cardinals ... and bishops confronting other bishops. The priests who venerate me will be scorned and condemned by their confreres; churches and altars will be sacked; the Church will be full of those who accept compromises and the demon will tempt many priests and religious to leave the service of the Lord ...** I alone am able still to help save you from the calamities which approach. Those who place their total confidence in me will be given necessary help." [21]

Mother Elena Patriarca Leonardi was told by St. Padre Pio on February 4, 1947 that the Virgin would entrust her with a great Mission.

Mother Elena Leonardi was born on November 4, 1910. She was married at age 20. Her husband died in 1934. She had a son and grandson. On April 22, 1968 she was run over by a car. **After that her life was completely devoted to the realization of the Work, pronounced by St. Padre Pio in the Confession of February 4, 1947 in San Giovanni Rotondo. From March 21, 1953 to October 9, 1983 she received many messages.**

Mother Elena Patriarca Leonardi was, it appears, actually given the Third Part of The Secret of Fatima by Our Blessed Mother, although Our Lady didn't tell her it was the Third Part of The Secret. The messages given to Mother Elena have both the Apostasy and the Great Chastisement for Mankind spelled out in some detail.

On March 26, 1978 Our Blessed Mother told Mother Elena Leonardi: "The time of the great trial will come also for the Church: **cardinals will oppose cardinals, bishops against bishops. Satan marches triumphantly in the midst of their ranks due to their hubris and lack of charity!** My daughter, there will be death everywhere because of the errors committed by the obstinate followers of Satan! Awareness of the terrible reality is urgent. Everyone must pray, do penance with the Holy Rosary, Holy Masses and Confessions. No sacrilegious Communions!" [16]

On February 12, 1979, Our Lady as the Mother of all Peoples, said to Mother Elena Leonardi: "My daughter, the time has run out; this is the Apocalyptic hour; if they do not return to my Heart, they will know only desolation. **Cardinals and bishops will confront the Pope who will be accused and mistreated, since the days of suffering are being prepared for the Holy Father.** Speak to him and tell him to be prudent and strong; I protect and watch over him." [16]

In His message of January 25, 1996, to Sadie Jaramillo, a visionary and locutionist from California, Jesus said: "Amongst those will be brother priests of Mine, for whom you suffer. The princes of the church now stand at odds, one against another, cardinal against cardinal, bishop against bishop and I behold all. The living fulfillment of prophecy becomes clearer and clearer with each passing moment." [6]

On November 7, 1996 St. Michael said to Janie Garza, a married visionary, mother and stigmatist from Austin, Texas: "The sufferings in your country will be manifested in many forms: Satan's attacks on the family will increase in great strength, **the persecution in the Church will be great, priests will turn against priests, bishops against bishops, cardinals against cardinals. The religious will also partake in this great division. There will be great slander and evil plots against the holy Vicar of Christ. Great will be his suffering.**

"The spirit of disobedience toward the holy Vicar will increase. **Only a few will remain obedient and united with the holy Vicar of Christ.** These few holy souls will be the ones who will carry the suffering of the Church through their prayers. Pray and fast for these holy priests of the Mother of God." [8]

Cardinals And Bishops Will Turn Against The Pope

Pedro Regis, Brazil

Pedro Regis, Angüera, Brazil has been receiving public messages from Our Blessed Mother since October 10, 1987. She first appeared to him September 29, 1987, and then again on October 1, 1987. On October 1, 1987 she appeared and introduced herself saying, **"Don't be afraid. I am the Mother of Jesus. I am here because I need you to help my poor children who need My assistance."** She asked him to **return to that place every Saturday.**

Don Silvério Albuquerque, former Bishop for the Archdiocese of Feira de Santana said about the apparition that had been occurring in Angüera for a few years, "I know the family very well, and I have already talked to all of its members, including to Pedro, who declares to be the visionary." The Bishop said, "I have already reached the conclusion that, from the pastoral point of view, the meeting in Angüera is valid, because it has been doing good. I believe that many conversions have occurred."

May 9, 1995. Message 951 (in Venice) – Dear Sons and Daughters, I invite you to pray for the conversion of sinners and lovingly live the messages I have already transmitted to you! And **pray in a special way for My first beloved son, Pope John Paul II! Know, all of you, that the Church of my Son will pass through a crisis such as has never been seen. Cardinals and bishops will turn against the Pope, many will lose the faith, but as I have said, hear the voice of him who is truly the successor to the chair of Peter. The Pope is betrayed by his closest collaborators. There are few who have the courage of Peter, but many who have the courage of Judas. Pray! I repeat, Pray! The decisive time is coming. Those who are with the Lord will come out the better. All this must happen, but in the end the Lord will conquer.** Courage! You are not alone. My Son goes with you. This is the message that I transmit to you in the name of The Most Holy Trinity. Thank you for permitting me to reunite you here once more. I bless you in the name of the Father, and of the Son, and of the Holy Spirit. Amen. Be at peace.

May 28, 1996. Message 1117 – Dear Sons and Daughters, **I also invite**

you to obey your ecclesiastical superiors. Don't back away! Go to meet my Son Jesus. Pray! Pray for my beloved firstborn son, the Pope John Paul II. I want to tell you that the Church of my Jesus will pass through a crisis such as has never been seen since its foundation....

My Son's Vicar Soon Will Fall
Under The Oppositions Force

Sadie Jaramillo was told on September 8, 1997 by Mary: "I have asked you specifically to pray for the Princes of the Church, for soon they will stand one against another openly. Whereas now, the division occurs where the heart of that shepherd is closed to the Vicar of Christ.... Pray for my Son's Vicar, for soon he will fall under the oppositions force...." [6]

Jennifer – Words From Jesus

Priests Will Be Against Priest And Nun Against Nun

On July 1, 2001 Jesus said to Jennifer, a mid-western United States visionary and locutionist, the mother of four, "I am He who came to shed the sins of the world." On March 3, 2003 Jesus said to Jennifer, "My child, I want you to write down this message for the world for you are My chosen instrument. Do not fear for fear does not come from Me for I have been preparing you for this mission." Since then she has been receiving messages from Jesus for the world. She has a spiritual director, a priest in good standing.

12/25/03
7:45 PM
My people the hour is drawing closer and these messages are to help guide you through these events that are about to unfold. You have begun to see the division in My church for too many of My chosen sons have fallen to the ways of the world. For as I have told you, priests will be against priest and nun against nun. You will see countries that have enormous power fall into ruins and the rise of

the antichrist.

Apostasy In The Church

Pedro Regis

August 6, 1988. Message 64 My beloved Sons and Daughters. Today I invite all of you to make a courageous public witness. **All of you should give a witness of union by a strong adhesion to the Pope and bishops united to him. Be courageous defenders of the pontiff and openly denounce those who are against his magisterium by teaching contrary to what he says. Today, a great number of bishops, priests, religious, and laity no longer believe. They have already lost the true faith in Christ and His Gospel. The church of Christ is wounded by the malevolent contact by the immorality and apostasy that now spread themselves within it. An increasing number of my innocent children walk in the darkness of denial of God, lack of faith, immorality, and impiousness. Bishops and priests of the Holy Church of God, go back to teaching the true catholic morality.** I encourage and bless all of you in the name of the Father, and of the Son, and of the Holy Spirit. Amen. Be at peace.

A Great Number Of Priests Who Celebrate The Eucharist No Longer Believe: Many Deny, Others Restrict The Real Presence Or Reduce It To A Spiritual Or Symbolic Presence.

August 13, 1988. Message 66 – My beloved Sons and Daughters. **My Church is in darkness. My adversary is working always more clearly against the Holy Catholic Church. Today a great number of priests who celebrate the Eucharist no longer believe. Many deny the real presence of my Son Jesus, and others restrict it to the moment of the celebration of the Holy Mass or reduce it to just a spiritual or symbolic presence. The church of Christ is overshadowed by the smoke of satan. He darkens the thoughts and intelligence of many of you, my dear sons, leading you to deceit, mistrust, pride, and apathy, and through these, darkens the Holy Church of God....**

March 3, 1998. Message 1394 – Dear Sons and Daughters, **There will**

28

be a terrible crisis of faith. **A great apostasy will shake the Church and the antichrist will spread his errors and false teachings throughout the whole world....**

January 1, 2000. Message 1681 – Dear Sons and Daughters, I am the Queen of Peace. I am the Mother of God the Son and your Mother. **I ask you to intensify your prayers for the Church of my Son Jesus, which is passing through difficult moments. What I foretold in the past is about to happen. Pray. The apostasy in the Church has become very clear. Many consecrated souls have lost the faith and the captain of this great ship will suffer much. The moment of agony of the Church is coming. The faithful will go through great trials, but in the end the Lord will conquer. Don't you lose hope. I am your Mother and I am with you. Tell everyone that the decisive moment in the struggle between the Woman clothed with the sun and the red dragon has begun. Open your hearts and receive the Grace of The Lord. Courage. Those who are with the Lord will win.** This is the message that I transmit to you in the name of The Most Holy Trinity. Thank you for permitting me to reunite you here once more. I bless you in the name of the Father, and of the Son, and of the Holy Spirit. Amen. Be at peace.

April 4, 2000. Message 1721 – Dear Sons and Daughters, sin has penetrated the heart of My poor children, bringing them to a sad spiritual blindness. **Contamination has even entered into the heart of my Church. Today many of my consecrated souls no longer accept true doctrine. They have even come to deny what the successor of Peter, Pope John Paul II is saying. The number of those who celebrate a Eucharist they no longer believe in is increasing daily. Apostasy has become clear within the Church and so my poor children go to false doctrines. Your time has come. Be defenders of the truth.... What prophets announced in times gone by is now being fulfilled. I ask you to pay attention....**

Janie Garza

On December 17, 1993 St. Joseph said to Janie Garza, "My little one, you have a generous heart, and your heart is full of love for priests. Pray for all priests, for these are hard times for the Church. **The Church is in the midst of great turmoil. Many priests are struggling with their**

29

faith. **Priests in great numbers are separating themselves from the Vicar on earth. There is much division in the Church among the priests and religious.**

Many priests are not living their priestly vows of poverty, chastity, and obedience. Many priests have separated from God and have lost reverence and love for the Eucharist. The apostasy is growing strong within the Church. Holy priests suffer much because of all the turmoil and the apostasy in today's Church.

Many priests have stopped practicing the sacrament of Reconciliation. Their souls are stained and dark with sinfulness. **The world is in need of holy priests that will help guide their people back to God.** Many priests alienate themselves from God due to their lack of commitment to follow the true doctrine of the Church. They choose to be a part of the world instead of being holy and belonging to God's Kingdom.

Many priests are not feeding the flock entrusted to them, and the flock leaves their shepherd, looking elsewhere to be fed. **Many priests have been responsible for their flock leaving the Catholic faith.** The Church is in need of much prayer.

My little one, offer up all your sufferings and prayers for the purification of the Church. **Pray unceasingly for all priests. Invite others to pray and fast for the Church.** Pray and ask the intercession of St. Michael for the protection of the Church. **Share this message, for the Church is in need of purification and conversion.** Many priests live in darkness and much prayer is needed for enlightenment of the Holy Spirit. Now, my little one, you know what you must do to help the priests.... [8]

Apostasy Leads To Schism

Janie Garza

On September 23, 1994 St. Joseph said to Janie Garza: "My little one, the chastisement is already upon the world. You can see its manifestation in the sinfulness of the world, the great apostasy, the

schism that is destroying many priests and consecrated souls, the violence in the family, the bloody massacre of the innocent infants, the increase in false prophets that are misleading many, the destruction of the youth through drug abuse and unhealthy relationships, the deadly plague, the pestilence that sweeps throughout the world taking the lives of many, the increase in homosexuality, the broken marriages that end in divorce, the destruction in natural disasters, the corrupted world leaders who are bringing destruction upon their countries, and the blasphemies against God by those who hate God. These are some of the signs of the chastisement and the only refuge is the refuge that you will find in the Immaculate Heart of Mary." [8]

On January 27, 1995 St. Joseph said to Janie Garza: "I, St. Joseph, wish to invite all families to pray everyday for the conversion of the world. **Through your prayers you will stamp out much of the evilness that exists in the world.** Learn to forgive your loved ones and love those who wound you the most.

The world is in need of much prayer and love. **Pray especially for the apostasy and schism that is growing strong within the Church and that is destroying and dividing the Church of God."** [8]

Pedro Regis

January 1, 1997. Message 1210 – Dear Sons and Daughters, **Pray for the Church of my Jesus. It will suffer because of great persecutions. Many of my beloved children will turn against the Pope. There will be a great schism. True doctrine will be denied even by members of the hierarchy. Pray. The Church of my Jesus will be attacked, it will be the target of great attacks. Only the faithful, the true faithful, will remain firm.** Don't be frightened by what I say. You need to hear this so that when it happens you will remember that I foretold it. Don't lose hope. You who are with me will be supported and protected....

31

Saint John (Don) Bosco's Vision:
Popes, Pillars Of The Eucharist And Our Lady

Saint John Bosco was born in 1815, the youngest son of a Peidmontese farmer. At age nine he had a dream that showed him his life's mission. Jesus and Mary appeared to him and asked him to devote his life to helping poor boys. He established the Salesian Society. Saint John Bosco died in 1888.

"On 30 May 1862 Don Bosco at his 'Good Night' talk told his boys, and the clerics he was training, about a dream he had dreamt a few nights previously: he actually described it as a parable or allegory. Strictly speaking a parable is a general story with a deeper meaning, but one in which the points of the story may not all be significant, while in an allegory every detail is important and meaningful. In the case of Don Bosco's dream it is difficult to know just how significant each point is. After some preliminary remarks he went on to describe what he had seen."

"Try to picture yourselves with me on the seashore, or, better still, on an outlying cliff with no other land in sight. The vast expanse of water is covered with a formidable array of ships in battle formation, prows fitted with sharp spear-like beaks capable of breaking through any defense. All are heavily armed with cannons, incendiary bombs, and firearms of all sorts – even books – and **are heading toward one stately ship, mightier than them all.** As they try to close in, they try to ram it, set it afire, and cripple it as much as possible.

This stately vessel is shielded by a flotilla escort. Winds and waves are with the enemy. *In this midst of this endless sea, two solid columns*, a short distance apart, soar high into the sky: **one is surmounted by a statue of the Immaculate Virgin at whose feet a large inscription reads: Help of Christians; the other, far loftier and sturdier, supports a (Communion) Host of proportionate size and bears beneath it the inscription Salvation of believers.**

The flagship commander – the Roman Pontiff (the Pope) – seeing the enemy's fury and his auxiliary ships in a very grave predicament, summons his captains to a conference. However, as they discuss their strategy, a furious storm breaks out and they must return to their ships. When the storm abates, the Pope again summons his captains as the flagship keeps on its course. But the storm rages again. Standing at the helm, the Pope strains every muscle to steer his ship between the *two columns* from whose summits hang many anchors and strong hooks linked to chains.

The entire enemy fleet closes in to intercept and sink the flagship at all costs. They bombard it with everything they have: books and pamphlets, incendiary bombs, firearms, cannons. The battle rages ever more furious. Beaked prows ram the flagship again and again, but to no avail, as, unscathed and undaunted, it keeps on its course. At times a formidable ram splinters a gaping hole into its hull, but, immediately, a breeze from the *two columns* instantly seals the gash.

Meanwhile, enemy cannons blow up, firearms and beaks fall to pieces, ships crack up and sink to the bottom. In blind fury the enemy takes to hand-to-hand combat, cursing and blaspheming. **Suddenly the Pope falls, seriously wounded. He is instantly helped up but, struck down a second time, dies. A shout of victory rises from the enemy and wild rejoicing sweeps their ships. But no sooner is the Pope dead than another takes his place. The captains of the auxiliary ships elected him so quickly that the news of the Pope's death coincides with that of his successor's election.** The enemy's self-assurance wanes.

Breaking through all resistance, the new Pope steers his ship safely between the *two columns* and moors it to the *two columns*; first to the one surmounted by the Host, and then to the other, topped by the statue of the Virgin. At this point something unexpected happens. **The enemy ships panic and disperse, colliding with and scuttling each other.** Some auxiliary ships which had gallantly fought alongside their flagship are the first to tie up at the *two columns.*

Many others, which had fearfully kept far away from the fight, stand still, cautiously waiting until the wrecked enemy ships vanish under the waves. Then, they too head for the *two columns,* tie up at the swinging hooks, and ride safe and tranquil beside their flagship. A great calm now covers the sea."

At this point Don Bosco asked one of the priests present for his views. He replied that he thought that the flagship symbolized the Church headed by the Pope, with the ships representing mankind and the sea as an image of the world. The ships defending the flagship he equated with the laity and the attackers with those trying to destroy the Church, while *the two columns represented devotion to Mary and the Eucharist.*"

He did not mention the death of the Pope and neither did Don Bosco in his reply, in which he agreed with what the priest had said, while adding **that the enemy ships symbolised persecutions: "Very grave trials await the Church. What we have suffered so far is almost nothing compared to what is going to happen. The enemies of the Church are symbolized by the ships which strive their utmost to sink the flagship. Only two things can save us in such a grave hour: devotion to Mary and frequent Communion.** Let us do our very best to use these two means and have others use them everywhere."

Not surprisingly the contents of this dream amazed all those listening, and four of those present wrote down what they had heard. Two wrote the next day, 31 May and two some time later, but all four narratives agree substantially. Such small differences as were found can be explained on the basis that it is impossible to get every detail when remembering and writing a spoken narrative.

One point that did cause some argument amongst those who had been present was over whether there had been _two popes_ as commander of the flagship as in the above account, or, as some thought, _three._ This point was made clearer in 1886 when one of those who had heard the dream recounted in 1862 returned to the Oratory.

At dinner with Don Bosco he began to narrate the dream and was quite certain that **_two popes_** had fallen, since he was sure that after the first was struck down the captains of the other ships had said, 'Let's hurry. We can quickly replace him'; on the second occasion he maintained that they had said nothing. **Don Bosco seemed to back up this version of events by calling attention to what was being said, and so its probable that we are dealing with _three popes_ in the account.**

Those who had written down the dream were convinced that it was a genuine vision and prophecy, although Don Bosco's immediate aim was probably to encourage his boys to pray more fervently for the Church and the Pope, as well as to indicate the importance of devotion to Mary and the Blessed Sacrament." [9]

Living Through St. John Bosco's Vision

We may be living part way through Saint John (Don) Bosco's vision, but as in all genuine prophecy before its fulfillment, there is quite a degree of uncertainty and ambiguity, and it would be foolish to attempt to come to definite conclusions at this stage. Two or three Popes? It appears from Saint John (Don) Bosco's comment that there may possibly have been three popes in his vision. If there were three popes, could they be Pope St. John Paul II, Pope Benedict XIV and Pope Francis. Pope St. John Paul II and Pope Benedict XVI brought the Church back to a proper philosophical and theological belief based on a proper interpretation of Vatican II rather than the "false spirit of Vatican II"? This "false spirit of Vatican II" which caused so much confusion within the clergy, religious and lay members of the Catholic Church had led to the loss of the Faith in a generation or two of the children brought up and educated under this false interpretation. Could Pope Francis be the third Pope of the vision as a pastoral and missionary Pope in the evangelization of the world?

The important point is the way in which the end of the vision points to what would seem to be the worldwide triumph of the Church, a triumph which will be recognized by all, but one which is only gained after much suffering.

The emphasis in St. John Bosco's vision on the role of *Mary, Help of Christians*, and the *Blessed Sacrament*, is also significant, especially with regard to the message given at Fatima. Mary promised a period of peace for the world following troubled times. Could this be the 'great calm' of Saint John (Don) Bosco's dream?

Chapter 3

Satan Reigns In The Highest Places In The Church And The World

Pope Leo XIII is reported to have had an ecstasy on October 13, 1884, in which he heard Satan ask God for permission to try to destroy the Church and **heard God grant to Satan 100 years** to try to accomplish this.

On November 5, 1983, Mirjana, a visionary at Medjugorje, Yugoslavia, confided to Fr. Tomislav Vlasic revelations received prior to December 26, 1982. He in turn on December 16, 1983 confided them in a letter to Pope John Paul II: **"I am reporting here what Mirjana told me in a conversation of November 5, 1983.** I summarized the essentials of her account, without literal quotation."

Father Vlasic said that the Blessed Virgin gave Mirjana the following message in substance, "Excuse me for this, but you must realize that **Satan exists. One day he appeared before the throne of God and asked permission to submit the Church to a period of trial. God gave him permission to try the Church for one century. This century is under the power of the Devil, _but when the secrets confided to you come to pass, his power will be destroyed._** Even now he is beginning to lose his power and has become aggressive. **He is destroying marriages, creating division among priests and is responsible for obsessions and murder. You must protect yourselves against these things** _through fasting and prayer, especially community prayer._ **Carry blessed objects with you. Put them in your house, and restore the use of holy water."**

Satan Was Thus The Uncontested Dominator
Of The Events Of The 20th Century

At Fatima on May, 13, 1990, the Anniversary of the First Apparition, in message # 425 Our Blessed Mother told Fr. Gobbi, Marian Movement of Priests, in locution that Satan has been the uncontested dominator of the events of this century of yours. She stated that Satan has brought all humanity to the rejection of God, his law of love, division, hatred, immorality and wickedness. She said that Satan had brought about and legitimating everywhere divorce, abortion, obscenity, homosexuality and recourse to any and all means of obstructing life.

In this message Our Lady revealed that the Church will know the hour of its greatest apostasy, the man of iniquity will penetrate into its interior and will sit in the very Temple of God, while the little remnant which will remain faithful will be subjected to the greatest trials and persecutions.

At La Salette, on September 19, 1846, (Leece version that had the Imprimatur of the local Bishop), Melanie revealed that she was told by Our Blessed Mother: "Rome will lose the faith and become the seat of the Antichrist.... The Church will be in eclipse.... Pagan Rome will disappear." [7]

The Red Dragon, Freemasonry And Islam

On June 14, 1998 Mary said to Sadie Jaramillo: "I tell you again, the Mercy will descend amidst fire and turmoil! The symbols shown to you on your trip indicate **the red dragon will rear its ugly head and align itself with those of the race of the Orient!** So too will **the Freemasons make their move to accomplish their one-world order. Islam is a sleeping giant ready to awaken.** Thus for many in the coming days; they will pray for death, for these have not prepared for this battle of all battles! The preparations are spiritual ones and many have spent precious time in only the cares of the world. They will find, as with the princes of the Church, that there is a God. A God of Love who only asked for their heart! All that has been foretold to you and many others is on the point of being fulfilled. Know that I your Mother and the Mother of God, ask now from you the total focus of your heart on My Son Jesus, **for this apostasy which is eclipsing the Church will soon bring darkness and the fulfillment of Daniel's prophecy.** (Daniel Chapter 12). The one who has prepared snares and traps for humanity prepares for his unveiling to the world. Peace, security and wealth, he will promise, order to a world filled with disorder! The message you proclaim is to awaken the dead souls of my children to the truth...." [3]

Attack On The Eucharist And
The Holy Church In Darkness

Marie-Julie Jahenny, born February 12, 1850, died 1941, was a stigmatist from La Fraudais near Blain in Brittany. During her ecstasy of the 3rd of June 1880, Our Lord describes how Lucifer will proceed. He will address priests: "You will dress in a large red cloak. ... We will give you a piece of bread and a few drops of water. You can do with everything that you did when you belonged to Christ. ... ("But," says Our Lord, "they do not add: *Consecration* and *Communion*").

And hell had added: "We will permit you to say it in all houses and even under the firmament." [42]

Marie-Julie saw that "there will not remain any vestige of the Holy Sacrifice, no apparent trace of faith. *Confusion* will be everywhere." The preceding 1st of June: "All the works approved by the infallible Church will cease to exist as they are today for a time. In this sorrowful annihilation, brilliant signs will be manifested on earth. **If, because of the wickedness of men Holy Church will be in darkness, the Lord will also send darkness that will stop the wicked in their search of wickedness...."** [42]

April 9, 1998 in Message 1409 Pedro Regis was told by Our Lady Dear Sons and Daughters, **Today remember the institution of the Eucharist and the priesthood. Because these sacraments are a great force for the Church of my Son, Satan has tried to destroy them in every possible way. See how many sacrileges are committed against**

39

the Eucharist. See how many scandals involve priests. The great plan of the devil is to end the Eucharist and destroy the true meaning of the consecrated life. By accepting false doctrine, many will say that Jesus is just symbolically present, and with this the devil will drag a great number of consecrated people and faithful into error. Now is the time of great confusion.... My Son is really in the Eucharist, body and blood, soul and divinity. Those who teach the contrary are sent by the antichrist. Pay attention. This is the message that I transmit to you in the name of The Most Holy Trinity. Thank you for permitting me to reunite you here once more. I bless you in the name of the Father, and of the Son, and of the Holy Spirit. Amen. Be at peace.

How The Church Was Brought To This State

Modernism, Freemasonry, The Great Apostasy

Modernism

St. Pius X in 1907 condemned Modernism in the encyclical *Pascendi Dominici Gregis*. He defined Modernism as "the synthesis of all heresies." He told us that the trinity of parents responsible for the perversion known as modernism are: 1) Its religious ancestor is the Protestant Reformation; 2) Its philosophical parent is the Enlightenment; 3) Its political pedigree comes from the French Revolution. The Enlightenment produced rationalists who placed reason over faith.

He recognized Modernism as the most dangerous revolution the Church has ever had to face and that it was scourging her severely.

He stated that Modernism leads to pantheism and atheism. Modernists place the foundation of religious philosophy in that doctrine called agnosticism.

The modernists hold dogma (religious formulas) as arising as

40

secondary propositions based on primitive and simple formulas. They consider them **to be symbols and instruments;** that is, images and vehicles of truth which are **subject to change and ought to evolve and be changed.**

St. Pius X stated that **they admit that all religions are true. He recognized that they seize upon chairs in the seminaries and universities, gradually making them chairs of pestilence. St. Pius X stated that Modernists try in every way to diminish and weaken authority.**

They propose to remove the ecclesiastical Magisterium itself by sacrilegiously falsifying its origin, character, rights, and by freely repeating the calumnies of its adversaries.[35]

St. Pius X suppressed Modernism in the seminaries and universities, where it went underground to resurface after Vatican II as neo-modernism, which masquerades under "The Spirit of Vatican II," feminism in the Church, liberation theology, and the conciliar Church.

Freemasonry Is A Religion

Masonry is a religion with the characteristics of a religious cult. Worship is practiced in separate phases or periods:
- **Adoration of the Great Architect of the Universe.** (the true Masonic Divinity is concealed)
- **Adoration of Nature.** The idea of the Great Architect of the Universe is translated into that of the God-Nature, universal cause of things, as conceived by the materialist, the pantheist, or the theosophist, who only disagree on the name but not on the idea which is formed of the first principal cause of things. Albert Pike, the author of *Morals and Dogma of the Ancient and Accepted Scottish Rite of Freemasonry,* written in 1871, called by Haywood 'the Scottish Rite Bible', states of the worship of Nature. "There is merely formal Atheism, which is the negation of God in terms, but not in reality." *There is a worship of the flesh which Masonry has inherited from the ancient pagans.*
  In the worship of Nature, the sun is taken as its representative and

most characteristic symbol of the God-Nature, which Masons adore. This worship is referred to in the many symbols or ceremonies in the lodges. The circumambulation or procession around the altar in the lodges according to Albert G. Mackey, author of *Encyclopedia of Freemasonry* is an imitation of the course of the sun. The worship of the sun represents a restoration from death to life. To the sun also, as a regenerator and vivifier must be attributed the phallic cult of worship which formed a principal part of the mysteries.

- **Worship of Satan or Lucifer** in some lodges at least. **According to the Masonic laws Satan is the good god or angel of light who came to teach Eve the secret which was to make human beings like God, seducing her carnally, a knowledge which she shared afterwards with Adam.** [11]

Illustrious Masons speak of the goddess-reason. [11]

Freemasonry is the modern-day continuation of Gnosticism and of the ancient secret societies.

Albert Pike who by 1859 had risen in Freemasonry to the titled position of M.P. Sovereign Grand Commander of the Supreme Council for the Southern Jurisdiction of the United States on page 626 of his book *Morals and Dogma* stated: "The Kabalah is the key to the occult sciences and the Gnostics were born of the Kabalists."

In 1870 Pike reached an agreement with Mazzini and was called the Supreme Pontiff of Universal Freemasonry.

The Kabalah is found principally in two books called the *Book of Creation* and *Aohar*, [11]

Masonry has or pretends to have a relationship with the more ancient sects, the Egyptian, the Chaldeans, the Indo-Brahmins, the Greeks, the Persians, etc. ... From these sources comes also its doctrines of pantheism, materialism, the dualism or bisexualism of god, the emanation of souls, etc. "In the Masonic legends of certain degrees it is customary to say that **Masonry .... comes from Satan himself**, who for them is the good god, the eternal enemy of Jehovah, the God of the Bible and of the Christians." [11]

The Knights Templar, a military and religious order was first established in 1118 AD in Jerusalem. It grew rapidly and in the year 1128 was taken under the special protection of the Pope. They became extremely wealthy through gifts of land and money.

The order of Knights Templar degenerated. In 1312 Pope Clement V abolished the Order. [12]

"Evidence suggests that the surviving Knights either founded or merged with an existing secret order in the early 1300s, later referred to as the Order of the Rose Croix (The Rosicrucians)." [12]

The Rosicrucians in progressing to their goal of establishing a New World Order "decided to take on the appearance of a benevolent organization of good works in order to continue their occult traditions within. They merged with and finally took over the stone mason guilds of Europe, retaining many of their symbols from the building trade." The *stone masons* who were actually employed in the building profession were known as *Operative Masons*, unlike the occult adepts who took over their guilds, who became known as *Speculative Masons*. [12]

The transition from Operative to Speculative Masonry took several decades, the move beginning in the 1640s and culminating in the formation of the world's first Grand Lodge in London in 1717. In this gradual takeover, "the torch was passed to the Masonic Order, with the Rosicrucian's embedding themselves deep within its structure and hierarchy to become the Adepts, or the Princes of Freemasonry." [12]

This "new" order expanded rapidly. [12]

The Illuminati

A new ultra secret society known as the Illuminati was formed as an Order within the Masonic Order.

Albert G. Mackey describes the Illuminati as a "secret society

founded on May 1, 1776, by Adam Weishaupt, who was professor of canon law at the University of Ingolstadt."...[12]

"John Robinson, an 18th century historian and a prominent Mason, was entrusted with some of the original documents and correspondence of the Illuminati." In his book *Proofs of a Conspiracy*, 1798, he wrote: *"The express aim of the Order, was to abolish Christianity, and overturn all civil government."* He quoted Weishaupt as saying that the plan for *a New World Order* can succeed "in no other way but by secret associations, which will by degrees, and in silence, possess themselves the government of the States, and make use of those means for this purpose...." Mackey commented that the order extended rapidly into other countries, and its Lodges were found in France, Belgium, Holland, Denmark, Sweden, Poland, Hungary, and Italy. [12]

At the Masonic Congress of Wilhelmsbad on July 16, 1782, the Illuminati solidified itself as the undisputed leader of the occult one-world movement. The decision was made to move the headquarters of illuminized Freemasonry from Bavaria to Frankfurt, which was already becoming the stronghold of the Rothschilds and the international financiers. An alliance was forged between illuminized Freemasonry and the growing Rothschild network. [12]

The tenets of Illuminati were:
- **Abolition of monarchies and all ordered government.**
- **Abolition of private property and inheritance.**
- **Abolition of patriotism and nationalism.**
- **Abolition of family life and the institution of marriage, and the establishment of communal education of children.**
- **Abolition of all religion.** [13]

The novice in the Illuminati was taught that "the ends justify the means, that evil methods were justifiable if the ultimate outcome was for good." In the higher degrees he was told that: "This is our 'Great Secret'. *Once the impediment of religion is dispensed with, the way is open for a world dictatorship, ruled by Illuminism.* [13]

After the exposure of the Illuminati plot by the Bavarian government, after only 10 years of existence, and revelation of it to

the leaders of Europe, some of whom were under the Order's influence, most of the initiates got away and were taken in by various European leaders. Although the Illuminati officially ceased to exist the continuation of its efforts were ensured through the Grand Orient Lodge of France. Working through the Grand Orient and the network of illuminized Masonic Lodges already put in place by Weishaupt, high-Freemasonry continued its agenda for world domination. [12]

The first major "accomplishment" of illuminized Freemasonry was the French Revolution through the Jacobin Society and Napoleon Bonaparte who was one of their men. Illuminized Freemasonry received help from Voltaire, Robespierre, Danton and Maat, all of whom were prominent Masons. The Jacobin Society named Weishaupt as its "Grand Patriot."

"Weishaupt was as much the founder of revolutionary Communism as was Karl Marx....

Weishaupt adopted the teachings of radical French philosophers such as Jean Jacques Rousseau (1712-1778) and the anti-Christian doctrines of the Manicheans. He was indoctrinated in Egyptian occultism in 1771 by a merchant of unknown origin named Kolmer, who was said to have traveled Europe in search of converts. For the next five years Weishaupt formulated a plan by which all occult systems could be reduced to a single, powerful organization. On May Day, 1776 Weishaupt launched his order of the Illuminati." [13]

"The plan of the Illuminati was to replace Christianity by a religion of reason." [13]

"British historian, Nesta Webster, author of World Revolution, observed that Rousseau's writings embodied all of the principles which would later be known as Communism." [13]

"Weishaupt had already decreed bringing women into the order should be a goal, so that the philosophy of the new liberated women could be developed. This concept was devised to aid in his plan for the breakup of the family by generally developing rationales which would sow discord between men and women. He initially achieved this by painting the plight of women as a downtrodden class." [13]

Although the Illuminati's efforts had officially ceased to exist, unofficially **its agenda continued to move forward throughout the network of illuminated Masonic Lodges that had already been set in place. The main catalyst for this continued drive seemed to come from the Grand Orient Lodge of France, and later on, from the Masonic leaders of Italy and the United States.**

On July 14, 1889 Albert Pike as the leader of Freemasonry, issued his instructions to the 23 Supreme Councils of the World:

"To you, Sovereign Grand Inspectors General, **we say this, that you may repeat it to the Brethren of the 32nd, 31st, and 30th degrees – The Masonic religion should be, by all of us initiates of the high degrees, maintained in the purity of the Luciferic Doctrine....**

That is why the intelligent disciples of Zoroaster, as well as, after them, the Gnostics, the Manicheans and the Templars have admitted, as the only logical metaphysical conception, the system of two divine principles fighting eternally, and one cannot believe one inferior to the other. Thus, the doctrine of Satanism is a heresy; and the true and pure philosophic religion is the belief in Lucifer, the equal of Adonay; but Lucifer, God of Light and God of Good, is struggling for humanity against Adonay, the God of Darkness and Evil." [13]

Communism, Illuminized Freemasonry, And International Banking

In the Stalin Showcase Trials of 1938 - 1939 the role of the financiers of Communism was revealed. The role of "They", Wall Street was revealed. In 1938, the Russian Ambassador to Paris, Christian G. Rakovsky, a founding member of the Russian Communistic State, a member of "Them", the hidden forces behind Freemasonry, was arrested. Gavriil G. Kusmin (known as Gabriel) was sent by Stalin to question him. [14]

The interview was witnessed by Dr. Landowsky, a Russianized Pole who lived in Moscow. He kept a copy of the interview which was published in the booklet, *The Red Symphony*, by J. Landowsky, Excerpts from this interview were published in *Towards World Government, New World Order* by Deirdre Manifold. [14]

Rakovsky said: "You know that according to the unwritten history known only to us, **the founder of the First Communist International is indicated – of course secretly – as being Weishaupt**.... **he was ordered to found a secret organization which was to provoke and push the French Revolution to go further than its political objectives with the aim of transforming it into a social revolution for the establishment of Communism....**" [14]

Rakovsky said what is **not** known **are the relations between Weishaupt and his followers with the Rothschilds.** The secret of acquisition of wealth of the best known bankers could have been explained by the fact that **they were the treasurers of the first Comintern. There is evidence that when the five brothers spread out to the five provinces of the financial empire of Europe, they had some secret help for the accumulation of these enormous sums; it is possible that they were the first Communists from the Bavarian Catacombs who were already spread all over Europe. But others say, and I think with better reason, that the Rothschilds were not the treasurers, but the chiefs of that first secret Communism. The opinion is based on the well known fact that Marx and the highest chiefs of the First International – already the open one – were controlled by Baron Lionel Rothschild, whose revolutionary portrait was done by Disraeli, the English Premier, who was his creature.... He described him in the character of Sidonia,** a man who, according to the story, was a multimillionaire, knew and controlled spies, Carbonari, Freemasons, ... Gypsies, revolutionaries, etc.. [14]

Rakovsky brought out that he thought we could determine that the inventor of the Financial International and the Revolutionary International was the same person. He stated it is an act of genius: to create, with the help of Capitalism, accumulation of the highest degree, to push the proletariat towards strikes, to sow hopelessness, and at the same time create an organization which must unite proletarians with the purpose of driving them into revolution. This is to write the most majestic chapter of history. Even more – **remember the phrase of the mother of the five Rothschild brothers: "If my sons want it, then there will be no war." This means they were the arbiters of peace and war, but not emperors....** Is not war already a revolutionary function? War – the Commune. **Since that time every war was a giant step towards Communism.** [14]

The Alta Vendita – Its Role In Taking Over The Church

When Weishaupt passed away, the Alta Vendita or highest lodge of the Italian Carbonari exercised the supreme government of all the secret societies of the world. It ruled the blackest Freemasonry of France, Germany and England under a nobleman called Nubius until Giuseppe Mazzini wrenched the scepter away. Mazzini functioned for many years as the head of Italian Masonry and joined in 1870 with Albert Pike the head of Masonry in the United States to form the new supreme rite the *New and Reformed Palladian Rite* **in Masonry. Membership in this essentially Luciferian rite was very limited. This rite held that divinity was dual with Lucifer the equal of Adonay. The whole Masonic world was set up in Charleston, the sacred city of the Palladium.**

The Conspiracy To Take Over The Church

In the permanent instructions of the Alta Vendita we have the conspiracy to take over the Church. They were to give bad names to faithful Prelates who may be too knowing or too good to do the work of the Carbonari against conscience, God and the souls of men. **The instruction stated,** the Pope, whoever he may be, will never come to the secret societies. It is for the secret societies to come first to the Church, in the resolve to conquer the two. **The work which we have undertaken is not the work of a day, nor of a month, nor of a year. It may last many years, a century perhaps, but in our ranks the soldier dies and the fight continues....** That which we ought to demand, that which we should seek and expect, as the Jews expected the Messiah, *is a Pope according to our wants.... It is to the youth we must go.* **It is that which we must seduce; it is that which we must bring under the**

banner of the secret societies.... Now then, in order to secure to us a Pope in the manner required, it is necessary to fashion for that Pope a generation worthy of the reign of which we dream. The instructions told them to never speak in the presence of the youth a word of impiety or impurity. You ought to present yourself with all the appearance of a man grave and moral. Once your reputation is established in the colleges, in the gymnasiums, in the universities, and in the seminaries – once that you have captivated the confidence of professors and students so act that those who are principally engaged in the ecclesiastical state should love to seek your conversation.

Nourish their souls with the splendors of ancient Papal Rome.... Offer them at first, but always in secret, inoffensive books, poetry resplendent with national emphasis; then little by little you will bring your disciples to the degree of cooking desired.... you will obtain for yourselves the reputation of good Catholics and pure patriots. That reputation will open the way for our doctrines to pass to the bosom of the young clergy, and even to go into the depths of convents.

In a few years the young clergy will have, by the force of events, invaded all the functions. They will govern, administer, and judge. They will form the council of the Sovereign. They will be called to choose the Pontiff who will reign; and that Pontiff, like the greater part of his contemporaries, will be necessarily imbued with the Italian and humanitarian principles which we are about to put in circulation. It is a little grain of mustard which we place in the earth, but the sun of justice will develop it even to be a great power; and you will see one day what a rich harvest that little seed will produce. [15]

Let the clergy march under your banner in the belief always that they march under the banner of the Apostolic Keys.... Lay your nets like Simon Barjona. Lay them in the depths of sacristies, seminaries, and convents, and if you precipitate nothing you will give yourself a draught of fishes more miraculous than his. The fisher of fishes will become fishers of men. You will bring yourselves as friends around the Apostolic Chair. You will have fished up a Revolution in Tiara and Cope, marching with Cross and banner – a Revolution which it will need but to be spurred on a little to put the four corners of the world on fire.... [15]

The first leader of the Alta Vendita was a corrupt nobleman who took the name Nubius. He was sacrificed by the party of Mazzini, and managed in revenge to communicate documents to the authorities of Rome. Piccolo Tigre, a member of the Alta Vendita, was the most active agent of Nubius. The letter of Piccolo Tigre stated that they should isolate a man from his family, to cause him to lose his morals. They were to then recruit him for affiliation with the nearest lodge. [15]

"The main advice of the permanent instruction is to seduce the clergy. ... The ecclesiastic is to be deceived, being led on by patriotic fervor, and blinded by a constant, though, of course false, and fatal popularity.... The seduction of the foremost ecclesiastics, prelates, and bishops was the general policy of the sect at all times." [15]

When Nubius passed away, Lord Palmerston of England, for the greater part of his career, was the real master, the Grand Patriarch of the Illuminati, and as such, the Ruler of all the secret societies of the world. [15]

Henry John Temple, Viscount Palmerston (Lord Palmerston), twice served as Prime Minister of England: February 6, 1855 to February 19, 1858 and June 12, 1859 to October 18, 1865.

Pope Leo XIII's April 20, 1884 Encyclical
Humanum Genus

Pope Leo XIII April 20, 1884 wrote *Humanum Genus* an encyclical on Freemasonry, condemning it as Popes before him had done. He said, **"Let no man think that he may for any reason whatsoever join the Masonic sect, if he values his Catholic name and his eternal salvation as he ought to value them.** Let no one be deceived by a pretense of honesty."

The encyclical teaches that the fruit produced by Freemasonry is pernicious and bitter for it is nothing less than the overthrow of the

Christian social and political order, and the substitution of a new state of things founded on Naturalism. **This means in Masonry human nature and human reason are supreme, and that there are no truths revealed by God that men are bound to believe.** The Pope notes that the Masons want to bring back after a lapse of eighteen centuries the manners and customs of the pagans. **The Masons hold all religions to be alike, and the Catholic religion as equal to other religions.** *They have plotted the destruction of the papacy, holding that the sacred power of the Pontiffs must be abolished, and the Pontificate must be utterly destroyed. Pope Leo XIII calls this a "fatal plague."* Pope Leo XIII ratified and confirmed by his Apostolic authority, what the Roman Pontiffs his predecessors, had decreed for the purpose of opposing the undertakings and endeavors of the Masonic sect, and whatsoever they had enacted to deter or withdraw men from societies of this kind. [41]

Past Attempts To Capture The Roman Catholic Church From Within

In his book *The Keys of This Blood*, 1990, on pages 535-536 and page 678, **Fr. Malachi Martin informed us that the Papacy was almost captured after the death of Pope Leo XIII when his Cardinal Secretary of State (Cardinal Rampolla), in the Conclave of 1903, received the votes to pronounce the *Accepto*, but was never allowed to do so.** Emperor Franz Joseph of Austria, at that time had the privilege from the Vatican of vetoing any pope-elect whom he did not fancy. The Emperor did not fancy him. The ostensible reason given was the Cardinal Secretary of State's record of political opposition to Austria and his support of France. So, on August 2, 1903, the Polish born Jan Cardinal Puzyna of Austria-Hungary stood up in the Conclave and announced the Emperor's veto of the Cardinal Secretary of State. [23]

The Church then elected Cardinal Sarto (Italian for tailor), whose father was a polish born tailor named Jan Krawiec (Polish for tailor) and his mother Margherita a seamstress. **Cardinal Sarto took the name Pope Pius X.** His father had moved to Italy for political asylum when Poland fell into Prussian hands. [23]

Pope Pius X was later declared a Saint. It was St. Pius X who

51

condemned Modernism as the Synthesis of All Heresies.[35]

In the book *The Secret Archives of The Vatican*, by Maria Luisa Aambrosini with Mary Willis, 1969, on page 266, we are told that **Charlemagne's son Louis the Pious acquired an imperial veto over whatever choice was made in Papal elections – a right not abrogated until 1904 after it had swayed a papal election.**[10]

The Communist Infiltration Into The Church

In the book *AA-1025 – The Memoirs of an Anti-Apostle* it was revealed how a French nurse in the 1960's attending **an auto crash victim, who died** with no identification on him, found **in his briefcase biographical notes which contained information about how the Communist Party commissioned him to enter the priesthood to subvert and destroy the church from within. He was the 1,025th man in the program when he was recruited.** [40]

Ms. Bella Dodd, who had been a member of the Communist Party for most of her life, defected and revealed that as one of her jobs as an agent was to encourage young radicals to enter Catholic seminaries and religious orders. She revealed that *in the 1930s they had put eleven hundred men into the priesthood* to advance to become monsignors and bishops and destroy the Church from within. In the 1950s during a lecture she said that *"right now they are in the highest places, and they are working to bring about change in order that the Catholic Church will no longer be effective against Communism."* She also said that the changes would be so drastic that *"you will not recognize the Catholic Church."* [32]

Freemasonry and Modernism have so much in common that they are of the same threat to the Catholic Church and to all of society.

The False Church Of These End Of The Times

Freemasonry In The Church

On February 12, 1979, Our Lady as the Mother of all Peoples said to Mother Elena Leonardi: "Communism will triumph because of the godless rulers; many magistrates will perish; **freemasonry in the churches, prelates without dignity....** My daughter, the time has run out; this is the Apocalyptic hour; if they do not return to my Heart, they will know only desolation. **Cardinals and bishops will confront the Pope who will be accused and mistreated, since the days of suffering are being prepared for the Holy Father.** Speak to him and tell him to be prudent and strong; I protect and watch over him." [16]

Vision Of Priest And Clergymen With Faces Like Heads Of Foxes, Wolves And Hyenas

On May 31, 1978, Ida Peerdeman, a visionary in Holland, at the Consecration heard: **"Be faithful to its True Doctrine. Bring My People to Me and I will feed their souls."** At Holy Communion Ida had a vision of the whole world before her and heard, **"They have ravaged My Church and chased My followers into wilderness."** The Voice said, **"Watch well, and understand rightly everything I'll show you." Ida saw several large buildings. She recognized them as the side wall of the Vatican. The other buildings were seminaries and universities. From all these buildings she saw priests and clergymen coming out. She became frightened because their faces looked like heads of foxes, wolves and hyenas. They came along skulking and moved around searching like these animals. Ida heard the Voice say, "They are those who have led My people into wilderness and have broken up My Church."** [17]

False Ecumenism – Modern Ecumenical Christianity

Blessed Katherine Emmerick, (1820s) in visions, saw the Church of St. Peter in ruins and so many of the clergy busying themselves in the work of this destruction, but not openly in front of others. **She saw that everything that pertained to Protestantism was gradually gaining the upper hand, and the Catholic religion fall into complete decadence. She saw many pastors allowing themselves to be taken up with ideas dangerous to the Church. They were building a great, strange, and extravagant Church in which everyone "was to be admitted in order to be united and have equal rights: Evangelicals, Catholics, sects of every kind; such was to be the new Church."** [18]

On September 13, 1992 Josyp Terelya had an apparition from Our Blessed Mother in Marmora, Ontario. She told him that the final times are near. You are on the threshold of the day of judgment.

Our Blessed Mother said, "Remember Satan has infiltrated the very womb of the Church, and is spreading the idea of his *ecumenical Christianity*, of his new interpretations of the faith. This has led to today's indifference and neglect in the religious education of children and the youth. There is a loss of awareness of the true Catholic faith. The dangerous ideology of a *modern ecumenical Christianity* is spreading. Satanists are attempting to destroy Holy Sunday, so that modern Christians cannot discern between good and evil. Sunday is the greatest day in the Church of Christ. Defend it against Satan."

Chapter 4

The Co-Rulers Of Evil
The False Prophet And
The Antichrist

The False Pope Will Spread A False Doctrine
And Will Persecute The Church

Julia of Yugoslavia on February 28, 1976, in a conversation with Our Lord Jesus Christ about Pope Paul VI and the false Pope, who according to the prophecies will come, **was told: "The false Pope has not yet come! One day, when the false shepherd rules he will spread a false doctrine and will persecute the Church. You will recognize him by the persecution of the Church.** He will not have much time at his disposal. **His rule will be short but strong.** The good Christians and My true servants will have to hide themselves.... The safest is to be with one's relatives... **Once the false Peter is in, he will persecute My Church and My Flock will be dispersed...."** [33]

The Masonic Black Pope – The False Prophet

On March 3, 1976 Julia had a vision of the Antipope. Julia said, "In Rome, in the Square of Saint Peter's, very many people were crowded. Over their heads flew a great white flag, with four red bands, lengthwise. **From the entrance of the Basilica of Saint Peter a priest appeared with a tall cylinder on his head and a strange coat over his shoulders.** His robust face and the cylinder were surrounded for some moments by a white mist. But on the top of the cylinder the mist was not joined. **This priest radiated no mildness and goodness. He watched**

the crowd with a gloomy face. **Above the priest a Voice was heard, 'This will be the false Pope.'** He did not remain for long; after a short time he disappeared." [33]

Ida Peerdeman, Holland, during her tenth vision on June 9, 1946, saw stars everywhere in the air, then **suddenly in front of her, a cardinal's hat. A sign in the form of an X appeared and covered it over. Rome was shown to her. There was a dispute over the pope. She saw numerous bishops who were not Roman Catholics. A voice rang out:** *"What A Pity!"* [1]

A Short Time After The Warning

We Will Have A Masonic Pope – The Black Pope
Of Sadie Jaramillo's Vision

Sadie Jaramillo, on June 16, 1996, had a vision during Mass, after communion, as she was giving her thanksgiving. She states, "I saw something very strange. **There was this man, dressed in black, in black pontifical robes, with a black miter, the type the Pope wears."** [6]

At 7:00 P.M., June 16, 1996, Sadie was told by Our Blessed Mother, "This man exists and awaits his moment to take the seat of Vicar of Christ, though he, along with many, are the *wolves in sheep clothing.* This day is near. This storm will break, not only in the Body of Christ, but then onto the world." [6]

On March 20, 1997, Sadie had an interior vision of Jesus, as in the Image of Divine Mercy, an illuminated cross above Him, a great chain, like the ones that anchor ships, and Our Lady standing on Satan's head. Sadie said: "I see myriads and myriads of angels. I also see a capital A with another A upside down resting on the first A. I later learn that **this is a Masonic lodge symbol. Above this a Pope's Miter in black."**

Sadie, writing about her understanding of this vision, **said: "The Masonic symbol, with the black Pope's Miter above it, represents the Antipope who will reign with the Antichrist.** The fact that these two

56

visions are side by side represents the **short length of time from the Warning to the revelation of the antipope and Antichrist."** [6]

The Black Pope's Reign Will Be Shortened

On March 31, 1997, Jesus told Sadie: "The black Pope will soon be seated and reign with the one who opposes Me. From the time of the illumination of your souls to the time of the revelation of this man of perdition will be short. (I hear the Number 6). And he will reign 6 and 6 and 6 more. **Of this be assured: The Queen of Mercy has obtained the shortening of his reign. Scripture says 'if this time had not been shortened, not one would survive.'"** [6]

My Vicar Will Go Into Exile Until His Martyrdom

Jesus told Sadie Jaramillo on July 5, 1996: "My Vicar will go into exile until his martyrdom. My final act of Mercy, that which My Faustina prepared the world for, through that image, will be fulfilled .... all you who will accept My Teachings and Words of everlasting life, who still look towards the Chair of Peter, My Vicar, as your true representative of Me, you are anchored safely in My Heart and the Heart of My Mother, two yet one, and the storm will not prevail.... **I have never left My Church, though in many churches I have been put out.** I will see you through the storm, and you will increase in courage and in strength, for **it will be by the very power of God those destined to be My Remnant will go through these final dark moments. Just as I opened the way, in many other times of persecution, so it will be again."** [6]

On August 12, 1996, Jesus told Sadie Jaramillo, "There will be intense changes in the weather soon. Prepare! *The wolves who hide in sheep's clothing* **are known to Me as they prepare to remove My True Vicar from the Chair of Peter. Prepare for the priests who will flee."** [6]

On December 9, 1996, Our Blessed Mother told Sadie: "For the souls of my priests lie perilously in danger. Some have not the courage to fight and stand against the errors of disobedience. The darkness that comes will reveal the True Light. It will separate My faithful from those who will gleefully embrace **the great Apostasy of the Church.** Up to now changes have been through rebellious acts of disobedience, but **very soon the cry will resound from East to West – No to Rome! (No to the Holy Father!)"** [6]

St. Pius X (d. 1914): "I saw one of my successors taking flight over the bodies of his brethren. He will take refuge in disguise somewhere; and after a short retirement he will die a cruel death. The present wickedness of the world is only the beginning of the sorrows which must take place before the end of the world." [18]

Pedro Regis

Two Popes (Two Kings), Only One The True Successor Of Peter

The Existence Of Two Kings Will Spread Great Confusion Throughout The World

March 19, 2005. Message 2497– Dear Sons and Daughters – **A great ship will be on the high seas, and all aboard will be surprised by Christ in front of them. A divided reign and an empty chair. The existence of two kings will spread great confusion throughout the world, but God will come to the aid of His people. His chosen ones will not be left helpless. Trust in the Lord.**

March 29, 2008. Message 2977 – from Our Lady of Peace. Dear Sons and Daughters – You live in the moments of great tribulations. Don't go away from The Lord. **A great ship will split in two, and the hour of great sorrow will come to My poor children....**

June 28, 2008. Message 3016 – from Our Lady of Peace. Dear Sons and Daughters – *When the reign is divided, a king will go with science and deny God and His works.* **Many men of faith will become indifferent and there will be great suffering for the Church....**

July 8, 2008. Message 3020 – from Our Lady of Peace, Anguera, Bahia,

58

Brazil. Dear Sons and Daughters – **When the reign is divided, there will be great disorder among religious leaders. Many faithful men and women will wander aimlessly, full of doubts. They won't know what side to be on.** A wound will be opened in the heart of the Church....

December 23, 2008. Message 3098 – from Our Lady of Peace, given in Maceió, Brazil. Dear Sons and Daughters – The Church of My Jesus will carry a heavy cross. **The day will come when there will be two thrones, but only on one will be the true successor of Peter. It will be a time of great spiritual confusion for the Church.** Stay with the truth. Listen to what I say and remain firm in the faith....

The Antichrist

Satan, Antichrist And New World Order
The Man Of Iniquity Will Establish Himself
Within The Church

On September 19, 1846, at La Salette, Leece version, Our Blessed Mother, in an apparition approved by the Church, **stated: "Rome will lose the Faith and become the seat of the Antichrist."** [7]

The identities of Antichrist are discussed by St. Augustine and St. Thomas: a.) a church, the mass of people, the whole body of Satan, the false church and false christ, and b.) the real person, the Antichrist possessed by Satan.

The Antichrist And The Temple Of God

Is the temple in which the Antichrist sits to be adored as God the rebuilt Temple of God in Israel (as some of the Fathers of the Church such as St. Irenaeus and St. Cyril believed), or is it a Church, a question raised by St. Augustine?

St. Augustine held: "It is not certain what temple the Antichrist will use to accept divine worship, whether the ruined and restored temple of Solomon or a Church. Yet the Apostle, it would seem, would not call a temple of an idol or demon the temple of God. Some think therefore, that the Antichrist in this passage refers not specifically to the prince of evil himself, but to his whole body, the mass of people who adhere to him as their prince. Others think that the Antichrist will act as if he were the temple of God himself, as if he were the Church itself."

St. Thomas said: "that others maintain that never will Jerusalem or the temple be rebuilt and that he (Antichrist) will sit in the Church in the sense that many from the Church will receive him. St. Augustine says that he (the Antichrist) with his adherents will form a church just as Christ and his followers are a Church."

No Valid Public Mass

Except for an underground Church, subject to intense bloody persecution, worse by far than any prior persecution of the Church, **there will be no valid public Mass, no valid public sacrifice for 1290 days, until the fall of Antichrist, when he will be cast into Hell with his false prophet for all eternity.**

A False Religion Will Appear

Jeanne Le Royer, Sister Mary of the Nativity, born 1731, died 1798, a visionary, **said that she saw that "when the Second Coming of Christ approaches, a bad priest will do much to harm the Church.... When the time of the reign of Antichrist is near, a false religion will appear which will be opposed to the unity of God and His Church. This will cause the greatest schism the world has ever known."[32]**

My People Numbered Like Sheep For The Antichrist

Jennifer – Words From Jesus

5/11/04
3:30 PM
My people, do you not see how the earth is showing you the signs of the depth of your sins? **You have seen storm after storm and there will be catastrophic earthquakes that will separate the land.** My people, you are living in historic times and so many of you are spending your time speaking righteously for the ways of the world and deny My laws, My ways. Speak for the world and your punishment will be severe and swift for your willingness to live for the immorality of the world.

You have tried to simplify your lives with your latest means of communication, yet I warn you to be on guard for these latest tracking devices will soon track your movement for you will become like numbered sheep to the authorities of this false messiah, this antichrist. The battle has begun to escalate and you will not be spared for the more you strive for holiness the greater the fight for Satan seeks your soul. *Do not lose hope or become discouraged for I will never abandon My people.*

You are here to fulfill your mission not to live a life of comfort by worldly possessions.

10/27/04
5:30 PM
My people, you will be gathered and numbered by the authorities for the antichrist. Do not yield to his ways for he speaks a language that is not of Me. Do not be fooled by this false messiah for he is soon to rise and his eyes speak evil. He will come to you at the point when you are weak and claim to be the one who comes to save you by his miracles.

Again, I say to you, it is I, Jesus, who was and is and is to come. I do not come to promise you things of this world, rather your reward will come in the kingdom.

61

Do not become one of his numbered sheep for he is a false shepherd led by the true prince of darkness. The times are upon you for *My Church is going to undergo great persecution* for many will be martyred for their willingness to follow Me. Do not shy away from the truth for all who live the truth will be saved.

My Chosen Sons, Prepare And Guide Your Flock, Defend My Church

Jennifer – Words From Jesus

2/15/05
9:00 PM
My chosen sons, prepare for your flock will soon come running. Take heed to your brother, the Holy Father, by being obedient to his guidance. *It is time to defend the truth for there is no middle line.* There is a time to be obedient and a time to be obedient to the truth and the true teachings of My Church.

Days of great change are upon you. **You will be tried in the fire by the authorities who represent this false messiah, this antichrist. You will be called to your time of crucifixion of martyrdom.** This is not a time to run in fear for **this is why you were called, just as Peter, to defend My Church, to guide your flock closer to the kingdom.**

Modern Revelations About The Appearance Of The Antichrist

Eileen George, a housewife and mother from Massachusetts, who has the support of her diocesan bishop, several cardinals and bishops, and many priests, is reported as receiving visions and messages from God the Father and Jesus.

On February 20, 1982, God the Father told Eileen George: "There will be a World War III and it will be started by a man who wears

the turban of the faith, a Moslem. He will be an anti-Christ put on earth by Lucifer. Yet there is a more powerful one to rise in Syria, when this one has accomplished his work. He will cause destruction and pain. He will cause heartbreak and tears, and a great persecution of Christians. The earth will tremble with earthquakes. He will be a great ruler of Satan." [29]

Christina Gallagher states she has seen visions of the Antichrist. She relates: "I was seeing this man time and time again. I had no idea who he was at first. I just saw his face and his head. I saw him a number of times and I didn't think there was anything wrong with him, but I used to feel from him a sort of horror. There was something different about his eyes. His eyes were so piercing. I could feel his eyes penetrate me and I didn't like it. Now, I didn't know what to make of this so I asked God one day, talking in prayer. I said: 'Dear God, who is this?' much like the way I had asked Catherine of Siena who she was. The next thing I knew I heard an echo of the Virgin Mary's voice saying: 'Antichrist.' I got the shock of my life. I've seen this man a number of times since then, but I just ask the Precious Blood of Jesus to cover me.

He's a man in his fifties. But he has a round face and he's bald on top with very short black hair, in a fine haircut. He would remind me of somebody like a bishop. There's something very strange and very peculiar about his eyes. They were dark brown or black. I'd say he was not a bad looking man. From what I can understand of what Our Blessed Mother has said about antichrist, there will be a number of them; a number in the world right now who are 'anti-christs' or 'anti' of Christ.

If he's not the Antichrist, I wonder why the Lord permitted me to see him and hear the words 'antichrist'. Because I didn't know anything about the antichrist at that particular stage in my life. I don't think it would be given to me otherwise. The Virgin Mary said to me: 'Few realize how soon the Antichrist will raise himself up.' There are many antichrists now, but one, as time goes on, will be elected at the top. I have recently been told by the Heavenly Father, in the course of a message, 'He who is anti of Me is now in the flesh'"....

In another description of this antichrist Christina stated: "His face has a sallow complexion. His hair was cut short and it was very black. He had a roundish bold-looking face with very dark eyes. He was broad-shouldered. His looks were piercing and penetrating. They were unusual. He did not smile. He seemed to be a priest or a bishop, I'm not saying he was. I've seen him twenty, twenty-five times; always the same. I would know him instantly if I saw him on television or in reality. I would know him instantly." She says she was shown this man and during each apparition, she heard Our Blessed Mother's voice repeat the word '**Antichrist**'."

Christina in late 1991 was given three dates and told to observe what would happen on those dates. "The three dates are all linked with the power of the antichrist to get control of the governments of the world, and so the money of the world, and to render it almost impossible for people to exercise their own rights and freedom." Christina added: "I know it is linked up to the Maastricht Treaty and the uniting of the currencies. This is through the Maastricht Referendum." [36]

The Mark Of The Beast

Don't Take The Mark Of The Beast
The Mark Of Antichrist

Sadie Jaramillo, on August 13, 1997, received a message from Jesus after He told her to write Jeremiah Chapter 25, verses 4 - 7 and 29 - 35, which she did from Douay - Rheims Bible.

Jesus said: "It is so! I have sent My prophets to proclaim the impending events and many refuse to hearken to My plea, to My requests, the request to return one and all to the Lord Your God that you would know salvation, peace and joy!

My Mother, assumed into the Glory of Paradise, has left countless signs among all God's children from one corner of this earth to the

64

other. And they still have not believed! **Amidst great confusion, amidst great turmoil, amidst great signs shown forth in the heavens, many will come to believe.**

And those who refuse will not believe those whom I have sent, but will believe he who comes to say he is Christ. His signs they will believe and accept. But woe to them who receive his mark. You shall seek death, but death will not come. And when you die, you will condemn yourself to the eternal fires of hell...." [6]

**My Churches Will Soon Be Silenced
And The Division Will Multiply
Leading Up To The Coming Of Antichrist**

Jennifer – Words From Jesus

3/27/05
9:00 PM (Easter Sunday)
The bells of My churches will soon be silenced and the division will multiply leading up to the coming of the antichrist. You will see the coming of a war that will have nations rising up against one another. My people, I have warned you that it is because of the war in the womb that My Father's just hand is about to strike.

**Our Lady Has Worked To Prevent
As Long As Possible
The Reign Of Antichrist**

On the same day, August 13, 1997, Mary, Queen of Heaven said to Sadie Jaramillo: "I have ceaselessly and tirelessly worked to this end: To prevent as long as possible this justice, and the reign of the Antichrist.... Tell all to trust in Jesus because of His Mercy: **Protection is afforded My remnant**. 'For you have not seen, but believed,' Do not fear in the coming days for what you will see. **The decree of God is against His enemies, not His children**. There is Triumph soon and in the midst of great difficulties, Triumph reigns!...." [6]

Our Lady Has Shortened The Length Of Antichrist's Reign

On March 25, 1998, Our Blessed Mother told Sadie Jaramillo: My little sorrowful rose, ... "The time left now is nearly expired. My children do you not understand? Though the warning of man's conscience was to have come long ago, this would certainly have meant that the length of the Antichrist's reign would have been longer! As it is now, I have shortened the length of his reign....

The Fall Of Antichrist

Our Blessed Mother, at La Salette, France on September 19, 1846, in a vision with the local Bishop's Imprimatur, told Melanie about bloody wars, famines, plagues and infectious diseases, rain with a fearful rain of animals, thunderstorms which will shake cities, earthquakes which will swallow up countries, that the Church will be in eclipse, the world will be in dismay. Pagan Rome will disappear.

Our Blessed Mother told Melanie that Enoch and Eli will come and preach with the might of God, and are put to death, pagan Rome will disappear. "At that time the Beast will rise proudly in the air to go to Heaven. He will be smothered by the breath of the Archangel St. Michael, fall and the earth which will have been in a continuous series of evolutions for three days, will open up its fiery bowels; and he will be plunged for eternity with all his followers into the everlasting chasms of hell. And then water and fire will purge the earth and consume the work's of men's pride and all will be renewed. God will be served and glorified." [7]

Jeanne Le Royer, Sister Mary of the Nativity, stated: "With the fall of Antichrist will come severe earthquakes, thick darkness will cover the Earth, the ground will open in thousands of places under the feet of the inhabitants and cities, towns, castles and an immense number of people will be swallowed up. One-half of that immense crowd on Mt. Olivet will be cast in the abyss with Antichrist. The ocean will move frightfully and waves arise heavenward overflowing the coast

and inundate the earth. All these calamities are only to frighten the remaining into accepting the Grace and Mercy of God. Fifteen days after the ascension of Henoch and Elias into heaven, terrible catastrophes will come upon the earth: **most severe earthquakes, tidal waves inundating much of the earth's surface, culminating in a thick darkness over the entire earth."** [44]

Chapter 5

Medjugorje – The Fulfillment Of Fatima

Father Tomislav Vlasic's Letter To Saint Pope John Paul II On December 2, 1983

The following is a letter sent to the Pope by Father Tomislav Vlasic of Medjugorje on December 2, 1983, providing information to the Vatican on the apparitions and their messages. The letter reads as follows:

"After the apparition of the Blessed Virgin on November 30, 1983, Maria Pavlovic came to see me and said, 'The Madonna says that the Supreme Pontiff and the Bishop must be advised immediately of the urgency and great importance of the message of Medjugorje'."

"This letter seeks to fulfill that duty.

"1. Five young people (Vicka Ivankovic, Maria Pavlovic, Ivanka Ivankovic, Ivan Dragicevic, and Jakov Colo) see an apparition of the Blessed Virgin every day. The experience in which they see her is a fact that can be checked by direct observation. It has been filmed. During the apparitions, the youngsters do not react to light, they do not hear sounds, they do not react if someone touches them, they feel that they are beyond time and space.

"All of the youngsters basically agree that:
• "We see the Blessed Virgin just as we see anyone else. We pray with her, we speak to her, and we can touch her."
• "The Blessed Virgin says that world peace is at a critical stage. She repeatedly calls for reconciliation and conversion."

• "She has promised to leave *a visible sign* for all humanity at the site of the apparitions of Medjugorje."

• "The period preceding this *visible sign* is a time of grace for conversion and deepening the faith."

• "The Blessed Virgin has promised to disclose *ten secrets* to us. So far, Vicka Ivankovic has received eight. Marija Pavlovic received the ninth one on December 8,1983. Jakov Colo, Ivan Dragicevic and Ivanka Ivankovic have each received nine. Only Mirjana Dragicevic has received all ten."

• "These apparitions are the last apparitions of the Blessed Virgin on earth. That is why they are lasting so long and occurring so frequently."

"2. The Blessed Virgin no longer appears to Mirjana Dragicevic. The last time she saw one of the daily apparitions was Christmas 1982. Since then the apparitions have ceased for her, except on her birthday (March 18, 1983). Mirjana knew that this would occur.

"According to Mirjana, the Madonna confided the tenth and last secret to her during the apparition on December 25, 1982. She also disclosed the dates on which the different secrets will come to pass. The Blessed Virgin has revealed to Mirjana many things about the future, more than to any of the other youngsters so far. For that reason I am reporting below what Mirjana told me during our conversation on November 5, 1983. I am summarizing the substance of her account, without word-for-word quotations.

"**Mirjana said that before the *visible sign* is given to humanity, there will be *three warnings* to the world.** The warnings will be in the form of events on earth. Mirjana will be a witness to them. Three days before one of the admonitions, Mirjana will notify a priest of her choice. The witness of Mirjana will be a confirmation of the apparitions and a stimulus for the conversion of the world.

"After the admonitions, the *visible sign* will appear on the site of the apparitions in Medjugorje for all the world to see. The sign will be given as a testimony to the apparitions and in order to call the people back to the faith.

"The ninth and tenth secrets are serious. They concern chastisement for the sins of the world. Punishment is inevitable, for we cannot expect the whole world to be converted. The punishment can be diminished by prayer and penance, but it cannot be eliminated. Mirjana says that one of the evils that threatened the world, the **one contained in the seventh secret, has been averted**, thanks to **prayer and fasting**. That is why the Blessed Virgin continues to encourage **prayer and fasting**: 'You have forgotten that through **prayer and fasting** you can avert war and suspend the laws of nature.'

"After the first admonition, the others will follow in a rather short time. Thus, people will have some time for conversion.

"That interval will be a period of grace and conversion. **After the visible sign appears, those who are still alive will have little time for conversion. For that reason, the Blessed Virgin invites us to urgent conversion and reconciliation.** The invitation to prayer and penance is meant to **avert evil and war**, but most of all **to save souls**.

"According to Mirjana, the events predicted by the Blessed Virgin are near. By virtue of this experience, Mirjana proclaims to the world: 'Hurry, be converted; open your hearts to God.'

"In addition to this basic message, Mirjana related an apparition she had in 1982, which we believe sheds some light on some aspects of Church history. She spoke of an apparition in which Satan appeared to her disguised as the Blessed Virgin. Satan asked Mirjana to renounce the Madonna and follow him. That way she could be happy in love and in life. He said that following the Virgin, on the contrary, would only lead to suffering. Mirjana rejected him, and immediately the Virgin arrived and Satan disappeared. Then the Blessed Virgin gave her the following message in substance:

"Excuse me for this, but you must realize that Satan exists. One day he appeared before the throne of God and asked permission to submit the Church to a period of trial. God gave him permission to try the Church for one century. **This century is under the power of the devil; but when the secrets confided to you come to pass, his power will be destroyed.** Even now he is beginning to lose his power and has become aggressive. He is destroying marriages, creating divisions among priests and is responsible for obsessions and murder. **You must protect yourselves against these things through** *fasting* **and** *prayer*, **especially** *community prayer*. **Carry blessed objects with you. Put them in your house, and restore the use of holy water.**

"According to certain Catholic experts who have studied these apparitions, this message of Mirjana may shed light on the vision Pope Leo XIII had. According to them, it was after having had an apocalyptic vision of the future of the Church that Leo XIII introduced the prayer to Saint Michael which priests used to recite after Mass up to the time of the Second Vatican Council. **These experts say that the century of trials foreseen by Leo XIII is about to end.**

"Holy Father, I do not want to be responsible for the ruin of anyone. I am doing my best. The world is being called to conversion and reconciliation. In writing to you, Holy Father, I am only doing my duty. After drafting this letter, I gave it to the youngsters so that they might ask the Blessed Virgin whether its contents are accurate. Ivan Dragicevic relayed the following answer: 'Yes, the contents of the letter are the truth. You must notify first the Supreme Pontiff and then the Bishop.'

"This letter is accompanied by fasting and prayers that the Holy Spirit will guide your mind and your heart during this important moment in history."

Yours, in the Sacred Hearts of Jesus and Mary,
Father Tomislav Vlasic
Medjugorje, December 2, 1983

Life In The World Will Change.
Men Will Believe Like In Ancient Times

After a taped interview, Father Tomislav gave a little information about the secrets on August 15, 1983. They (the seers) say *that with the realization of the secrets entrusted to them by Our Lady, life in the world will change*! What will change and how it will change, we don't know, given that the seers don't want to say anything about the secrets."[3]

Father Tomislav continued, "**Life in the world will change. Afterwards men will believe like in ancient times**. These few words imply a lot about extraordinary events, that lie ahead and for which Our Lady came to prepare the world at Medjugorje."

Our Blessed Mother has continued to appear to these young people up to the present day. Each of them was told by Our Lady that he or she would receive ten secrets. **Mirjana, Ivanka, and Jakov have now received all ten secrets and only see Our Lady infrequently.** In 1982 Mirjana was the first visionary to receive all ten secrets. Then Our Lady said she would appear to Mirjana annually on Mirjana's birthday, March 18th. Our Lady said she would appear more frequently to Mirjana when we were closer to the events. Since August 2, 1987 Our Lady has been appearing regularly to Mirjana on the 2nd day of each month. Our Lady also appears on Mirjana's birthday. **Ivan, Vicka, and Marija each have nine secrets and still see Our Lady daily.**

Our Lady's main messages are prayer, fasting, faith, conversion, and peace. She stressed that peace can only come from conversion or reconciliation with God and with one's neighbor.

The messages have not changed in tone or substance nor have the secrets yet been revealed.

Our Lady's apparitions at Medjugorje are considered by many to be the fulfillment of Fatima. In the United States countless prayer groups and apostolates have sprung up as a direct result of Medjugorje.

After many years of Our Lady appearing as Queen of Peace, a war of diabolical ethnic cleansing broke out there. UN intervention brought the wars to a close. (Ten Day War Of Slovenian Independence, 1991), Croatian War of Independence (1991–1995), Bosnian War (1992–1995), Kosovo War (1998–1999). The war in Bosnia-Herzegovina was televised almost every night.

In the message of September 25, 1992, Mary explained how Satan was trying to destroy everything which she and her Son Jesus were building up, *"Dear children! Today also I wish to tell you: I am with you in these restless days in which Satan wishes to destroy everything which I and my Son Jesus are building up. In a special way he wishes to destroy your souls. He wishes to guide you as far away as possible from Christian life as well as from the commandments, to which the Church is calling you so you may live them. Satan wishes to destroy everything which is holy in you and around you. Therefore, little children pray, pray, pray, in order to be able to comprehend all which God is giving you through my coming!"*

Our Lady has appeared in Medjugorje every day since June 24, 1981 to the present.

Our Lady still appears to three of the visionaries daily (Marija, Vicka, and Ivan).

Beginning on March 1, 1984, Our Lady began giving Weekly Messages to St. James parish in Medjugorje and to the World.

On January 25, 1987, Our Lady began giving these Messages on the 25th of each Month.

The 25th of the month message is always given by Our Lady to the visionary Marija.

Some Of Our Lady's Teachings At Medjugorje In Messages Through The Years

Our Lady has given many messages over the years. Among these we have selected several to highlight some of her teaching.

January 10,1983
Mirjana shared with Father Tomislav Vlasic that during the year and a half that she had been receiving apparitions, she had experienced the maternal love and intimacy of Our Lady and questioned Her why God could so "Mercilessly" send sinners to Hell forever. Our Lady responded, **"Men who go to Hell no longer want to receive any benefit from God.** They do not repent nor do they cease to revolt and to blaspheme. They make up their mind to live in Hell and do not contemplate leaving it."

Regarding Purgatory: "In Purgatory there are different levels; the lowest is close to Hell and the highest gradually draws near to

74

Heaven. It is not on All Souls Day, but at Christmas, that the greatest number of souls leave Purgatory. There are in Purgatory, souls who pray ardently to God, but for whom no relative or friend prays on earth. God makes them benefit from the prayers of other people. It happens that God permits them to manifest themselves in different ways, close to their relatives on earth, in order to remind men of the existence of Purgatory and to solicit their prayers to come close to God who is just, but good. **The majority of people go to Purgatory. Many go to Hell. A small number go directly to Heaven."**

October 21, 1983 "The important thing is to pray to the Holy Spirit so that He may descend on you. When one has Him, one has everything. People make a mistake when they turn only to the saints to request something."

In 1983 Messages Our Lady Taught About Belief, Faith And Prayer

"The most important thing is to believe."
"Faith cannot be alive without prayer."
"All prayers are good, if they are said with faith."
"The most beautiful prayer is the Creed.""The Mass is the greatest prayer of God. You will never be able to understand its greatness. That is why you must be perfect and humble at Mass, and you should prepare yourselves for it."

April 3, 1986
"Dear children! I wish to call you to a living of the Holy Mass. There are many of you who have sensed **the beauty of the Holy Mass**, but there are also those who come unwillingly. I have chosen you, dear children, but Jesus gives you His graces in the Mass. Therefore, **consciously live the Holy Mass and let your coming to it be a joyful one. Come to it with love and make the Mass your own.** Thank you for having responded to my call."

July 5, 1984
"Dear children; Today I wish to tell you, **"Always pray before your work and end your work with prayer. If you do that, God will bless**

you and your work. These days you have been praying too little and working too much. Pray, therefore. In prayer you will find rest. Thank you for responding to my call."

August 14, 1984: This apparition was unexpected. Ivan was praying in his house and then started getting ready to go to church for the evening service, when Our Lady appeared to him and asked him to relate this message to the people:**"I ask the people to pray with me these days. Pray all the more. Fast strictly on Wednesday and Friday. Say every day at least one Rosary: Joyful, sorrowful and glorious mysteries."** Our Lady asked the people to accept this message with a firm will. She asked this in a special way from the parishioners and believers of the surrounding places.

October 18, 1984
"Dear children; Today I ask you to read the Bible in your homes every day and let it be in a visible place there so that it always encourages you to read and pray. Thank you for your response to my call."

August 25, 1996
"Dear children! Listen, because I wish to speak to you and to invite you to have more faith and trust in God, who loves you immeasurably. Little children, you do not know how to live in the grace of God, that is why I call you all anew, to carry the word of God in your heart and in thoughts. **Little children, place the Sacred Scripture in a visible place in your family, and read and live it.** Teach your children, because if you are not an example to them, children depart into godlessness. Reflect and pray and then God will be born in your heart and your heart will be joyous. Thank you for having responded to my call."

April 25, 2005
"Dear children! Also today, I call you to renew prayer in your families. By prayer and the reading of Sacred Scripture, may the Holy Spirit, who will renew you, enter into your families. In this way, you will become teachers of the faith in your family. By prayer and your love, the world will set out on a better way and love will begin to rule in the world. Thank you for having responded to my call."

76

Power Of Prayer And Fasting

July 21, 1982
Concerning Purgatory: **"There are many souls in Purgatory.** There are also persons who have been consecrated to God – some priests, some religious. **Pray for their intentions, at least The Lord's Prayer, the Hail Mary, and the Glory Be seven times each, and the Creed. I recommend it to you. There is a large number of souls who have been in Purgatory for a long time because no one prays for them."**

Concerning fasting: **"The best fast is on bread and water. Through fasting and prayer, one can stop wars, one can suspend the laws of nature.** *Charity cannot replace fasting. Those who are not able to fast can sometimes replace it with prayer, charity, and a Confession; but everyone, <u>except the sick, must fast.</u>"*

November 6, 1986
"Dear children! Today I wish to call you to pray daily for souls in purgatory. For every soul prayer and grace is necessary to reach God and the love of God. **By doing this, dear children, you obtain new intercessors who will help you in life to realize that all the earthly things are not important for you, that only Heaven is that for which it is necessary to strive.** Therefore, dear children, pray without ceasing that you may be able to help yourselves and the others to whom your prayers will bring joy. Thank you for having responded to my call."

Through Prayer And Fasting Wars Can Be Stopped

January 25, 2001
"Dear children! Today I call you to **renew prayer and fasting** with even greater enthusiasm until prayer becomes a joy for you. Little children, the one who prays is not afraid of the future and the one who fasts is not afraid of evil. **Once again, I repeat to you: only through** *prayer and fasting* **also wars can be stopped – wars of your unbelief and fear for the future.** I am with you and am teaching you little children: your peace and hope are in God. That is why draw closer to God and put Him in the first place in your life. Thank you for having responded to my call."

January 2, 2006
"Dear children, my Son is born. Your Savior is here with you. What prevents your hearts from receiving Him? What all is false within them? Purify them by *fasting and prayer*. Recognize and receive my Son. He alone gives you true peace and true love. The way to eternal life is He – my Son! Thank you."

Through Your Prayers You May Stop Satan's Plan

October 25, 2008
"Dear children! In a special way I call you all to pray for my intentions so that, through your prayers, you may stop satan's plan over this world, which is further from God everyday, and which puts itself in the place of God and is destroying everything that is beautiful and good in the souls of each of you. Therefore, little children, arm yourselves with *prayer and fasting* so that you may be conscious of how much God loves you, and carry out God's will. Thank you for having responded to my call."

March 2, 2011
"Dear children! My Motherly Heart suffers tremendously as I look at my children who persistently put what is human before what is of God, at my children who, despite everything that surrounds them and despite all the signs that are sent to them, think that they can walk without my Son. They cannot! They are walking to eternal perdition. That is why I am gathering you, who are ready to open your heart to me, you who are ready to be apostles of my love, to help me; so that by living God's love you may be an example to those who do not know it. May *fasting and prayer* give you strength in that, and I bless you with the Motherly blessing in the name of the Father, and of the Son, and of the Holy Spirit. Thank you."

October 25, 2012
"Dear children! Today I call you to pray for my intentions. Renew *fasting and prayer* because satan is cunning and attracts many hearts to sin and perdition. I call you, little children, to holiness and to live in grace. Adore my Son so that He may fill you with His peace and

love for which you yearn. Thank you for having responded to my call."

Pray The Rosary To Defeat Satan

August 8, 1985
"Dear children, today I call you especially now to advance against satan by means of prayer. Satan wants to work still more now that you know he is at work. Dear children, put on the armor for battle and with the Rosary in your hand, defeat him! Thank you for having responded to my call."

June 12, 1986
"Dear children! Today I call you to begin to pray the Rosary with a living faith. That way I will be able to help you. You, dear children, wish to obtain graces, but you are not praying.

I am not able to help you because you do not want to get started. **Dear children, I am calling you to pray the Rosary and that your Rosary be an obligation which you shall fulfill with joy.** That way you shall understand the reason I am with you this long. I desire to teach you to pray. Thank you for having responded to my call."

Complete Surrender To God

February 25, 1988
"Dear children, today again I am calling you to prayer and complete surrender to God. You know that I love you and am coming here out of love, so I could show you the path of peace and salvation for your souls. I want you to obey me and not permit satan to seduce you. Dear children, satan is very strong and, therefore, I ask you to dedicate your prayers to me so that those who are under his influence may be saved. Give witness by your life, sacrifice your lives for the salvation of the world. I am with you and I am grateful to you, but in Heaven you shall receive the Father's reward which He has promised you. Therefore, little children, do not be afraid. If you pray, satan cannot injure you even a little, because you are God's children and He is watching over you. Pray, and let the Rosary

always be in your hands as a sign to satan that you belong to me. Thank you for having responded to my call."

In Prayer You Shall Perceive The Greatest Joy And The Way Out Of Every Situation That Has No Exit

March 28, 1985
"Dear children! Today I wish to call you to pray, pray, pray! **In prayer you shall perceive the greatest joy and the way out of every situation that has no exit.** Thank you for starting up prayer. Each individual is dear to my heart. And I thank all who have urged prayer in their families. Thank you for having responded to my call."

Blessed Objects

July 18, 1985
"**Dear children! Today I call you to place more blessed objects in your homes and that everyone put some blessed objects on their person.** Bless all the objects and thus Satan will attack you less because you will have armor against him. Thank you for having responded to my call."

Love

November 7, 1985
"**Dear children! I am calling you to the love of neighbor and love toward the one from whom evil comes to you.** In that way with love you will be able to discern the intentions of hearts. Pray and love, dear children! **By love you are able to do even that which you think is impossible.** Thank you for having responded to my call."

April 25, 1995
"**Dear children! Today I call you to love. Little children, without love you can neither live with God nor with brother.** Therefore, I call all of you to open your hearts to the love of God that is so great and open to each one of you. **God, out of love for man, has sent me among you to show you the path of salvation, the path of love. If you do not first love God, then you will neither be able to love neighbor nor the one you hate. Therefore, little children, pray and through prayer you will discover love.** Thank you for having responded to my call."

Let Holy Mass Be Your Life

April 25, 1988
"**Dear children!** God wants to make you holy. Therefore, through me He is inviting you to complete surrender. **Let holy Mass be your life.** Understand that the church is God's palace, the place in which I gather you and want to show you the way to God. Come and pray. Neither look at others nor slander them, but rather, let your life be a testimony on the way of holiness. Churches deserve respect and are set apart as holy **because God, who became man, dwells in them day and night.** Therefore, little children, believe and pray that the Father increase your faith, and then ask for whatever you need. I am with you and I am rejoicing because of you conversion and I am protecting you with my motherly mantle. Thank you for having responded to my call."

Pray For The Shepherds

April 2, 2013
"**Dear children; I am calling you to be one with my Son in spirit. I am calling you, through prayer, and the Holy Mass when my Son unites Himself with you in a special way, to try to be like Him; that, like Him, you may always be ready to carry out God's will and not seek the fulfillment of your own. Because, my children, it is according to God's will that you are and that you exist, and without God's will you are nothing. As a mother, I am asking you to speak about the glory of God with your life because, in that way, you will also glorify yourself in accordance to His will.** *Show humility and love for your neighbor to everyone.* **Through such humility and love, my Son saved you and opened the way for you to the Heavenly Father. I implore you to keep opening the way to the Heavenly Father for all those who have not come to know Him and have not opened their hearts to His love. By your life, open the way to all those who still wander in search of the truth. My children, be my apostles who have not lived in vain.** *Do not forget that you will come before the Heavenly Father and tell Him about yourself. Be ready!* **Again I am warning you, pray for those whom my Son called, whose hands He blessed and whom He gave as a gift to you. Pray, pray, pray for your shepherds. Thank you.**"

81

Prayer Of Consecration To Heart Of Jesus, And To Mary's Immaculate Heart,

October 25, 1988
"Dear children! My invitation that you live the messages which I am giving you is a daily one, specially, little children, because I want to draw you closer to the Heart of Jesus. **Therefore, little children, I am inviting you today to the prayer of consecration to Jesus, my dear Son, so that each of you may be His. And then I am inviting you to the consecration of my Immaculate Heart. I want you to consecrate yourselves as parents, as families and as parishioners so that all belong to God through my heart.** Therefore, little children, pray that you comprehend the greatness of this message which I am giving you. I do not want anything for myself, rather all for the salvation of your soul. Satan is strong and therefore, you, little children, **by constant prayer, press tightly against my motherly heart.** Thank you for having responded to my call."

May 25, 2004
"Dear children! Also today, I urge you to consecrate yourselves to my Heart and to the Heart of my Son Jesus. Only in this way will you be mine more each day and you will inspire each other all the more to holiness. **In this way joy will rule your hearts and you will be carriers of peace and love.** Thank you for having responded to my call."

Find Yourself A Special Time When You Could Pray In Peace And Humility

November 25, 1988
"Dear children! I call you to prayer, to have an encounter with God in prayer. God gives Himself to you, but He wants you to answer in your own freedom to his invitation. **That is why little children during the day, find yourself a special time when you could pray in peace and humility, and have this meeting with God the creator.** I am with you and I intercede for you in front of God, so watch in vigil, so that every encounter in prayer be the joy of your contact with God. Thank you for having responded to my call."

I Call You To Peace

December 25, 1988
"Dear children! I call you to peace. Live it in your heart and all around you, so that all will know peace, peace that does not come from you but from God. Little children, today is a great day. Rejoice with me. Glorify the Nativity of Jesus through the peace that I give you. **It is for this peace that I have come as your Mother, Queen of Peace.** Today I give you my special blessing. Bring it to all creation, so that all creation will know peace. Thank you for having responded to my call."

Satan Is Strong And Wishes To Destroy
Human Life, Nature And The Planet

January 25, 1991
"Dear children! Today, like never before, I invite you to prayer. Let your prayer be a prayer for peace. **Satan is strong and desires to destroy not only human life, but also nature and the planet on which you live.** Therefore, dear children, pray that through prayer you can protect yourselves with God's blessing of peace. God has sent me among you so that I may help you. If you so wish, grasp for the rosary. *Even the rosary alone can work miracles in the world and in your lives. I bless you and I remain with you for as long as it is God's will.* Thank you for not betraying my presence here and I thank you because your response is serving the good and the peace."

I Invite You To Become Missionaries Of My Messages

February 25, 1995
"Dear children! Today I invite you to become missionaries of my messages, which I am giving here through this place that is dear to me. God has allowed me to stay this long with you and therefore, little children, I invite you to live with love the messages I give and to transmit them to the whole world, so that a river of love flows to people who are full of hatred and without peace. I invite you, little children, *to become peace where there is no peace and light where there is darkness*, so that each heart accepts the light and the way of salvation. Thank you for having responded to my call."

I Invite You To Conversion

February 25, 1996
"Dear children! Today I invite you to conversion. This is the most important message that I have given you here. Little children, I wish that each of you become a carrier of my messages. I invite you, little children, to live the messages that I have given you over these years. **This time is a time of grace. Especially now, when the Church also is inviting you to prayer and conversion.** I also, little children, invite you to live my messages that I have given you during the time since I am appearing here. Thank you for having responded to my call."

Put Prayer In The First Place In Your Families

April 25, 1996
"Dear children! Today I invite you again to put prayer in the first place in your families. Little children, when God is in the first place, then you will, in all that you do, seek the will of God. In this way your daily conversion will become easier. Little children, seek with humility that which is not in order in your hearts, and you shall understand what you have to do. **Conversion will become a daily duty that you will do with joy.** Little children, I am with you, I bless you all and I invite you to become my witnesses by prayer and personal conversion. Thank you for having responded to my call."

The Holy Spirit

May 25, 1998
"Dear children! Today I call you, through prayer and sacrifice, to prepare yourselves for the coming of the Holy Spirit. Little children, this is a time of grace and so, again, I call you to decide for God the Creator. Allow Him to transform and change you. **May your heart be prepared to listen to, and live, everything which the Holy Spirit has in His plan for each of you. Little children, allow the Holy Spirit to lead you on the way of truth and salvation towards eternal life.** Thank you for having responded to my call."

84

You Are Concerned Too Much About Material Things And Little About Spiritual Ones

April 25, 2000
"**Dear children! Also today I call you to conversion. You are concerned too much about material things and little about spiritual ones. Open your hearts and start again to work more on your personal conversion.** Decide everyday to dedicate time to God and to prayer until prayer becomes a joyful meeting with God for you. Only in this way will your life have meaning and with joy you will contemplate eternal life. Thank you for having responded to my call."

Renew Prayer In Your Families And Form Prayer Groups

September 25, 2000
"**Dear children!** Today I call you to open yourselves to prayer. May prayer become joy for you. **Renew prayer in your families and form prayer groups. In this way, you will experience joy in prayer and togetherness. All those who pray and are members of prayer groups are open to God's will in their hearts and joyfully witness God's love.** I am with you, I carry all of you in my heart and I bless you with my motherly blessing. Thank you for having responded to my call."

I Desire To Call You To A Renewal Of Family Prayer

May 20, 2011
"**Dear children, today more than ever I desire to call you to prayer. Dear children, satan wants to destroy today's families, therefore I desire to call you to a renewal of family prayer. Pray, dear children, in your families with your children, do not permit access to satan. Thank you, dear children, for also today responding to my call.**"

Youth Today Called To Participate In The Evangelization Of The World And Families

August 5, 2011

"**Dear children, also today, in this my great joy, when I see you in such a large number, I desire to call you, and to call all the youth, to** participate in the evangelization today of the world; to participate in the evangelization of families. Dear children, pray, pray, pray, and the Mother prays together with you and intercedes before Her Son. Pray, dear children. Thank you, dear children, also today, for having responded to my call."

Pray With The Heart. Read And Meditate On Sacred Scripture

February 25, 2012
"Dear children! At this time, in a special way I call you: 'pray with the heart'. Little children, you speak much and pray little. Read and meditate on Sacred Scripture, and may the words written in it be life for you. I encourage and love you, so that in God you may find your peace and the joy of living."

Relation Of Fatima To Medjugorje

At Fatima, Mary said, "In the end, my Immaculate Heart will triumph. Saint Pope John Paul II believed that the Medjugorje apparitions were a continuation and fulfillment of the apparitions at Fatima.

Mirjana on October 3, 2009 said that Mary told her, "What I started in Fatima, I will finish in Medjugorje. My heart will triumph."

Phenomena At Medjugorje

- **Rosaries Turn To Gold**
- **Three Bursts Of Light Announce The Apparition Of Our Lady**
- **The Sun Spins, Dances, Scatters Rays Of Multicolored Light, Images**

From the beginning days of the apparitions and still continuing, millions of pilgrims coming to Medjugorje have witnessed: the spinning of the sun: at different times during the day, but especially during the evening Rosary, Apparition time and Croatian Mass each evening in Medjugorje.

86

Pilgrims have reported being able to look at the sun without hurting their eyes and seeing many different things:

- the Host spinning in the center of the sun
- the sun spinning and dancing all around, scattering rays of multicolored light, moving closer and farther away from them
- different figures around the sun, such as Our Lady, The Two Hearts, crosses and others

At The Fatima Apparitions Of Our Lady

- **Our Lady Came With A Flash Of Light**
- **The October 13, 1917 Miracle Of The Sun**
- **Images Of the Holy Family, Our Lord Carrying His Cross With His Mother, Our Lady**

Fatima, Saturday, July 13, 1917

Our Lady appeared only to the children. Seeing Our Lady, Lucia asked, "What do you want of me?"

Our Lady responded, "I want you to come on the thirteenth day of next month and to continue to pray the Rosary every day in honor of Our Lady of the Rosary, in order to obtain peace for the world and the end of the war for she alone can help."

Lucia said, "I would like to ask who you are and to perform a miracle so that people will believe that you are appearing to us."

Our Lady replied, "Continue to come here every month. In October I will tell you who I am and what I want. And I will perform a miracle so that everyone may see and believe."...

Fatima, Saturday, October 13, 1917

More than 70,000 people, both believers and critics, had gathered in the field in terrible rainy weather. Many newspaper reporters and photographers were there to record the miracle or prove the children were lying. The crowd was standing in the relentless, pouring rain with mud up to their ankles. Many were praying the Rosary. Suddenly Lucia cried out, "Put down your umbrellas everyone!" **To Jacinta and Francisco she said, "Kneel down. Our Lady is coming! I have seen the flash!"** Lucia then said to Our Lady, "What do you want of me?"

Our Lady replied, *"I am the Lady of the Rosary*, I have come to warn the faithful to amend their lives and ask for pardon for their sins. They must not offend Our Lord any more, for He is already too grievously offended by the sins of men. People must say the Rosary. Let them continue saying it everyday."

She also said, "I would like a chapel built here in my honor." She added that "the war will end soon" and that the soldiers would not be long in returning to their homes.

As Our Lady was about to leave she pointed to the sun and Lucia cried out, "Look at the sun!" The rain had stopped and the black clouds parted and the sun began to whirl in the sky, scattering rays of multicolored light and lighting up the entire countryside. The sun whirled for three minutes, stopped and, then, resumed again a second and third time lasting a total of twelve minutes. The sun spun faster each time and at the end seemed to tear itself from the sky and began plunging to earth.

The crowd was on their knees, terrified, asking pardon for their sins fearing that the end of the world was at hand. **At the last moment the sun halted its descent and returned to its normal position. The miracle ended with the rain soaked earth and people's clothes now being completely dry. There were many reported healings. The miracle was seen over a 600 square mile area.** The Portugal newspaper reporters gave long and detailed accounts but newspapers in most other countries ignored the story.

As the crowd was witnessing the miracle of the sun, the children saw visions of the Holy Family, Jesus, Joseph and Mary. They also saw Our Lord carrying His cross with His Mother, Our Lady

of Sorrows. Lucia also saw **Our Lady of Mount Carmel who signifies the triumph over suffering.**

Mary Is Seen In Chapter 12 Book Of Revelation
As The Women Robed (Clothed) With The Sun

Chapter 11
[19] Then the sanctuary of God in heaven opened, and the ark of the covenant could be seen inside it. Then came flashes of lightning, peals of thunder and an earthquake and violent hail.

Chapter 12
[1] Now a great sign appeared in heaven: a woman, robed with the sun, standing on the moon, and on her head a crown of twelve stars.

Saint Pope John Paul II's Private Belief In Medjugorje

Saint Pope John Paul II did not discourage anyone regarding Medjugorje. Multiple times he pronounced his support and belief in Medjugorje in an unofficial status during private audiences at the Vatican.[49]

On April 21, 1989, Bishop Paul Hnilica, S.J., Auxiliary Bishop of Rome, reported that he had been admonished by the Holy Father for not stopping in Medjugorje on his return trip to Rome after a meeting in Moscow on behalf of the Pope. The Pope said to Bishop Hnilica, "If I wasn't the Pope, I'd be in Medjugorje already."[49]

In 1995 he said to Vicka who had brought 350 wounded servicemen to the Vatican, **"Are you not Vicka from Medjugorje? Pray to the Madonna for me, I pray for you."**[49]

"Let the people go there. They pray there." – in conversation with Archbishop Flores of San Antonio, TX when he asked, "Your Holiness, numerous persons from my diocese go to Medjugorje. I did not permit nor forbid them. What should I do?" And after further comment from the

Archbishop, "but they are inviting me to accompany them in the month of August," the Pope responded, "**Go and pray for me**." (1989)[49]

Saint Pope John Paul II had a long-standing devotion to Our Blessed Mother.

Saint Pope John Paul II was deeply committed to the messages of Medjugorje and their fruit. He sought to protect it. This happened on several occasions when the local bishop was not in favor of Medjugorje.

Saint Pope John Paul II and Cardinal Ratzinger who followed Saint Pope John Paul II as Pope Benedict XVI both protected the integrity of what was happening there in Medjugorje.

Medjugorje's Impact

In the modern era no place in the world can point to more conversions and the seeds of vocations of men and woman than in Medjugorje. It is a place of singular importance of grace for those willing to accept it.

Medjugorje's impact throughout the world is unprecedented in Church history with its fruits reaching peoples of all nations. It has been a great gift from Heaven with untold religious vocations born there.

Current Status Of Medjugorje

To date, Medjugorje has neither been approved by Roman Catholic authorities nor has it been condemned, but since March 17, 2010 it is being investigated by a Vatican Commission.

On March 17, 2010 – The Holy See Press Office published that, "An international investigative commission on Medjugorje has been constituted, under the presidency of Cardianal Camillo Ruini and dependent upon the Congregation for the Doctrine of the Faith. Said commission – made up of cardinals, bishops, specialists and experts -

will work privately, submitting the results of its work to the authority of the dicastery."

They have not come to any conclusion at the present time.

It may well be that no official approval or disapproval will be given until the secrets have been revealed. This would be the prudent course for the Church to take. Meanwhile we are free to go there and have been encouraged to go there to convert, to pray, to confess, to do penance and to fast.

Chapter 6

Divine Mercy

A Sign For The End Times
After It Will Come The Day Of Justice

Saint Faustina Kowalska

Saint Pope John Paul II, who made a pilgrimage to Saint Faustina's tomb in 1997, called her the "Great Apostle of Mercy in our day." Referring to his own connection with Saint Faustina's mission, **the Pope said at her tomb, "The message of Divine Mercy has always been near and dear to me.... (and it) in a sense forms the image of this Pontificate."**

Born on August 25, 1905 in the village of Glogowiec in Lodz County, Poland, Sister Faustina was the third of ten children. She received not quite three years of elementary school. At age 14 she went to work. **On August 1, 1925, she entered the Congregation of the Sisters of Our Lady of Mercy in which, as Sister Maria Faustina,** after a two-year novitiate **she made her first profession of vows on April 30, 1928. On May 1, 1933 she took her perpetual vows. She died on October 5, 1938.**

She began recording her mystical experiences in a diary; being nearly illiterate, it was written phonetically, without quotation marks or punctuation, and runs to nearly 700 pages.

This diary which was rewritten by Sister Xavier Olszamowska at the request of Mother General Michaela Moraczewska. This rewritten diary was not accurate or scholarly, since the copyist added or deleted certain little words and made grammatical changes and omitted certain words.

The diary was microfilmed in 1950's to safeguard it. In making copies neither the original nor the microfilm was used, only the transcript of Sr. Xavier Olszamowska. No one had compared the copied text with the original.

A bad translation reached Rome in 1958, and was labeled heretical. However, **when Karol Wojtyla (Saint Pope John Paul II) became Archbishop of K(C))rakow, he ordered a better translation made, and Vatican authorities realized that instead of heresy, the work proclaimed God's love.** It was published as *Divine Mercy in my Soul.*

Finally, a copy of the original was made and included in the Acts of the Informative Process in Cracow, certified by the Metropolitan Curia of Cracow on October 19, 1967 and signed by Fr. Stefan Marzowski. This text was verified in detail during the informative Process, and a French translation was made from this copy, included in the Informative Process and sent to Rome with the latest transcript and photocopies.

On October 21, 1965 Bishop Julian Groblicki, **specially delegated by Archbishop Karol Wojtylia (the future Saint Pope John Paul II)** began with a solemn session in the Archdiocese of Cracow, the Informative Process relating to the life and virtues of Sister Faustina.

On September 20, 1967 **His Eminence, Karol Cardinal Wojtyla,** with a solemn session, closed the Informative Process of the Servant of God in the Cracow Archdiocese.

On January 26, 1968 these Acts of the Informative Process were received in Rome by the Sacred Congregation for the Causes of Saints. On January 31, 1968 the Process of Beatification was formally inaugurated by decree of the Sacred Congregation for the Causes of Saints.

The Sacred Congregation for the Doctrine of the Faith, in its revision in 1978 withdrew the censures and reservations advanced earlier by the Holy See in relation to the writings of Sister Faustina.

Beatified on April 18, 1993 by Saint Pope John Paul II; her beatification miracle involved the cure of Maureen Digan who suffered Milroy's disease, a hereditary form of lymphedema that cost her a leg.

Canonized on April 30, 2000 by Saint Pope John Paul II; her canonization miracle involved the cure of Father Ronald P. Pytel's heart condition.

The Feast Of Divine Mercy

According to Jesus' wish, the Feast of Mercy is to be celebrated on the first Sunday after Easter. Jesus is showing us the close connection between the Easter mystery of man's Redemption and this feast. The Liturgy for this day extols God most fully in the mystery of His mercy.

The Feast of Mercy is to be but not only a day designated for the singular worship of God's Mercy, but also a day of grace for all people, particularly for sinners. Jesus attached great promises to this feast, the greatest of which is connected with the reception of Holy Communion on that day. It is the promise of complete forgiveness of sins and punishment. In other words, this grace is equal only to the one we receive in the Sacrament of Holy Baptism. The greatness of this feast lies also in the fact that everyone, even those converted that very day, may obtain any grace for the asking, if what they are asking is compatible with God's will.

I want this image, **Jesus told Saint Sister Faustina**, "... to be solemnly blessed on the first Sunday after Easter; **that Sunday is to be the Feast of Mercy**. I desire that the Feast of Mercy be a refuge and shelter for all souls, and especially for poor sinners. On that day the very depths of My tender mercy are open. I pour a whole ocean of graces upon those souls who approach the fount of My mercy. **The soul that will go to Confession and receive Holy Communion shall obtain complete forgiveness of sins and punishment**. On that day are open all the divine floodgates through which graces flow. Let no soul fear to draw near Me, even though its sins be as scarlet. The Feast of My Mercy has issued forth from My very depths for the consolation of the whole world and is confirmed in the vast depths of My tender mercies."

The preparation for this Feast is to be a Novena consisting of the recitation of the Divine Mercy Chaplet for nine days, beginning on Good Friday.

Saint Pope John Paul II's Homily April 30, 2000, During Canonization Mass For Saint Faustina

April 30, 2000, during Canonization Mass Saint Pope John Paul II in his homily said: Divine Mercy reaches human beings through the heart of Christ crucified: "My daughter, say that I am love and mercy personified", Jesus will ask Sr. Faustina (Diary, p. 374). **Christ pours out this mercy on humanity though the sending of the Spirit who, in the Trinity, is the Person-Love. And is not mercy love's "second name"** (cf. Dives in misericordia, n. 7), understood in its deepest and most tender aspect, in its ability to take upon itself the burden of any need and, especially, in its immense Capacity for forgiveness?

Today my joy is truly great in presenting the life and witness of Sr. Faustina Kowalska to the whole Church as a gift of God for our time. By Divine Providence, **the life of this humble daughter of Poland was completely linked with the history of the 20th century,** the century we have just left behind. In fact, **it was between the First and Second World Wars that Christ entrusted His message of mercy to her.** Those who remember, who were witnesses and participants in the events of those years and the horrible sufferings they caused for millions of people, know well how necessary was the message of mercy.

Jesus told Sr. Faustina: "Humanity will not find peace until it turns trustfully to divine mercy" (Diary, p. 132). Through the work of the Polish religious, this message has become linked forever to the 20th century, the last of the second millennium and the bridge to the third. It is not a new message but can be considered a gift of special enlightenment that helps us to relive the Gospel of Easter more intensely, to offer it as a ray of light to the men and women of our time....

Divine Mercy Expresses The Jubilee Spirit

The Holy Father's Remarks Before Imparting
The Final Blessing Of The Mass Of
Canonization Of Sister Mary Faustina Kowalska

April 30, 2000

1.   At the close of this celebration, in which our Easter joy is combined with that of Sr. Faustina Kowalska's canonization, I affectionately greet and thank all of you who have come from various parts of the world. I ardently hope that each of you can experience what Our Lady one day assured St. Faustina: *"I am not only the Queen of Heaven, but also the Mother of Mercy and your Mother"* (Diary, 141).

2.   The message of Divine Mercy and the image of the merciful Christ of which Sr. Faustina Kowalska speaks to us today are a vivid expression of the spirit of the Great Jubilee which the whole Church is celebrating with joy and fruitfulness. Many of you have come to honor the new saint. May her intercession bring abundant gifts of repentance, forgiveness and renewed spiritual vitality to the Church in your countries. May the thought of God's loving kindness stir up in your hearts new energies for works of faith and Christian solidarity. I cordially greet the French-speaking pilgrims, especially those who have taken part in the canonization of Sr. Faustina. Following her example, may you entrust yourselves totally to the Lord and praise him in the power of his mercy! May the renewing strength of the risen Christ fill your hearts!

3.   At the same time my thoughts embrace all my compatriots and I entrust them to the intercession of the saintly Sr. Faustina. In the new millennium may the message of the merciful love of God, who bends over all human poverty, be an endless source of hope for everyone and a

call to show active love to one's brothers and sisters. I cordially bless you all....

Decree Establishing The Sunday After Easter "Divine Mercy Sunday"

Merciful and gracious is the Lord (Ps 111:4), who out of the great love with which he loved us (Eph 2:4) and with unspeakable goodness, gave us his Only-begotten Son as our Redeemer, so that through the Death and Resurrection of this Son he might open the way to eternal life for the human race, and that the adopted children who receive his mercy within his temple might lift up his praise to the ends of the earth.

In our times, the Christian faithful in many parts of the world wish to praise that divine mercy in divine worship, particularly in the celebration of the Paschal Mystery, in which God's loving kindness especially shines forth.

Acceding to these wishes, the Supreme Pontiff John Paul II has graciously determined that in the Roman Missal, after the title "Second Sunday of Easter", there shall henceforth be added the appellation (or "Divine Mercy Sunday"), and has prescribed that the texts assigned for that day in the same Missal and the Liturgy of the Hours of the Roman Rite are always to be used for the liturgical celebration of this Sunday. The Congregation for Divine Worship and the Discipline of the Sacraments now publishes these decisions of the Supreme Pontiff so that they may take effect. Anything to the contrary not withstanding.

From the offices of the Congregation for Divine Worship and the
Discipline of the Sacraments, 5 May 2000.
Cardinal Jorge A. Median Estevez
Prefect
Francesco Pio Tamburrino
Archbishop Secretary

The Hour Of Mercy

As often as you hear the clock strike the third hour, immerse yourself completely in My mercy, adoring and glorifying it; invoke its omnipotence for the whole of the world, and particularly for poor sinners; for at that moment mercy was opened wide for every soul.

It is Jesus' desire that the moment of His Death on the Cross (3:00pm) be venerated every day; the hour which He said was the hour of grace for the whole world – mercy triumphed over justice. At this hour, we should meditate upon His sorrowful Passion because it reveals most fully the love God has for His people. At this time, Jesus wants us to worship and glorify the Mercy of God, and, by the merits of His Passion, to implore the necessary graces for ourselves and the whole world, especially sinners.

Divine Mercy

Saint Faustina Kowalska (1905-1938)
On The Second Coming
And Final Coming Of Jesus Christ

83 Write this: **Before I come as the just Judge, I am coming first as the King of Mercy.** Before the day of justice arrives, there will be given to people a sign in the heavens of this sort: *All light in the heavens will be extinguished, and there will be great darkness over the whole earth. Then the sign of the cross will be seen in the sky, and from the openings where the hands and the feet of the Savior were nailed will come forth great lights which will light up the earth for a period of me. This will take place shortly before the last day.*

625 In the evening, when I as praying, the Mother of God told me, **Your lives must be like Mine**: quiet and hidden, in increasing union with God, pleading for humanity and **preparing the world for the second coming of God.**

635 March 25. In the morning, during meditation, God's presence enveloped me in a special way, as I saw the immeasurable greatness of God and, at the same time, His condescension to creatures. **Then I saw the Mother of God, who said to me,** Oh pleasing to God is the soul that follows faithfully the inspirations of His grace! **I gave the Savior to the world; as for you, you have to speak to the world about His great mercy and prepare the world for the Second (91) Coming of Him who will come, not as a merciful Savior, but as a just Judge.** Oh, how terrible is that day! Determined is the day of justice, the day of divine wrath. The angels tremble before it. **Speak to souls about this great mercy while it is still the time for (granting) mercy.** If you keep silent now, you will be answering for a great number of souls on that terrible day. **Fear nothing.** Be faithful to the end. I sympathize with you.

793 1 am reliving these moments with Our Lady. With great longing, I am waiting for the Lord's coming. Great are my desires. I desire that all humankind come to know the Lord. I would like to prepare all nations for the coming of the Word Incarnate. O Jesus, make the fount of Your mercy gush forth more abundantly, *for humankind is seriously ill and thus has more need than ever of Your compassion. You are a bottomless sea of mercy for us sinners; and the greater the misery: the more right we have to Your mercy. You are a fount which makes all Creatures happy by Your infinite mercy.*

848 While I was saying the chaplet, **I heard a voice which said,** *Oh, what great graces I will grant to souls who say this chaplet; the very depths of My tender mercy are stirred for the sake of those who say the chaplet. Write down these words, My daughter. Speak to the world about my mercy; let all mankind recognize My unfathomable mercy. It is a sign for the end times; after it will come (230) the day of justice. While there is still time, let them have recourse to the fount of My mercy; let them profit from the Blood and Water which gushed forth for them.*

O human souls, **where are you going to hide on the day of God's anger? Take refuge now in the fount of God's mercy. O what a great multitude of souls I see! They worshiped the Divine Mercy and will be singing the hymn of praise for all eternity.**

965 Jesus looked at me and **said, Souls perish in spite of My bitter Passion. I am giving them the last hope of salvation; that is, the Feast of My Mercy. If they will not adore My mercy, they will perish for all eternity.** Secretary of My mercy, write, tell souls about this great mercy of Mine, because **the awful day, the day of My justice, is near.**

1146 (39) *(Let) the greatest sinners place their trust in My mercy. They have the right before others to trust in the abyss of My mercy. My daughter, write about My mercy towards tormented souls. Souls that make an appeal to My mercy delight Me. To such souls I grant even more graces than they ask. I cannot punish even the greatest sinner if he makes an appeal to My* **compassion, but on the contrary, I justify him in My unfathomable and inscrutable mercy.** Write, before I come as a just Judge, I first open wide the door of My mercy. He who refuses to pass through the door of My mercy must pass through the door of My justice....

The Spark That Will Prepare The World For My Final Coming

1155 *(43) The Lord gave me knowledge of His will under three aspects, so to speak, but it all comes down to one.* **The first is that souls separated from the world will burn as an offering before God's throne and beg for mercy for the whole world.... and by their entreaties they will obtain blessings for priests, and through their prayers prepare the world for the final coming of Jesus.**

1588 Today **I heard the words**: In the Old Covenant I sent prophets wielding thunderbolts to My people. **Today I am sending you with My mercy to the people of the whole world. I do not want to punish aching mankind, but I desire to heal it, pressing it to My Merciful Heart. I use punishment when they themselves force Me to do so; My hand is reluctant to take hold of the sword of justice. Before the Day of Justice I am sending the Day of Mercy.** I replied. "O my Jesus. Speak to souls Yourself, because my words are insignificant."

1732 As I was praying for Poland, **I heard the words: I bear a special love for Poland**, and if she will be obedient to My will, I *will exalt her in might and holiness.* **From her will come forth the spark that will prepare the world for My final coming.**

Other Messages About Divine Mercy

Sadie Jaramillo

The Outpouring Of Mercy Before Final Justice

On January 25, 1996, Jesus told Sadie Jaramillo: "The conversion of My Apostle Paul was a precedent set in My word. It was his experience of private revelation! As he was blinded by My light, he knew he could no longer deny the One whom he persecuted.

And now all will be caught in this moment of Mercy as My light reveals once again My persecution! For what is sin, no matter what kind, if not My persecution....

As you are illuminated in My light and this moment (that) will be just you and Me, you will see your persecution of Me, but even more you will see My great mercy and love. And this day, which will be to many as a night of terror, will pass and *then many, for whom you and others have suffered, will be brought into the harvest....* **there yet remains the outpouring of Mercy before final justice...."** [6]

The Greatest Moment Of Divine Mercy

On February 19, 1995, Our Blessed Mother told Sadie Jaramillo: "My little sorrowful rose, I request that you take down my words. ... For **the greatest moment of Divine Mercy will bring many to the foot of my Son's glorious Cross.** It will also be a time of chaos and confusion. I clarify to you, to prepare for a shortage of food items upon the arrival of this moment. And then for the control of famine which will follow.

It is the illumination of man's heart and soul. The heavens will crack with God's thunder. It will be the most awesome, holy fulfillment of Calvary; a moment to choose the path to eternal life, or to be led to eternal damnation.

The moment which will lead my remnant to begin harvesting in God's vineyard. You will tire, but you will work ceaselessly...." [6]

The Great Prodigy Of Grace And Divine Mercy

On October 13, 1999 Jesus told Sadie Jaramillo: You will see my True Church broken in two! You will see them try to stamp out belief in My True Presence! **This will happen as a result of the crowning title given to My Mother, Mary: Co-redemptrix, Mediatrix and Advocate of all Graces!**

Behold the doors open and you will see great destruction, chaos, and devastation. **But you will also behold great wonders of God and the greatest prodigy of Grace and Divine Mercy to transform those who will accept this grace!...**" [3]

The Warning Is Our Lord's Final Act Of Mercy

On July 5, 1996, Jesus told Sadie Jaramillo: "My Vicar will go into exile until his martyrdom. My final act of Mercy, that which My Faustina prepared the world for, through the image, will be fulfilled. But in the end, for My enemies, fire will rain down from heaven and the Mighty hand of God will seek you out and destroy you, every last one, and you will be no more.... I will see you through the storm, and you will increase in courage and strength, *for it will be by the very power of God those destined to be My Remnant will go through these final dark moments.*" [6]

I Am The King Of Mercy

On August 10, 1996 - 10:00 A.M. Jesus told Sadie Jaramillo: "I am the King of Mercy and mercy I desire to bestow. For the last moment before justice I call you and all to be apostles of Divine Mercy. The will of God the Father has called many, and few have responded. **Yet for the sake of those few, their prayers of the heart have been heard and much has been mitigated, so great is God's love....** [6]

Mercy Will Be Fulfilled And Justice Will Reign

On November 9, 1996 - 4:30 A.M. Jesus told Sadie Jaramillo: "Now. Nature will mirror the fury of God's anger and many will be brought to their knees. *Great confusion and chaos will abound*. This nation will soon be under martial law and many even now see the signs.

But the persecution of ethnic groups will increase, but I will have My own in the eye of the storm and it will not overtake you!

The stage is set for the fulfillment of great and wondrous things. The light that will break through the hardness of man's heart and conscience will suddenly break through, but their woes are yet to begin!

But you, My Mother's faithful..., you are My own and these I will protect as My own. You will bring in a great harvest of souls for My Father's kingdom....

But you, oh enemies of God, tremble, for God will seek you out and destroy you! Repent before it is too late! Great mercy have I shown you for justice to be postponed so many times, but no longer will this be. Mercy will be fulfilled and justice will reign!..." [6]

In The Light Of Mercy, All Will See
The Darkness Of Their Soul

Jesus told Sadie Jaramillo on September 29, 1994: "The heavens will shake, the earth will tremble, all of creation will resound with this knowledge. In the light of Mercy, all will see the darkness of their soul. The moment is here." [6]

Saint Pope John Paul II Entrusted The World To The Divine Mercy

In August 2002 Saint John Paul II entrusted the world to the Divine Mercy when he dedicated the new shrine erected in Lagiewniki a suburb of Krakow.

The Pope explained that this pilgrimage center, built over three years near the convent where Faustina Kowalska (1905-1938) lived and died, will spread the message of that Polish mystic "to all the inhabitants of the earth."

Saint John Paul II said during his homily: "In this shrine, I wish solemnly to entrust the world to Divine Mercy. I do so with the burning desire that the message of God's merciful love, proclaimed here through St. Faustina, may be made known to all the peoples of the earth and fill their hearts with hope.

How greatly today's world needs God's mercy! In every continent, from the depth of human suffering, a cry of mercy seems to rise up.

Where hatred and the thirst for revenge dominate, where war brings suffering and death to the innocent, there the grace of mercy is needed in order to settle human minds and hearts and to bring about peace.

Wherever respect for life and human dignity are lacking, there is need of God's merciful love, **in whose light we see the inexpressible value of every human being**.

Mercy is needed in order to ensure that every injustice in the world will come to an end in the splendor of truth."

Jesus' words as recorded in Saint Faustina's Kowalska diary:

"From here, there must go forth 'the spark which will prepare the world for his final coming."

This spark needs to be lighted by the grace of God.

This fire of mercy needs to be passed on to the world. In the mercy of God the world will find peace and mankind will find happiness!"

All Of Us By Praying
The Divine Mercy Chaplet
Can Avert
The Great Chastisement

March 25, 2003

(Mitigation of Chastisement is still possible. All of us by praying the Divine Mercy Chaplet can avert the Great Chastisement, as noted by Saint Pope John Paul II in a document he signed on March 25, 2003).

Chapter 7

THE WARNING

(The Illumination Of Consciences)
(A Judgment In Miniature)

Heaven's Great Intervention Of Divine Mercy

Blessed Anna Maria Taigi – The Warning

Anna Maria Taigi, Beatified in 1920 as a model of women and mothers, was not only a prophetess of our time, but one of the most extraordinary mystics in the history of the Church.

Blessed Anna Maria Taigi spoke of a great chastisement which would come to the world before which there would be an illumination of the conscience of men by which suddenly everyone would see themselves as God sees them. She indicated that this illumination of conscience would result in the saving of many souls because many would repent as a result of this "Warning". . . . this miracle of "self illumination". [18]

THE WARNING – Garabandal, Spain, 1961–1965

During the apparitions from 1961 – 1965 at Garabandal, Spain, four young children saw and received messages from Our Blessed Mother. These apparitions occurred during the period of Vatican Council II, and just after the failure of the Church to reveal the Third

Part of the Secret of Fatima, which those of us who were living at the time and who had been following the Fatima apparitions expected would be done by Saint Pope John XXIII in 1960.

At Garabandal, Conchita, Mary Loli and Jacinta received messages about The Warning. Mary Loli was told the year of the Warning. Within a year following the Warning there would be a Great Miracle. Conchita was told the date of the Great Miracle.

In June 1962 these three visionaries experienced the "Night of the Screams" (actually over two nights that so terrified the people of the hamlet that almost all went to confession and Communion). **During these two nights they were shown the Warning and the Great Chastisement. The first night, during which only Mary Loli and Jacinta were present, was about the Warning. On the second night, during which Conchita was present as well, they were shown the Chastisement (which at that time was conditional). Mary Cruz did not share in either event.**

On January 1, 1965, at the pines, The Blessed Virgin Mary told Conchita about the Warning. She was told what the warning would be, but does not know the day or the date.

The Warning – Conchita

Conchita told us that the Warning will be like two heavenly bodies or stars colliding that make a lot of noise and a lot of light, but they don't fall. We are going to see it. It will horrify us because at that very moment we will see our souls and the harm we have done. In that moment we are going to see our conscience, **everything wrong that we are doing, and the good that we are not doing.** It will be as though we are in agony, but we will not die by its effects, but perhaps we will die of fright or shock to see ourselves. **The Warning is like a purification for the Miracle. Conchita said that it is sort of a catastrophe.** It will make us think of the dead, that is, we would prefer to be dead than to experience the Warning. **Conchita revealed to us that it would be very fearful, a thousand times worse than earthquakes. It will be like fire. It will not burn our flesh, but we will feel it bodily and interiorly. It is a thing from heaven. People in every part of the**

world will suffer from it. **None of us will escape this:** the good, so that they may draw nearer to God; the evil, so that they may amend their lives. **Conchita said that if she did not know what the Chastisement was, she would say that the Warning was worse than the Chastisement.**

In an interview in October 1968, in answer to a question about the Warning, Conchita said: **"The Warning is something supernatural and will not be explained by science. It will be seen and felt."**

According to Conchita: **"The Warning will be a purification, a preparation for the Miracle,** and everyone will see it. It will make people aware of the evil that they do with their sins."

The Warning – Mary Loli

Mary Loli said: **"When the Warning occurs everything will stand still, even planes in the sky, but just for a few moments. At the moment everything stops, the Warning will occur. The Warning will last just a few minutes.** It is very close and it is important we prepare ourselves because it is a terrible thing. It will make us feel all the wrong we have done."

Mary Loli told us: **"Everyone will experience it** wherever they may be, regardless of their condition or their knowledge of God. **It will be an interior personal experience. It will look as if the world has come to a standstill**, however, no one will be aware of that as **they will be totally absorbed in their own experience.** It is going to be something like an interior feeling of sorrow and pain for having offended God. **God will help us see clearly the harm we are causing Him and all the evil things we do.** He will help us to sense this interior pain because often when we do something wrong we ask the Lord's forgiveness with our lips, **but now He will help us sense physically that deep sorrow."**

Mary Loli said that it would look like the Communists had taken over the world and it would be very hard to practice religion, for priests to say Mass or for people to open the doors of the churches at the time of the Warning. It would be as though the Church had disappeared.

The Warning – Jacinta

Jacinta stated: "**The Warning is something that is first seen in the air everywhere in the world and immediately is transmitted into the interior of our souls. It will last for a very little time**, but will seem a very long time because of its effect within us. It will be for the good of our souls, in order to see in ourselves our conscience, the good and the bad we've done. Then we will feel a great love toward our heavenly parents and ask forgiveness for all our offenses. **The Warning is for everybody because God wants our salvation. The Warning is in order for us to draw closer to Him and increase our faith.** Therefore, one should prepare for that day, but not await it with fear because God doesn't send things for the sake of fear but rather justice and love and **He does it for the good of all His children that they might enjoy eternal happiness and not be lost.**"

The Miracle And Its Relation To The Warning

Conchita knows the date of the Miracle, and eight days before the Miracle occurs she will announce the date to the world. The Miracle is to occur during the months of March, April or May, between the 8th and the 16th of the month, at 8:30 P.M. Garabandal time on a feast day of a little known Martyr of the Eucharist, at the time of a rare ecclesiastical event, unrelated to the Miracle.
(Editor's Note: Some people believe that this same ecclesiastical event could be the Consecration of Russia to the Immaculate Heart of Mary. Others believe this event could be the proclamation of the Final Marian Dogma, Our Lady is Co-Redemptrix, Mediatrix of All Graces, and Advocate.)

Conchita was told what the Miracle would be, and said: "It will be a miracle of the love of God, something that will prove and manifest His love to us in an outstanding way." The Miracle, Conchita has stated, will coincide with an event in the Church, a singular event that happens very rarely and had not (as of 2013) occurred in Conchita's lifetime. Conchita said that **it is not new or stupendous, only rare, like a definition of a dogma – something like that in that it will affect the entire Church. It will happen on the same day as the**

110

Miracle, but not as a consequence of the Miracle, but only **coincidentally.**

There will be healing of those present in Garabandal at the time of the Miracle. The sick who are present will be cured, the incredulous will believe, and the sinners will be converted.

Our Lord told Conchita, on July 20, 1963, that the purpose of this Miracle is: "to convert the whole world". Conchita asked Our Lord if Russia would be converted. Our Lord answered: "Yes, she will be converted, and thus everybody will love Our Hearts."

On February 7, 1974 Conchita said: "For the words of the Blessed Mother to be complete, there must be the Warning and the Miracle. It is all one message."

(The fourth visionary, Mary Cruz, who later denied that these apparitions occurred, will, we are told, again believe that she did have them, but only after the Miracle.)

The Permanent Sign At Garabandal After The Miracle

After The Miracle There Will Be A Permanent Sign Left At Garabandal

On September 14, 1965, Conchita said: "The Sign that will remain forever at the pines is something that we will be able to photograph, televise and see, but not touch. It will be evident that this is not a thing of this world, but from God."

Conchita revealed that although the sign can be compared to a "pillar of smoke" or to "rays of sunlight" it will not actually be either of these things.

At Garabandal we were told that after these events have occurred there will be a short period of time for mankind to convert. If mankind doesn't, then there will be a Great Chastisement.

The Illumination (Warning) In Messages Given To Janie Garza, Austin, Texas, Visionary And Stigmatist

May 13, 1994 *The illumination of the soul*

St. Joseph: I, St. Joseph, bring God's blessings to you and to your family.

Janie: Thank you, beloved St. Joseph. Praised be the Eternal Father for His goodness forever and ever. Amen.

St. Joseph: My little one, I, St. Joseph, know that you have been struggling with the seriousness of the messages that you have received from Most Holy Mary and St. Michael. I am here to help you to understand these messages. **You see, my little one, the people of God have ignored His warnings.** The world does not understand the darkness that surrounds them.

Many people continue to live in sin, and forget that the day is coming when they will be allowed to see the state of their souls. What a terrible time this will be for many, many souls. Many will die, for they will not be able to withstand knowing the truth about the condition of their souls...." [8]

September 9, 1995 *The Illumination*

"Jesus: Good morning, Our humble servant. We are here to bless you and your family. We are here to comfort you in your suffering.

Janie: Good morning, My Lord and My Lady. Thank You so much for blessing us and for bringing comfort to my heart.

Our Lady: Our sweet angel, you are suffering, for you've seen all the evil in the world through the visions which God allows you to see. You have seen many of the things that are to come. You have seen the suffering in the families and the suffering in the Bride of my Son. These visions which you embrace with your heart and make reparation for, this is the reason for your great suffering.

Janie: Blessed Mother, I don't mind my suffering, but I am affected by knowing of all the suffering youth, the children and the killing of the unborn babies. Please pray so that I will pray unceasingly for the poor sinners in the world. **Could you tell me about the illumination which St. Joseph talked to me about. Will people suffer much?**

Jesus: Our humble servant, the illumination that will take place will be for a short period. During this time My Father will allow all of humanity to see the state of their souls as My Father sees their souls. This will be a time of great grace when many souls will repent and return to My Father. Those souls that die will die from great shock to see the state of the darkness which exists in their souls.

Janie: Beloved Savior, will the illumination scare people?

Jesus: The fear that will inflame their hearts is the holy fear of the immense power of My Father, especially for those many souls that have continued to deny the existence of My Father. These will be the souls that will experience tremendous fear.

Janie: Will all people convert?

Jesus: Many will convert, but many will not.

Janie: Oh, Jesus, will this happen very soon?

Jesus: Our humble servant, **this will happen within a short period.** Do not be distracted with dates, but **prepare everyday with strong prayer. Many who worry about these times will not live to see these things take place. This is why Holy Scripture warns everybody not to be concerned about tomorrow, for tomorrow is promised to no one. The present day has enough trials and crosses.**

Know that when **We speak about such things to come; this is for the** people to convert and abandon their evil ways. Everyday is an opportunity for souls to convert. People should not wait for such things to come to convert, but they should convert now, before it's too late! The very fact that such judgments will come is because people refuse to convert and continue to live in darkness.

Janie: Oh Beloved Savior, please continue to pour Your love and mercy into our souls so that we accept You as our Savior truly in our lives. I love You both.

Jesus: We love you, and all your prayers, your sacrifices and your little ways are pleasing to Us. We give you Our blessings. Until tomorrow, remain in the spirit of prayer as a family.

Janie: We will, we truly will." [26]

The Warning And Preparation For The Warning

On March 19, 1996 St. Joseph, appeared to Janie Garza and gave her a message on *The Illumination*

Janie: St. Joseph came with two big angels and many smaller angels. He was dressed with a golden tunic and an olive mantle that had golden designs on the edge of the hem. He blessed all the people with his presence. He had a beautiful, gentle smile. There was great light around him, and all the angels were in brilliant light. St. Joseph had two white roses in his hands. He knows that roses are my favorite flowers, because they have the fragrance of Our Lady....

Janie: Oh, we are so blessed to have you as Protector of the Family. Praised be God forever and ever.

St. Joseph: My little one, God's love for humanity is immense. He appeals to the world every second of the day to turn away from their sins. He gives them His love and mercy to help souls to convert. God will continue to appeal to His children to return back to His love and mercy.

The time is coming when God will allow all His children to look deep into their souls and see their sins as God sees their sinful hearts. God will send an illumination throughout the world. This will be a time of great grace and conversion to many souls. Shortly after this great illumination of souls, God will send a great miracle for the world to see.

After this great sign, the world will know peace. There will be great joy for all the faithful people of God. His children will be happy. There will be love in families everywhere. People will benefit from their labor, and they will build their homes and live to enjoy them. They will see their children's children, and all will live long lives.

Janie: Beloved St. Joseph, what should we do to prepare for this?

St. Joseph: Pray, my little one, pray. Remain faithful to all that the Holy Spirit directs you to do. Act in everything that Most Holy Mary is calling you to. Be a strong messenger of living her messages of *peace*, *prayer*, *Holy Mass*, *fasting*, *conversion* and *reading Holy Scripture*. Do this as a family. Do not reject God's Most Holy Name, so that He will not reject you. Decide to be a holy family, to pray together, to love, and to forgive one another. This is a time of decision for all of God's children.

Live as God's people, leading good, simple and just lives. Open your hearts to God's love and mercy. **Every family must consecrate themselves to the Sacred Heart of Jesus, to the Immaculate Heart of Mary, and to my intercession and protection, that We may lead you closer to God. We will prepare you for the things to come. Live as children of the Lord, and you will live through all these troubled times.**

Janie: Please help us, beloved St. Joseph, we need your help.

St. Joseph: My little one, **be prepared by living all that I, St. Joseph, have shared with you on a daily basis, living each day as if it was your last day. This is God's Holy Will for His children. Do not fear anything, but abandon yourself to the Holy Spirit who will help you to do the Holy Will of God.**

Janie: Thank you for this, most humble St. Joseph.

St. Joseph: I give you my blessing. Live in God's peace.

Janie: Later on this evening I was thanking God for St. Joseph, and my guardian angel said to me, "St. Joseph is the splendor of the interior life." I understood that both Our Lady and St. Joseph are the splendor of the interior life.[8]

Janie Garza's Vision Of The Warning

On March 19, 1997, Janie Garza had a vision and a message from St. Joseph. *This light pierced every heart at the same time*

St. Joseph: Greetings, my little one. God's peace to you and all who are present here.

Janie: Peace to you, beloved St. Joseph, on your feast day. I've waited for this time to spend with you.

St. Joseph: My little one, today will be a day of great joy for you, for on this day my foster Son, Jesus, will come to you as well.

Janie: Oh, beloved St. Joseph, I am so happy!

St. Joseph: My little one, today, I, St. Joseph, ask that you open your heart to what I share with you. It is important that you continue to pray and fast as a family. Offer your prayers and sacrifices to God in reparation for all the sins of the world. This is a time of great preparation. The call to conversion is urgent! There is no time for procrastination! *Families must turn to God and abandon their sinful lives. The time for repentance is now, tomorrow may be too late!* **Know that God is already much offended, and His justice will come upon the world like a thief in the night!**

Janie: Beloved St. Joseph, is God angry with us?

St. Joseph: No, my little one, **God is not angry, but much offended for**

all the evilness that exists in many hearts. Know that God loves all His children, but many continue to reject His love. Behold, my little one, and see the love and mercy of God.

Janie: At this time I saw a bright light up in the sky. Then, this light was absorbed by yet a much brighter light, an immense light. My heart was pounding so fast. *Then, I saw a huge Cross across the sky that covered every corner of the world. The Cross was like a neon light.*

Then, Jesus, Our Lord, appeared on the Cross. I could see His wounds, His Sacred Heart. Then, before my eyes I saw rays of light that came from His wounds and His Heart down upon all the people in the world. These rays of light appeared to be like laser beams of light that pierced every heart. Then I heard horrible screams. I said to Our Lord, "Why are the people screaming?"

Jesus: Through divine grace all of humanity is absorbed with seeing all the sin which lies in the very core of their souls.

Janie: I understood that perhaps some souls would die from seeing their sinfulness. **Then I saw people running in all different directions.** I asked Our Lord, "Where are they going?"

Jesus: Behold the goodness of My Father.

Janie: I saw a multitude of angels all in the sky. Great light came from them. Their light was coming upon thousands of what appeared to be Cathedrals. These Cathedrals were beautiful. The people were racing to these beautiful Cathedrals. I understood that these were the souls that had repented after seeing their sinful souls. They were seeking Reconciliation.

This great light that penetrated all souls happened all at once. Perhaps the duration was between five to ten minutes; I am not sure. It seemed to me like all time stood still. This great light from Jesus pierced every soul in the world at the very same time. I understood that this was truly a time of great grace. Before the vision ended, Our Lord said these words to me.

Jesus: The world must trust in the intercession of St. Joseph, for he has been chosen by My Father to help the world in these troubled times. *Devotion to St. Joseph is most important. He will lead many to the Two United Hearts that are One with the Father.*

Janie: Then the vision was gone.

St. Joseph: My little one, hold dear to your heart all that you saw today. Know that I, St. Joseph, will help all who seek my intercession. Peace, my little one, peace.

Janie: Thank you, beloved St. Joseph, and peace to you.[8]

Maria Esperanza

The Fourth Message Of Betania

There Is Coming The Great Moment Of A Great Day Of Light

"Little children, today, healthful for your souls you must contribute to helping me build my house in this place. **A refuge of a Mother with the title, 'Mary, Reconciler of People and Nations:** Pray, meditate, and nourish yourselves with the bread of the Eucharist which gives you supernatural life. Be what you are: strong souls, healthy and strong, to combat with the weapons of love since it is love by which you are going to penetrate hearts and the consciences of all my children, dwellers of these lands, in a summons, an outcry shouting: **'Rise up, the hour has come for rebuilding the moral values of a People of God.'**

"I want to be known, I repeat to you, under the name of Virgin and Mother, Reconciler for the People because man needs to find himself. He needs to see in each human being his or her own brother or sister. Ideologies may be respected because it is respect that is due to one's self, to each one, to recognize each one as a member of one same family, the family of God.

118

"Little children, all rise to a single ideal, struggle for the poorest and the most abandoned, struggle for the new generation that must grow and develop in a healthy environment.

"Yes, my children, learn the value of each person in his or her own milieu where he or she lives and moves, with his or her way of thinking as well as in the negative side of their surroundings. Learn to value these people in order to help them to fight against the evil that surrounds them, drawing them forward to live in a healthy atmosphere in spiritual peace as God, the Father, wishes to save you all by faith. It is man's answer in the midst of the structure of society, being sure that God has created you.

"Little children, I am your Mother, and I come to seek you so that you may prepare yourselves to be able to bring my message of reconciliation. *There is coming the great moment of a great day of light. The consciences of this beloved people must be violently shaken so that they may 'put their house in order' and offer to Jesus the just reparation for the daily infidelities that are committed on the part of sinners.*

"Little children, I want to take possession of your hearts! To give you in the Holy Spirit the gift of understanding that you may find the profound significance of my presence among you. I am offering you the opportunity of the great promise that one day my Divine Son will make known to you. It is essentially important in these times: **'The Reconciliation of the Universe.'** Oh may it be.... people with God, and people with each other!

"Lo, this Mother who is pleading as the poorest of women, the littlest, the most humble, but the most pure; she wishes to transmit to you again the purity of heart, simplicity, loyalty, obedience to the service of your brothers and sisters, prudence, and still more, constant zeal for the works of our Mother, the Church. Today there is need of giving testimony with your life and your faith in God so that this Mother may be able to prepare you for the apostolate. Prepare you, yes, and the invitation is commendable and assuredly valid if you desire it. With a recommendation for perseverance, proceed and put it into practice." [31]

Christina Gallagher – The Warning

Everyone Will See Themselves As They Really Are In The Sight Of God

Christina said: "There will come a sign, which everyone in the world, in an interior way, will experience – and it is not far away. Everyone will experience an inner awareness and they will know that this is from God, and they will see themselves as they really are in the sight of God. It is up to each one of us to help as many people as we can by our prayers, so that when this supernatural sign comes, they will change, and will be able to respond to that sign and be saved by God."

The Coming Sign

On December 14, 1996 Christina Gallagher had a vision and message from Jesus, Our Lord.

Jesus said: "Those who desire to live in the justice of the world, will receive the justice of My Hand.

"Soon the world will receive a Sign to know of My Reign, for all things are desired through My heart and the heart of My Father. Know that Justice will be served. So many shout of truth and that they know the truth. They neither know nor serve the truth...."

In reference to the coming Sign, Jesus said:

"*Soon the sign that will be given will be My Face. My Face will radiate in the skies and throughout the world more brilliantly than a thousand suns, to show the triumphant glory of the Son of God and the Immaculate Heart of My Mother.* For She Is Immaculate – ever honored in grace before My Father, for truly I tell you, the fruit of Her womb brought the Light of God into the world."
(Christina understood that this was Our Lord bringing His mother for the triumph of her Immaculate Heart).

120

When Christina asked when this Sign would come, Jesus responded: "Soon, child, soon, the world will recognize its Creator! **Soon the heavens and earth will change in its seasons.**

The birth pangs rage in the world, but will multiply – calamity after calamity, storm after storm."

Light From Heaven

Christina is then shown the heavens open. As the sky opens, there is a huge outpouring of light. It comes down and goes out all over the world. She sees the Face of Jesus, luminous and yet transparent, in huge form, coming forth. Gradually, His hands form and then His feet. From the wounds In His hands and feet, brilliant light shines down, so that these stand out more than the rest of His Body, which can be seen in outline in the light.

Christina can see His Heart living and beating. Within His Sacred Heart can be seen Our Blessed Lady, with her own Immaculate Heart beating and angels are to be seen moving everywhere. As the Light radiates, it penetrates everything.

Christina could see billions of enormous, loathsome black "lizards" fleeing in all directions to escape, but in vain. No matter where they attempted to hide, in houses, under rocks, it is impossible to escape the Light, which seems to penetrate the very earth itself.

The world is saturated with the Light.

Christina is also aware that the darkness which will come before this heavenly Illumination will plunge everything into a dense obscurity."
(From Christina Gallagher's official internet site.)

121

The Bright Cross In The Heavens During The Warning

Paola Albertini, Italy – A Great Cross In The Sky

It has been reported that **The Blessed Mother has also said to Paola Albertini, Italy**, the visionary instrumental in healing Mother Angelica, among others, during her trip to the United States, that **"there will appear a great cross in the sky. All will see it. Some will be converted. Some will be so frightened that they will die. And others will be indifferent to it. There will be a test, and then there will come this sign....** Jesus and Mary will help us. Let us not be afraid."

Saint Sister Faustina Kowalska (1905-1938)

Before I Come As The Just Judge, I Am Coming First As The King Of Mercy

Jesus told Saint Sister Faustina Kowalska in Notebook I, #83: "Write this: before I come as the just Judge, I am coming first as the King of Mercy. Before the day of justice arrives, there will be given to people a sign in the heavens of this sort:

All light in the heavens will be extinguished, and there will be great darkness over the whole earth. Then the sign of the cross will be seen in the sky, and from the openings where the hands and feet of the Savior were nailed will come forth great lights which will light up the earth for a period of time. This will take place shortly before the last day." [20]

The Heavenly Body Of The Warning

Amparo Cuevas, the Spanish visionary at El Escorial, during an ecstasy in 1982 received the message: "Soon a Warning will be given which will affect all people everywhere.

"**Each and every person will see the Warning and will understand its meaning. When the Warning comes there will be those who will be so terrified that they will die from sheer fright.**

A star, the Asteroid Eros, will illuminate the earth causing it to appear to be surrounded by flames during a period of some twenty minutes, an event which will spread panic everywhere. All those who believe in God and the Holy Virgin will remain in a kind of ecstasy during this period. This will occur in the near future.

When Eros lights up the earth making it appear that the whole world is in flames, many people will wish to die at that moment in that shower of fire, which will strike fear in everyone, a fear which will in fact cause the death of many people; those who are just and who believe, will not suffer." [45]

Sadie Jaramillo

The Warning Will Be The Most Awesome, Holy Fulfillment Of Calvary

On February 19, 1995, Our Blessed Mother told Sadie Jaramillo: "My little sorrowful rose, I request that you take down my words. ... **For the greatest moment of divine mercy will bring many to the foot of my Son's glorious Cross. It will also be a time of chaos and confusion.** I clarify to you, to **prepare for a shortage of food items upon the arrival of this moment. And then for the control of famine which will follow.**

"It is the illumination of man's heart and soul. The heaven will crack with God's thunder. **It will be the most awesome, holy fulfillment of Calvary**; a moment to choose the path to eternal life, or to be led to eternal damnation.

"**The moment which will lead my remnant to begin harvesting in God's vineyard.** You will tire, but you will work ceaselessly...." [6]

123

The Warning Is Our Lord's Final Act Of Mercy

On July 5, 1996, Jesus told Sadie Jaramillo: "My Vicar will go into exile until his martyrdom. **My final act of Mercy, that which My Faustina prepared the world for, through the image, will be fulfilled.** But in the end, **for My enemies, fire will rain down from heaven** and the Mighty hand of God will seek you out and destroy you, every last one, and you will be no more.... I will see you through the storm, and you will increase in courage and strength, for it will be by the very power of God those destined to be My Remnant will go through these final dark moments." [6]

On August 10, 1996 – 10:00 A.M. Jesus told Sadie Jaramillo: "I am the King of Mercy and mercy I desire to bestow. For the last moment before justice I call you and all to be apostles of divine mercy. The will of God the Father has called many, and few have responded. Yet for the sake of those few, their prayers of the heart have been heard and much has been mitigated, so great is God's love...." [6]

On November 20, 1996, Jesus told Sadie Jaramillo: *"Soon you will behold the greatest prodigy in the heavens. You will behold this with your eyes and feel it in your soul. You will see Me on the Cross in the heavens and the weight of your sins will be revealed in your soul.* By a means of your consecration to My Most Sacred Heart, I have truly placed you there in My Heart.

You will behold this great manifestation of Mercy from within My Heart, and the flames of My purifying Love will raise and will consume all that is left, that keeps you from totally loving Me." [6]

The Greatest Act Of Mercy Since
The Beginning Of Creation

On January 31, 1997, Jesus told Sadie Jaramillo: "The rumblings within the Church are signs leading up to the revealing of this Man of Perdition, this Man of Destiny, this Man: the Antichrist....

124

This I tell you now, child, I have spoken once of a light that will brighten a night and will announce to you and to all, the greatest act of Mercy since the beginning of creation You are going to live through this tremendous evidence of My love. Tangible, physical evidence of God's infinite love for every creature alive on the face of this earth. You will be pierced with the sword of truth when all is revealed....

Very soon, as many events will follow another quickly, you will soon be in the midst of the chaos, confusion and turmoil....

Do not let yourselves be deluded into thinking nothing will happen. It should have happened long ago, but I have desired to show mercy and, through the great intercession of the Queen of Heaven, great acts of God's Justice have been averted.

But we are in the final hours....

The economic ruin of this nation will come swiftly....

I implore My priests: Return your hearts to Rome, the Chair of Peter, My Vicar John Paul II and all that he stands for. It is the Truth, the Life and the Way." [6]

Sadie Jaramillo's Vision Of The Warning

Vision Of A Large Flaming Ball With A Tail

Sadie Jaramillo was told about the three visions of a large flaming ball with the tail, that she had on August 18, 1994. Jesus said: "This ball of light will explode in the conscience of man and he will see the dread of his soul. He will fall to his knees and My enemies will curse Me to their perdition." [6]

Sadie Jaramillo had had a vision on August 18, 1994 of a flaming object with a tail of flames hurling through space downwards in total blackness; same object with planet in the distance; object and the planet ready to collide. **Jesus said: "I have just shown you what will cause Man to fall on his knees and know the dread of his soul."** [6]

On August 14, 1996, Jesus revealed to Sadie Jaramillo: "As the darkness envelops totally this created world, your light will give light to others. When the light comes in the darkness, it will bring the darkness that will reveal the Light."

Sadie said: *"While receiving these words, I had an interior vision: I saw first a dark night with stars in the sky, then a burst of light like a fireball with a tail, which I have been shown before; then I see daylight suddenly growing darker until there is nothing but total blackness; then appears the Cross with Jesus Crucified."* [6]

On November 20, 1996, Jesus told Sadie Jaramillo: "Soon you will behold the greatest prodigy in the heavens. You will behold this with your eyes and feel it in your soul. *You will see Me on the Cross in the heavens and the weight of your sins will be revealed in your soul. By a means of your consecration to My Most Sacred Heart, I have truly placed you there in My Heart.*

You will behold this great manifestation of Mercy from within My Heart, and the flames of My purifying Love will raise and will consume all that is left, that keeps you from totally loving Me." [6]

"Concerning the three visions of the large flaming ball with a tail that Sadie had on August 18, 1994, **Jesus told Sadie Jaramillo on January 5, 1997: "This ball of light will explode in the conscience of man and he will see the dread of his soul. He will fall to his knees and My enemies will curse Me to their perdition."** [6]

The Warning – A Day of Thunder – Cosmic Disturbance

On August 13, 1997, Jesus told Sadie Jaramillo: "There is quickly coming this day of thunder, this cosmic disturbance.... For disturbance will come, plagues will come, famine will come, the sword will come...." [6]

Two Heavenly Bodies

Jesus said to Sadie Jaramillo on September 8, 1997: "The storms of God's justice brings to many the loss of your home, to many the loss of your means of employment and, at the height of tribulation, once the man of iniquity is revealed, you will lose your means of providing food and external provisions, for the mark of this man will be required. Therefore I ask you now to prepare as best as you are able. Heed well what I say, for then God will do the rest. Iniquity and his reign must abound for a short time more. But to you who hold fast and persevere, great is your reward. *The nations will soon be one. Your money will be one. Man's religion will be one, but in My Own, the Truth of the Gospel will be the light that will dispel the darkness. My light will keep you secure in the Refuge of My Heart. And soon, you will all know this by means of the two heavenly bodies which will cause such cosmic disturbance, then you will see what I have called in the past the dread of your soul....*" [6]

The Day Of Thunder Is A Type Of Second Pentecost

On March 24, 1994 – 9:00 A.M. Our Blessed Mother said to Sadie Jaramillo: "This day of thunder is upon My children! To My own (the children of light), it is an awesome and wonderful thing! To the godless, their hearts will be filled with terror!

It is a type of second Pentecost. My Divine Spouse will descend and, in a swift but thorough sweep, convict those souls of the truth and those souls will be brought into the Mystical Body of Christ. Others will know also, this is of God and though they resist, it will be a type of warning for them...." [6]

The Day Of Thunder – A Day Of Reckoning

On March 28, 1994 - 8:30 A.M. Our Blessed Mother said to Sadie Jaramillo: "You see once more a little, but a little, of the devastation and death that still awaits this humanity that refuses to see the call of God, the hand of God and the mercy of God. Very soon now, this day of thunder is upon you and will be the signal dispatched to the

four corners of the world.

The Holy Spirit of God will be, once again, the power which will renew the face of this earth; will cleanse, and will purify. The children of light will be filled with wondrous awe at this advent of His arrival, and the godless will know their dread and truth of their souls! Have I not requested of My children, 'Pray the Holy Spirit come?'" [6]

On September 1, 1994 Our Blessed Mother told Sadie Jaramillo: "I have made reference to this day before to you as **the day of thunder. It will be a day of reckoning, everyone with their sins in clear view, just as they are seen by God. No longer will the darkness that has pervaded every inch of the world, be able to blind these souls.**" [6]

The Warning Comes Amidst Great Confusion And Turmoil

September 21, 1995 – 1:41 A.M., Feast of St. Matthew, Sadie received a message from Our Blessed Mother: "My little sorrowful rose,... **Know that the greatest prodigy of the Holy Spirit is upon mankind. It will be the unveiling of one's soul, before the omnipotent light of Christ in whose light, perfect and true, all darkness of sin and guilt will be revealed! Many now are in that valley where the decision for or against God will be made!...** *Amid great confusion and turmoil, will the great warning come.*

Many of the faithful now will lose faith! The interior of the Church will go very dark. The enemies will rage and persecute truth and those who follow it...." [6]

This Warning Will Be Man's Last Chance And Hope For Salvation

On December 30, 1994 -7:15 A.M. Jesus told Sadie: "**This time of My warning is My gift to this poor humanity that has chosen to live in disregard of their God and each other. The laws of God are profaned and dissolved by your nation's courts.**

Therefore, I will turn your nation over to captivity. **This warning, this light into your soul that will penetrate the impenetrable, will be man's last chance and hope for salvation;** and for you, daughter and others, the ceaseless work begins...." [6]

After The Warning

On March 4, 1997, Jesus told Sadie Jaramillo: "Thus the importance of My promises for Mercy Sunday must be propagated far and wide!

The time for souls to respond after the illumination will be quick to end and it is during this time that My chosen instruments and persons will and must work tirelessly and unceasingly, for the one who opposes Me will swiftly be brought to the revealing and unveiling!" [6]

Sadie's Vision Of And Her Own Experience Of The Warning

On December 30, 1997, at 1:45 A.M., Sadie Jaramillo received a message. Sadie was awakened and **asked by Our Lord to write of her recent visions.... Sadie stated: "On Sunday, December 28, the feast of the Holy Innocents, I'm making my thanksgiving after receiving Holy Communion, when I see a brilliantly illuminated cross against a very dark sky. It seems as if this cross is beaming rays of light down towards the earth.** There is some light and I see people prostrate in adoration, like the kneeling Magi in my nativity scene. This is very intense and seems to be occurring for each person individually. **It seems that this cross is close enough that I could reach out and embrace the foot of it.**

Even where there is no light, I can see silhouettes of people, cowering back in intense fear, almost to the point of despair, hands up to their faces, crying, and then some falling to their knees. I have been shown this before.

At this point, I begin to see scenes of my own life from early childhood, beginning around seven years of age. It seems as if I am seeing a series of still photos of many scenes that lead to the time of my conversion. I feel intense shame and I begin to cry uncontrollably (yet silently for I am still in Mass). Through all of these scenes I did not see Our Lord, but I felt His Presence of Love. Though I did not hear these words, this understanding was given: **'I beheld all these things of your life and I still love you. For I do not remember them ever. I reveal them to you, for I place you in the crucible of My Love.'"**

Jesus told Sadie: "Yes child, it is I, Jesus. Born as a child to walk among men, to be crucified and die, so that many could live and experience the Glory of My Resurrection!

The hour is late and I have told you, 'I am going to place you in the crucible of My Love,' to experience, if you will, a mini-judgment.

The illuminated cross all will see, and if it seems you could embrace the foot, it is because on Calvary I saw each and all and it is a personal experience for those who finally surrender unto Me in their heart."... [6]

Jennifer – Words From Jesus

Jennifer's Vision Of The Warning

"My child, you are witnessing a vision of the warning to come."

The sky is dark and it seems as though it is night but my heart tells me it is sometime in the afternoon. **I see the sky opening up and I can hear long, drawn out claps of thunder.** When I look up I see Jesus bleeding on the cross and people are falling to their knees.

Jesus then tells me, **"They will see their soul as I see it."** I can see the wounds so clearly on Jesus and Jesus then says, **"They will see each wound they have added to My Most Sacred Heart."**

To the left I see the Blessed Mother weeping and then Jesus speaks to me again and says, **"Prepare, prepare now for the time is soon approaching. My child, pray for the many souls who will perish because of their selfish and sinful ways."**

As I look up I see the drops of blood falling from Jesus and hitting the earth. I see millions of people from nations from all lands. Many seemed confused as they were looking up toward the sky.

Jesus says, *"They are in search of light for it should not be a time of darkness, yet it is the darkness of sin that covers this earth and the only light will be that of which I come with for mankind does not realize the awakening that is about to be bestowed upon him. This will be the greatest purification since the beginning of creation."*

I see people crying and some with horrifying screams when they see Jesus bleeding on the cross.

Jesus says, "**It is not the sight of My wounds that causes their suffering; it is the depth of the soul knowing that he has placed them there. It is not the sight of My wounds bleeding that causes their suffering; it is knowing that man's rejection of Me has caused My wounds to bleed.**

My child, so many will perish for their souls have become so far from Me yet it is I, Jesus, that will show the great depth of My mercy.

My child you see that the earth has been trembling for as this hour of purification of enlightenment draws near, the fury of the lion will be prowling amongst My people. The temptation will multiply for he seeks his many victims. *It will be the greatest spiritual battle man has ever endured. My child, tell My people that today I am asking that they take heed to My words for the sign in the east is about to rise.*

Tell My people that this is the hour for I am Jesus and all will be done according to My will."

As I look up I continue to see Jesus bleeding on the cross. I continue to see the Blessed Mother weeping to the left. The cross is bright white and illuminated in the sky, it looks suspended. As the sky is opening up I see a bright light come down on the cross and in this light I see the resurrected Jesus appear in white look up toward heaven raising His hands, He then looks down at the earth and

131

makes the sign of the cross blessing His people.

In His Messages To Jennifer Jesus Tells Us About Many Of The Reasons For The Warning

On May 23, 2004 Jennifer was told by Jesus "My Church, the true Church will be brought to light.

Jennifer was told by Jesus on May 23, 2005 that the division in My Church will soon come to light.

On January 1, 2006 Jennifer was told by Jesus, *"My warning is the final act of mercy that will be given to mankind." Jesus told Jennifer that the events that follow will change this world as you have come to know it. And as the storms, disease and wars follow there will only remain a small remnant. There will be war over money, food and medicine. Brother will hand over brother for your true obedience to My commandments will be tested.*

A List Of Reasons For The Warning Given To Jennifer By Jesus

- I come at this time as your merciful savior to reach out to My lost children.
- Evil can no longer be.
- I am warning those of My people that are of this world.
- The reign of Satan is coming to an end.
- A Warning out of love for My people.
- You are being fed with false promises by a world that can be washed away.
- To correct My disobedient children.
- The heart of the family is being diminished and humanity cannot survive.
- Actions for which there is no justification – diminishing My

132

Commandments.

- You will come to know who is your true Messiah.
- To prepare the world for the time of My visitation.
- The truth will come out when the fullness of My mercy is poured out.
- I will soften hardened hearts and yet some will only become harder.
- Have faith and courage for you can overcome evil.
- The judgment and punishment of your Heavenly Father is about to fall upon mankind.

Signs, Secrets And Prophecies – Road To The Triumph

Chapter 8

Islam Rising Against Christianity And The West

The Islamic Mahdi, The Islamic Jesus
The Caliphate Restored
The Islamic One World Government

Islam, with nearly 1.6 billion adherents, is the fastest growing religion in the world. The two main divisions are Shiites and Sunnis, the smaller being the Shiites. Islam is now awakening. Apparently spontaneous uprisings throughout much of the Eastern Mediterranean and in Yemen have resulted in the overthrow of governments in Tunisia, Libya, Egypt, ongoing uprisings in Yemen, Syria, an uprising of Shiites in Bahrain. In Iraq the Shiites and Sunnis are waging guerrilla warfare. Iran is supporting the Iraqi Shiites to settle their differences. The Islamic nation of Afghanistan is the site of an United Nations – United States war against the radical Islamic Taliban which has been using an area of neighboring Pakistan, an Islamic Nation, which has been sympathetic with their religious agenda.

The Mahdi – The Islamic Messiah And Savior

The Muslims hold that the Mahdi is the messiah and savior to come on the scene in the end times to restore the Caliphate, which would bring all nations and people under the Islamic religion and preside over a worldwide government under Islamic Law. The Mahdi they believe will be assisted by Jesus, the Mahdi's religious subordinate in this. The Mahdi will be a political, military figure, and after three and a half years of waging war to convert nations to Islam will demand worship from all people as God. He will reign in this capacity, i.e. as the Antichrist.

The Jesus Of Islamic Belief

The Jesus whom Muslims believe in, is not the Jesus of Christianity. The Muslims hold that Jesus was not crucified and did not die on the cross. Jesus according to them was taken up to Allah, the Islamic name for their God, who they claim is the God of Abraham. They believe that for these two thousand years since Jesus lived on this earth, having never died, he will return to earth to correct what Christians believe about him, saying that, as the Muslims believe, he is not divine, not the Son of God, and that Islam is the true faith and all must convert or die. The Poll tax paid by subjugated people which has allowed them to live under Islamic rule will be abolished by this Muslim Jesus. These subjugated people must then convert to Islam or die. Beheading is the method of killing according to the instructions and life of Mohammed.

Mohammed, The Spread Of Islam, And The Ottoman Empire

Mohammed taught that deception, or lying in achieving the goals of Allah is permissible, even to denying that one is a Muslim if necessary.

Under Mohammed the Islamic religion and government spread rapidly by means of wars with neighboring nations.

After Mohammed's death, his associates, who were called Caliphs, continued these wars. They almost succeeded in destroying Christianity. It was only through the Pope's and Our Lady's intervention that their goal of destroying Christianity and all other religions was halted, on the sea in the Naval Battle of Lepanto on October 7, 1571, and on land in the Battle of Vienna on September 12, 1683. A rosary crusade called by the Pope led to the intercession of Our Lady and the miraculous defeat of the Turkish fleet which greatly outnumbered the christian fleet. These two battles prevented Europe and the world from falling under the rule of Islam which had the expressed goal of instituting a world-wide Islamic government under Islamic (Shariah) law and the destruction of all other religions other than Islam.

In World War I the Turkish/Ottoman empire entered on Germany's side and was defeated. In 1923 the Turkish Republic was declared, and on March 3, 1924 the Caliphate was abolished.

Islamic Desire To Re-establish A Worldwide Islamic Empire

The beast that was, the Islamic empire which was until 1923, then from 1923-1924 until now is not, and according to prophecy which will be again, would be accomplished, if this Islamic plan is realized, by means of the restoration of the Caliphate under a man recognized by them as the expected Mahdi. This Mahdi as Caliph would rule this worldwide Islamic empire and decree that he be worshipped as God under pain of death.

The September 11, 2001 morning attack by radical, fundamentalist Muslims on the World Trade Center in New York and the Pentagon in Washington, D.C. occurred on a day in the United States that is the anniversary of the beginning of the 1683 battle of Vienna which began in the early hours of September 12, 1683 at a time when it was still September 11, 1683, in New York City and Washington, D.C. areas. The Ottoman Turks, with an overwhelming sized army suffered a demoralizing defeat, which saved Europe and Christianity from Muslim subjugation, a defeat that still bothers radical Muslim fundamentalists who want a worldwide caliphate under Shariah Law in which all nations and people are Muslims worshiping Allah.

Iran, a Shiite Muslim nation, wants to reestablish the Caliphate. The former secular President of Iran, **Ahmadinejad, had said that he expects both Jesus and Imam Mahdi to return and wipe away oppression.** He was awaiting the return of the Mahdi, who would conquer the entire world for Islam, making Islam the only World religion.

There has been an apparently spontaneous, sudden unrest in the

Islamic world, *the Arab Springtime*, which has produced the rapid, unexpected overthrow of the Islamic governments, of Egypt, Libya, Tunisia, and ongoing civil strife in Syria, Iraq, Yemen, and strife in Bahrain promoted by Iran and opposed by Saudi Arabia which could lead to the reestablishment of the Caliphate under a nuclear armed Iran.

The Shiites, the smaller of the great division of Islam into Shiites and Sunnis, believe the Imam Mahdi disappeared as a child in 941 AD and will return to reign on earth for seven years before bringing about a final judgment and the end of the world.

The former President of Iran, Ahmadinejad, believed that his main mission, according to a speech he gave in Tehran on November 16, 2005, was to pave the path for the glorious reappearance of Imam Mahdi.

Ahmadinejad had described the Holocaust as a Myth and had called for Israel to be wiped off the map. On October 14, 2010, while visiting in southern Lebanon he said, "The Mahdi will come here, accompanied by Jesus Christ" to liberate Palestine and allow the millions of Arabs of Palestine to move there in his wake.

There is much about Islamic beliefs that people in the Christian West either don't know or, if they do know, they ignore.

There is danger in dealing with Islam in a religious or a diplomatic setting because of the Islamic belief about lying and using deception to promote Islam.

Islam's Doctrines Of Lying

<u>Kithman</u>: hiding the truth and <u>Taqiya</u>: concealing or disguising one's beliefs, convictions, ideas, feelings, opinions, and/or strategies at a time of imminent danger to save oneself from physical and/or mental injury. [47]

The Qur'an teaches that Muslims who deny their faith will receive forgiveness as long as their true faith was not really shaken. "Allah

138

revealed the verse: 'Except under compulsion, his heart remaining firm in faith.... (Surah 16:106)." [47]

The Mahdi: Islam's Awaited Messiah

In Arabic al-Mahdi means "the Guided One. His coming is the crowning element of all Islamic end-time narratives. In general both Shi'a and Sunni sects of Islam believe in him, but some quarters of Sunnis reject him altogether. [47]

Those Muslims who believe in the Mahdi believe he is coming to save the world.

Their Tradition states that the Mahdi will descend from the family of Muhammad and will bear Muhammad's name.

In this present age, throughout the Islamic world, there is a call for the restoration of the Islamic caliphate.

The caliph is viewed by Muslims as the vice regent for Allah on earth.

All Muslims will be required to follow the Mahdi whom they believe is the future world leader who will rule over the Islamic world and non-Muslim world. They believe that this Mahdi by means of military campaigns or holy wars (jihad) will accomplish this world revolution. [47]

The Mahdi's ascendency to power is said to be preceded by an army from the East carrying black flags, flags of jihad, banners of war. [47]

An Islamic tradition places the Mahdi's ascendency to power at the time of a final peace agreement between Arabs and the Romans (Christians, the West), a peace agreement lasting the seven years during which the Mahdi reigns.

They believe that the Mahdi will ride on a white horse, a tradition coming from the Muslim interpretation of Christian Scriptures

Signs, Secrets And Prophecies – Road To The Triumph

(Book of Revelation). [47]

The Islamic Belief About Jesus Is Not The Christian Belief About Jesus

The Islamic Jesus according to Islamic traditions is usually described as descending at the white minaret in the eastern side of Damascus meeting the army of the Mahdi preparing for battle. The Islamic Jesus is subordinate to the Mahdi. The primary purpose of their Jesus is to oversee the institution and the enforcement of Islamic Shariah law all over the world.

Their tradition holds that Jesus will declare himself a Muslim, thus leading many Christians to convert to Islam. Their belief is that Jesus will convert the Christian world to Islam, and will execute those who do not. The Islamic Jesus will marry, have children, and remain on earth nineteen years after marriage. He will live on earth for forty years and then will die and be buried next to the prophet Mohammad. [47]

Pedro Regis

The Most Painful Event Of The Fifteenth Century Will Be Repeated

February 16, 2005. Message 2483 to Pedro Regis. Dear Sons and Daughters, God has spoken, but men have not received His message. **The most painful event of the fifteenth century will be repeated.** Humanity is heading towards self-destruction which men have prepared with their own hands. Pray. Lovingly hear My appeals and you can grow spiritually. Don't back away. This is the message I give you today in the name of the Most Holy Trinity. Thank you for permitting me to bring you here once more. I bless you in the name of the Father, and of the Son, and of the Holy Spirit. Amen. Be at peace.
(Editors Note: **This refers to the fall of Constantinople, the Byzantine Empire (the end of the Eastern Roman Empire) to Islamic forces. On May 29, 1453** (according to the Julian Calendar), **the city of Constantinople was conquered by the Ottomans.** This battle marked

140

the end of the Byzantine Empire, an empire which had lasted for over 1,100 years. **The city's fall was a massive blow for Christendom.** Pope Nicholas V ordered an immediate counter-attack, but his death soon after marked the end of the plan.)

This painful event marked not only the final destruction of the Eastern Roman Empire, and the death of Constantine XI, the last Byzantine emperor, but also the strategic conquest crucial for Ottoman rule over the Eastern Mediterranean and Balkans. The city remained capital of the Ottoman Empire until the empire's dissolution in 1922. In 1923 the Turkish Republic was declared. **On March 3, 1924 the Caliphate was abolished. Constantinople was officially renamed Istanbul by the Turkish Republic in 1930.**

Radical Islamic believers have been estimated by some at about 10 percent of Moslims. This may seem to be small, however in absolute numbers it would be about 160,000,000 persons who hold radical beliefs.

On September 11, 2011 The United States Came Under Attack By Those Who Held These Radical Beliefs

Christina Gallagher And Maria Esperanza

While in New York to address a Rosary Rally at Battery Park on September 11, 1999 Christina Gallagher, a mystic and stigmatist from Ireland, prophesied that the Twin Towers would be destroyed.

Michael H. Brown stated on August 20, 2003 that, "It was (Maria) Esperanza (of Venezuela) who in 1992 publicly told a group of pilgrims that she had seen "two huge towers with black smoke all around them"- an apparent prophecy about terrorism at the Trade Center.

He also stated that in December 2000 and again in the following March she publicly warned that something big was about to happen in the U.S. involving foreign interests. On August 25, 2001 Michael Brown received a fax of a message Maria was given by St. Peter that "A great event will be happening in 3 weeks or 3 months." The attack occurred in the third week.

On September 11, 2001 Maria Esperanza was personally present in the New York City area – the third week after the prophecy.

Pedro Regis

The Terrorist Attack Of September 11, 2001 In New York Will Yet Cause Great Damage For Humanity

January 1, 2002. Message 1995 to Pedro Regis, a mystic living in Bahia, Brazil – from Our Lady Queen of Peace – Angüera, Bahia, Brazil. Dear Sons Daughters, I am the Queen of Peace. I come from heaven to offer you the grace of peace, which is the great treasure that humanity lost because of those who live without God and with hatred. I suffer because of my poor sons who live like the blind and do not know how to find the way of The Lord. I am your mother and come to lead you. I ask you to continue to pray, since you will have great tribulations. If you open yourselves to my call and live my messages, you will be transformed and will see peace reign on earth. Bend your knees in prayer, for only in this way will you contribute to the final triumph of my Immaculate Heart. **The prophecy that I announced to you last year (message of January 1, 2001) was fulfilled in the sad happening in the United States. Pray much, for all this will yet cause great damage for humanity. For centuries I have come to the world to call men to conversion, but they prefer war, death, and lack of love.** I come to offer you a new life, a life of grace in the Lord. I ask you to be builders of peace and love. With your examples and your words, seek to bring God to those who are distant. The Lord confides in you and awaits your sincere and courageous witness. Whatever may happen, don't forget; the Lord loves you and is at your side. Courage. Fear not. Be united with Jesus in prayer and the sacraments. This is the message I give you today in the name of the Most Holy Trinity. Thank you for permitting me to

142

reunite you here once more. I bless you in the name of the Father, and of the Son, and of the Holy Spirit. Amen. Be at Peace.

Pedro Regis was interviewed by Maureen Flynn, Signs and Wonders for Our Times, in late 2012. The interview was conducted by phone with a Portuguese interpreter. Pedro said: "On January 1, 2001 Mary said a great treasure would be taken from men. The great treasure is the Twin Towers. That prophecy was only about the towers."

Sadie Jaramillo

Terrorism, Civil Unrest, Civil War In U.S.A.

Sadie Jaramillo on July 7, 1998 received a message from Jesus in which He told her to describe her visions.

Sadie said: "I have been shown for the last two and a half weeks a crescent moon with a star. Then I see the moon crack in half, the bottom half falling away from the top half, but still connected. I then see a river of blood begin to flow from the bottom half of the moon.

One week ago today, while praying in the cenacle, I see a flash of fire, or something that looks very hot. It is more straight than round and has fumes rising from it, like gas fumes rising. It is like a flare that they shoot to show a location. I don't know from where it has come for I can only see where it is headed, and that it is to earth. I see earth off in the distance. Please bear with me when describing these visions. It is very hard sometimes.

Jesus: Now I, Who Am the lover of your soul, will reveal the meaning of these visions. The symbol of Islam indicates the river of blood that will flow from the instigation of war by these nations. They will also cause here in this country racial and civil strife and unrest.

The second vision indicates the signs from the heavens as spoken of in Scripture that will cause these bursts of fire to fall upon a humanity out of sync with its God! (Mt 24:29) Humanity has reached the level of degradation that has surpassed that of any other time! By their "knowledge" they believe they have no need for their Creator....

Now child, recall the vision shown to you before:

Sadie Jaramillo said: I recall a time when I was shown an image of the world, a globe. Then I saw this globe move ever so slightly from its normal position.

Jesus: These atomic bombs which have been set off, cause the very bowels of the earth to shift. Thus the world will suffer for the foolishness of man. The weather ceases to have seasons and unusual weather phenomena will become more and more prevalent! These are just the beginnings! The earth will shift and give vent to the just anger of God!...

Christina Gallagher

On March 29, 2009 Christina Gallagher received this message about civil war in the United States of America: The birth-pangs are over. The world is handed over to the antichrist.

Civil war will break out in the United States and many will fight and kill each other. 'Nests' of foreigners have already been placed in the U.S. Christina was shown a scene of what will take place, the weapons being used and the blood flowing. The horror was overpowering for her. Christina was then allowed to witness the explosion of a bomb which will be dropped on America. Its impact was horrific. She was shown that an earthquake will follow some time later.

The events in the U.S. will also filter throughout Europe and then throughout the world. A great suppression will come about....

Pestilence will accompany the civil war and the suppression. Mosquitoes will carry all kinds of new diseases. Locusts such as have never been seen before will form a plague; it will seem as those

themselves have an evil intent, almost as if they have an awareness that they are to wreack destruction.

Pedro Regis

Terrorists Led By One Who Looks Like A Prophet And The Land Of the Savior

April 30, 2005. Message 2516. Dear Sons and Daughters, bend your knees in prayer for peace in the world. Humanity lives in great stress and is heading towards self-destruction. **An arrogant man will make an agreement with Iran.** He will seem to want peace, but in truth he will be a thorn for many nations. **The terrorists, led by one who looks like a prophet, will bring suffering and pain to the nest of the eagle (U.S.A.) and to the land of the Savior.** Behold, the times predicted by Me have come. Pray. Pay attention. I am your Mother and I am with you. Forward with hope. This is the message I give you in the name of the most Holy Trinity. Thank you for permitting me to reunite you here once more. I bless you in the name of the Father, and of the Son, and of the Holy Spirit. Amen. Be at peace.

A Great Army Will Set Out From Mecca And Will Leave A Trail Of Destruction And Death

August 19, 2006. Message 2722. Dear Sons and Daughters, **a great army will set out from Mecca and will leave a trail of destruction and death wherever it passes.** The wickedness of men will be so great in this world that The Lord will anticipate the day of the last judgment. Be converted and return to Him Who is your One True Savior. Pray always. **The power of prayer will let you understand the plans of God for your lives.** Forward with courage. The Lord is waiting for you. This is the message I transmit to you today in the name of The Most Holy Trinity. Thank you for permitting Me to reunite you here once more. I bless you in the name of The Father, and of The Son, and of The Holy Spirit. Amen. Be in peace.

Nuclear And Biological Weapons
Will Be Used By Bearded Men

May 3, 2005. Message 2518. Dear Sons and Daughters, **nuclear and biological weapons will be used by bearded men and terror will spread over various nations.** The devil has managed to seduce a great number of my poor children and has taken them away from the grace of my Divine Son. Unhappy are those who cling to material goods. **Know that there will be a great chaos in the world economy, and only the meek and humble of heart will manage to survive.** I ask you to flee from all vanity. **Flee from the styles of this world. Learn to dress modestly. Take care of your body, for you are a temple of the Holy Spirit. Be careful. You belong to The Lord. Whoever offends The Lord with indecent styles runs the risk of eternal damnation. Truly free yourself from the claws of the devil.** Don't turn your soul over to condemnation. This is the message I give you in the name of the most Holy Trinity. Thank you for permitting me to reunite you here once more. I bless you in the name of the Father, and of the Son, and of the Holy Spirit. Amen. Be at peace.

A Weapon Of Great Destruction Will Be Prepared In A Laboratory

September 13, 2005. Message 2575. Dear Sons and Daughters, I suffer because of what awaits you. Bend your knees in prayer, for this is the only way you will have strength to bear the weight of the cross. **The men with big beards will act in a great city. A weapon of great destruction will be prepared in a laboratory.** Return quickly. Don't leave what you have to do for tomorrow. Don't back off. I am your Mother and I am at your side. Forward. This is the message I give you in the name of the Most Holy Trinity. Thank you for permitting me to reunite you here once more. I bless you in the name of The Father, and of The Son, and of The Holy Spirit. Amen. Be at peace.

March 4, 2006. Message 2648. Dear Sons and Daughters, I love you as you are, and I want to see you happy already here on earth, and later with Me in heaven. I ask you to conserve the flame of faith bright. Humanity has gone away from God and My poor children go as the blind leading

146

other blind people. Terror will come from a famous mountain range and death will pass through Mosselbai. Shouts of despair will be heard in Brmania and Messina. The power of prayer will lead you to peace. Don't forget; God loves you and is calling you. Don't lose heart. Courage. I will be with you always. **It will come from Iran, and men will fear it.** Japan will drink the bitter cup of pain. I suffer for My poor children. Pray. Pray. Pray. This is the message I give you today in the name of the Most Holy Trinity. Thank you for permitting me to bring you here once more. I bless you in the name of The Father, and of The Son, and of The Holy Spirit. Amen. Be at peace.

The Plague

May 10, 2005. Message 2520. Dear Sons and Daughters, God awaits you with the immense love of The Father. Return to Him for He is your Absolute Good and knows what you need. Free yourselves from sin and embrace the grace of The Lord. Don't let yourselves be contaminated by the poison of the devil. Humanity will confront difficult moments. Pray. **Russia will make an agreement, and from the agreement will arise something painful for men and women. The plague that will come will be such that those contaminated will not recognize themselves. Whoever is contaminated no longer will be able even to think.** Bend your knees in prayer. I am your Mother and I suffer because of what awaits you. This is the message I give you in the name of The Most Holy Trinity. Thank you for permitting me to reunite you here once more. I bless you in the name of The Father, and of The Son, and of The Holy Spirit. Amen. Be at peace.

Smallpox

June 4, 2005. Message 2531. Dear Sons and Daughters, belong to The Lord and you will have nothing to fear. Pray much and give your very existence to The Lord. Flee from sin and answer yes to the call of The Lord. **Smallpox will be used as a weapon against a nation by men with big beards. Many will suffer greatly.** Your Brazil will also suffer with the coming of a giant wave. A region of Brazil will live moments of anguish. Pray. You who are listening to Me should ask The Lord for mercy, and confide in My special protection. Don't back away. Fear not.

147

This is the message I give you in the name of The Most Holy Trinity. Thank you for permitting Me to reunite you here once more. I bless you in the name of The Father, and of The Son, and of The Holy Spirit. Amen. Be at peace.

Disease – Millions Of Cadavers Will Be Spread Everywhere

August 12, 2006. Message 2719. Dear Sons and Daughters, bend your knees in prayer and beseech your merciful Father for His grace. I am your Mother and I come from heaven to call you to conversion and holiness. Do not just cross your arms. **Humanity is heading for the abyss of destruction that men have prepared with their own hands.** Mankind will carry a heavy cross. **A disease will come, worse than all those that already exist. Men will be contaminated and millions of cadavers will be spread everywhere.** I suffer for what is waiting for you. **Repent. Repent. Repent.** This is the message I transmit to you today in the name of The Most Holy Trinity. Thank you for permitting Me to reunite you here once more. I bless you in the name of The Father, and of The Son, and of The Holy Spirit. Amen. Be in peace.

Israel

July 3, 2005. Message 2544. Dear Sons and Daughters, I am your Mother and I love you. Pray much in front of the cross for peace in the world and for conversion of sinners. Humanity has contaminated itself with evil and My poor children are heading on the way to self-destruction. **Israel will live the agony of one condemned, for it will be surprised by terrorists.** Know that God is saddened by your sins. Repent and return in order to be saved. I don't want to obligate you, but pay attention and listen to Me. Courage. Don't lose heart. I will speak to My Jesus for you. Forward. This is the message I give you in the name of the Most Holy Trinity. Thank you for permitting me to reunite you here once more. I bless you in the name of The Father, and of The Son, and of The Holy Spirit. Amen. Be at peace.

September 1, 2005. Message 2569. Dear Sons and Daughters, behold, the time of sorrows is coming. Now the time for great and sorrowful events is closer. **An earthquake will shock mankind.** Pray. Receive My appeals. **Something great will happen on Sinai. Know that men and women will drink the poison their own hands have prepared. You will see horrors before three great ones are honored. A Friday will go down in history forever.** Take care of your spiritual life. Be like Jesus in everything. Listen to man and obey God. Your salvation will come from The Lord. This is the message I give you in the name of the Most Holy Trinity. Thank you for permitting me to reunite you here once more. I bless you in the name of The Father, and of The Son, and of The Holy Spirit. Amen. Be at peace.

October 30, 2005. Message 2596. Tombador da Cima, Sento Se, Bahia. Dear Sons and Daughters, I come from Heaven to bless you and to tell you that you are important to The Lord. You are His people chosen and loved with a boundless love. I ask you to be courageous. Don't be disheartened by your difficulties. I am your Mother and I am at your side. Know that The Lord will send His angels to help you in your tribulations. There will be a great sign in the heavens of Brazil. It is the call of The Lord. Pay attention. **There will be great terror in Sinai.** In Assisi shouts of despair and great lamentations will be heard. Bend your knees in prayer. God expects much from you. Don't lose heart. You who are listening to Me, don't lose hope. Your reward will come from The Lord. This is the message I give you in the name of the Most Holy Trinity. Thank you for permitting me to reunite you here once more. I bless you in the name of The Father, and of The Son, and of The Holy Spirit. Amen. Be at peace.

December 17, 2005. Message 2616. Dear Sons and Daughters, pray. Humanity needs peace and you can contribute so that peace reigns in the hearts of men and women. **Israel won't take long before it encounters a great suffering.** France will grieve the death of its children and Los Angeles will be shaken. Behold the difficult times for humanity. Be converted and return to Him Who is your Way, Truth, and Life. Terrorists are preparing something painful for mankind. England will suffer. Georgia will also suffer a heavy cross. Remain firm on the way I have pointed out for you. Great pain will come to Alaska. I am your Mother and I am at your side. A swift bird shall fall. Don't just cross your arms. Forward. This is the message I give you in the name of the Most Holy Trinity. Thank you for permitting me to reunite you here once

149

more. I bless you in the name of The Father, and of The Son, and of The Holy Spirit. Amen. Be at peace.

July 17, 2008. Message 3027 – from Our Lady of Peace, given in Sorocaba, SP. Dear Sons and Daughters, I love you as you are and I want to see you happy already here on earth, and later, with Me in heaven. I ask you to be docile to My call. I come from heaven to offer you my love and to call you to a true conversion. Don't just cross your arms. God is calling you. Be faithful to His call. Humanity needs to accept the appeal of The Lord. Open your hearts and don't back away. Receive the Eucharist. Your victory will be in The Lord. **Be faithful to your church. A notice will come from Jerusalem that will call the attention of the world. It will be a great suffering for the Church.** What is waiting for you makes Me sad. Pray much. This is the message that I transmit to you in the name of The Most Holy Trinity. Thank you for permitting Me to reunite you here one more time. I bless you in the name of The Father, and of The Son, and of The Holy Spirit. Amen. Be in peace.

Jerusalem – A Frightening Event
Will Occur On A Hill In Jerusalem

June 17, 2006. Message 2695. Dear Sons and Daughters, I come from heaven to reveal to you the great happenings for these your times. I speak to you because I have permission of My Lord. Pay attention. **Humanity has fled from its Creator and is going towards the abyss of destruction.** Pray. God wants to save you, but you cannot live far from His Grace. **A frightening event will occur on a hill in Jerusalem.** Oh men and women, where do you want to go? Know that only Jesus is your Way, Truth, and Life. Return to Him and you will be saved. This is the message I give you today in the name of the Most Holy Trinity. Thank you for permitting me to bring you here once more. I bless you in the name of The Father, and of The Son, and of The Holy Spirit. Amen. Be at peace.

October 6, 2007. Message 2899 – from Our Lady of Peace. Dear Sons and Daughters, be courageous and testify that you belong to Christ. Flee from sin and seek the things from above. Know, all of you, that The Lord awaits you. Don't cross your arms. Be men and women of prayer. Humanity has withdrawn from God and has contaminated itself with sin. Be converted quickly. Don't stay in sin. **Israel will weep. Death will pass and the destruction will be great. A great city will be surrounded and its dwellers will experience a heavy cross.** I suffer because of what awaits you. This is the message I transmit to you today in the name of The Most Holy Trinity. Thank you for permitting Me to reunite you here once more. I bless you in the name of The Father, and of The Son, and of The Holy Spirit. Amen. Be at peace.

Atomic Holocaust In Middle East And Asia Third World War

A Great Earthquake Will Shake Iran And The Hidden Secret Will Be Hit.

June 9, 2007. Message 2848. Dear Sons and Daughters, return to The Lord. Don't just cross your arms. God is in a hurry. Bend your knees in prayer and beg The Lord for His loving kindness. **A great earthquake will shake Iran and the hidden secret will be hit.** I suffer because of what awaits you. Don't lose heart because of your difficulties. I will speak to My Jesus for you. Be good one to another. Love. Without love you cannot understand the plans of God for your lives. Forward. Thank you for permitting me to reunite you here once more. I bless You in the name of The Father, and of The Son, and of The Holy Spirit. Amen. Be at peace.

The Middle East Will Shake With Great Atomic Holocaust

January 28, 2010. Message 3272 – from Our Lady, Queen of Peace, Anguera, Bahia, Brazil. Dear Sons and Daughters, peace in the world is threatened. Bend your knees in prayer, for this is the only way you will attain true peace. Humanity is heading towards a great abyss and the moment has come for your return to The Lord. **The middle east will shake with great atomic holocaust.** The moments of pain for humanity is coming. I come from heaven to call you to conversion. Open your hearts and accept the will of God for your lives. Don't back out. Forward on the path I have pointed out. This is the message I give you today in the name of the Most Holy Trinity. Thank you for permitting Me to reunite you here once more. I bless you in the name of The Father, and of The Son, and of The Holy Spirit. Amen. Be at peace.

Iran Will Be Devastated By Israel

August 4, 2005. Message 2557. Dear Sons and Daughters, stay with The Lord. Oh men and women, where do you want to go? Know that there is no salvation outside of Christ. He is the Light of the world, and whoever is with Christ will have his life transformed. Don't let yourselves be contaminated. **Humanity is going towards destruction. The earth will be agitated and will tremble with a great atomic holocaust. Iran will be devastated by Israel.** Behold difficult times for humanity. Return to The Lord. Tell everyone that now is the favorable time for conversion. The day will come when many will have to repent for a life spent without God, but it will be late. Don't leave what you have to do for tomorrow. This is the message I give you in the name of the Most Holy Trinity. Thank you for permitting me to reunite you here once more. I bless you in the name of The Father, and of The Son, and of The Holy Spirit. Amen. Be at peace.

The Land Of The Savior Will Defend Itself When It Feels Defeat

March 26, 2005. Message 2501. Dear Sons and Daughters, the land of the Queen will be surprised and its enemies will cause great destruction. **The land of the Savior must suffer much, but when it feels defeat it will defend itself with weapons that spread fire in the sky.** Mankind will not find peace because it has gotten away from its Creator. Intensify your prayers and return to Him Who is your only great friend. The king will hurriedly leave his house, but must pass through blood flowing in his palace. Don't lose heart. Don't back away. You will be victorious with God. This is the message I give you in the name of the most Holy Trinity. Thank you for permitting me to reunite you here once more. I bless you in the name of the Father, and of the Son, and of the Holy Spirit. Amen. Be at peace.

Fire That Burns Fire, Cradle Of The Sun And Of Fire

October 28, 2006. Message 2752. Dear Sons and Daughters, I love you as you are, and I want to help you. Be strong and firm in the faith. Do not let the flame within you go out. Bend your knees in prayer and courageously live My appeals. Witness everywhere that you belong only to Christ. **Humanity is heading towards an abyss of destruction which men have prepared with their own hands. Fire that burns fire, cradle of the sun and of fire. Who understands will beseech the Mercy of The Lord.** Go forth on the way I have indicated to you. Whoever is with The Lord will not experience the weight of defeat. Courage. This is the message I transmit to you today in the name of The Most Holy Trinity. Thank you for permitting Me to reunite you here once more. I bless you in the name of The Father, and of The Son, and of The Holy Spirit. Amen. Be in peace.

City Of Jerusalem Will Be Destroyed

April 26, 2005. Message 2514. Dear Sons and Daughters, pray much for the conversion of men before the cross. You now live in most difficult moments for humanity. I ask you to return to The Lord as soon as possible. Humanity will suffer and men will have to lament a life lived without God. **The city of Jerusalem will be destroyed and when the great tribulation has passed it will not be recognizable; all that remains will be just a big desert.** Oh men and women, return. Receive God with love and flee from hatred. Humanity will drink the bitter cup that men have prepared with their own hands. This is the message I give you in the name of the most Holy Trinity. Thank you for permitting me to reunite you here once more. I bless you in the name of the Father, and of the Son, and of the Holy Spirit. Amen. Be at peace.

April 7, 2009. Message 3145 – from Our Lady of Peace, Anguera, Bahia, Brazil. Dear Sons and Daughters, your salvation is only in Jesus. You remember today (Good Friday) His total and conscious gift for the salvation of humanity. Confide in His love. He knows you by name and wants to save you. Don't refuse. Be courageous and give testimony everywhere that you belong only to Christ. When you feel the weight of the cross, call My Son Jesus, for He alone is your help in difficult moments. Days will come when there will be few men and women of faith. A great spiritual confusion will take many of My poor children from the way of God. Humanity will confront great trials. **Jerusalem and many neighboring cities will experience a heavy cross. The devastation will be great.** Bend your knees in prayer. Only by prayer will you be able to support the weight of trials that must come. This is the message I transmit to you today in the name of The Most Holy Trinity. Thank you for permitting Me to reunite you here once more. I bless you in the name of The Father, and of The Son, and of The Holy Spirit. Amen. Be at peace.

Palestine And The Holy Land

May 23, 2006. Message 2685. Dear Sons and Daughters, **a warning will come for Palestine which will be stricken, and my poor children will suffer in the Holy Land.** I am your Mother and I come from heaven to help you. Be courageous and give witness that you are of The Lord. Let your life speak of The Lord more than your words. Be strong. God is with you. Trust, and all will end up well for you. Don't lose heart. Courage. This is the message I give you today in the name of the Most Holy Trinity. Thank you for permitting me to bring you here once more. I bless you in the name of The Father, and of The Son, and of The Holy Spirit. Amen. Be at peace.

Amman

January 29, 2011. Message 3432 – from Our Lady of Peace, Anguera, Bahia, Brazil. Dear Sons and Daughters, don't lose heart. Be courageous. God is very close to you and you have nothing to fear. Open your hearts and accept the will of God for your lives. Be courageous and accept your true role as christians. Testify everywhere that you belong only to The Lord, and the things of this world are not for you. I am your sorrowful Mother, and I suffer because of your suffering. Don't back away. After all the trials The Lord will come and you will be rewarded for your courage and faith. **Humanity is heading towards an abyss of destruction that men have prepared with their own hands. Amman will tremble. The Orient will drink the bitter cup of pain.** Pray, pray,

154

pray. This is the message I transmit to you today in the name of the Most Holy Trinity. Thank you for permitting Me to reunite you here once more. I bless you in the name of The Father, and of The Son, and of The Holy Spirit. Amen. Be at Peace.

Syria

July 23, 2005. Message 2552. Dear Sons and Daughters, pray. Flee definitively from sin and return to Him Who is your Way, Truth, and Life. Humanity will not go many steps before it encounters destruction. Belong to The Lord. Seek holiness if you want salvation. **Syria will betray, but afterwards will drink its own poison.** Know that God is in a hurry. Don't wait for tomorrow to do what you have to do. This is the message I give you in the name of the Most Holy Trinity. Thank you for permitting me to reunite you here once more. I bless you in the name of The Father, and of The Son, and of The Holy Spirit. Amen. Be at peace.

Pakistan

September 7, 2007. Message 2886 – from Our Lady. Dear Sons and Daughters, **shouts for help will be heard in San Francisco and the same sorrowful things will be heard in Pakistan.** Bend your knees in prayer. Don't get away from prayer. Assume your true role as Christians and don't let the flame of faith within you go out. I am your Mother and I know what awaits you. I love you as you are, but I need your sincere and courageous yes, for this is the only way that I can transform you and lead you to Him Who is your one and only Savior. Forward. This is the message I transmit to you today in the name of The Most Holy Trinity. Thank you for permitting Me to reunite you here once more. I bless you in the name of The Father, and of The Son, and of The Holy Spirit. Amen. Be at peace.

July 17, 2007. Message 2864. Dear Sons and Daughters, pray. Only by prayer will you be able to grow in the spiritual life. Be strong in faith. Don't let the things of this world take you away from the way of God. You are entirely of The Lord. He loves you and is calling you. Humanity is heading toward an abyss of destruction, but you can change the situation. Be converted. Serve The Lord with love and fidelity. **Something sorrowful will happen in Pakistan** and will be repeated in

San Sebastian. Beseech the mercy of God for yourselves. This is the message I transmit to you today in the name of The Most Holy Trinity. Thank you for permitting Me to reunite you here once more. I bless you in the name of The Father, and of The Son, and of The Holy Spirit. Amen. Be at peace.

March 13, 2011. Message 3451 – from Our Lady of Peace, Maragigipe, Bahia, Brazil. Dear Sons and Daughters, I come from heaven to bless you and to tell you that now is the right time for your conversion. Don't cross your arms. Don't let the darkness of sin take you away from the way that will lead you to my Son Jesus. **You live in a time worse than the time of the flood. Bend your knees in prayer, for this is the only way you can contribute to the definitive triumph of my Immaculate Heart.** I suffer because of what is coming to you. People go away from God and the creature is valued more than the creator. My poor children go as the blind leading the blind. Repent and return to Jesus. He is your all and you can't do anything without Him. My poor children need to accept the love of God, for only in this way will you encounter peace. You are important for the realization of My plans. Tell everyone that God is in a hurry. **Terror will come to North Korea and my poor children will carry a heavy cross. Difficult days will come to India and Pakistan**. Pray. Only by prayer will you find strength to bear the weight of the cross. Courage. Don't back out. This is the message I transmit to you today in the name of the Most Holy Trinity. Thank you for permitting me to reunite you here once more. I bless you in the name of The Father, and of The Son, and of The Holy Spirit. Amen. Be at Peace.

Turkey

September 10, 2005. Message 2573. Dear Sons and Daughters, do your best in the mission The Lord has entrusted to you. Now is the time of the great spiritual battle. Be strong. Humanity is heading towards the abyss of destruction, and the moment has come for you to be converted.

Turkey will experience great pain. Great will be the suffering for many of My poor children. Don't get away from prayer. It will be on the east coast. A giant wave will cause great destruction. The eagle will suffer again. This is the message I give you in the name of the Most Holy

Trinity. Thank you for permitting me to reunite you here once more. I bless you in the name of The Father, and of The Son, and of The Holy Spirit. Amen. Be at peace.

February 25, 2006. Message 2646. Dear Sons and Daughters, love the Truth, and seek to imitate my Son Jesus in everything. Humanity has contaminated itself with sin and needs to be cured. Repent, for repentance is the first step to be taken on the road to conversion. I am your Mother and I suffer because of what awaits you. Many regions on earth will carry a heavy cross. Sorrowful happenings will afflict my poor children. Pray. Johannesburg will tremble. It will lose its glory and fame. **Death will pass through Turkey, and people will experience great sufferings.** In Oiapoque (north point of Brazilian shoreline) people will weep and lament. There will be great pain. Be brave and don't back away. God is with you. Happen what may, trust in The Lord. This is the message I give you today in the name of the Most Holy Trinity. Thank you for permitting me to bring you here once more. I bless you in the name of The Father, and of The Son, and of The Holy Spirit. Amen. Be at peace.

March 6, 2011. Message 3448 – from Our Lady of Peace, Anguera, Bahia, Brazil. Dear Sons and Daughters, I am always in your midst, even though you don't see me. Have confidence, faith, and hope. My Son Jesus loves you and awaits you with open arms. Now is the time of tribulations, but you can experience a great victory by living in the Grace of My Son Jesus. Don't lose heart. I encourage you to be men and women of prayer. I am in a hurry, and you cannot just stand still. Take care of your spiritual life. Give your yes to the call of the Lord Who sees what is hidden and know you by name. Humanity is on the track to destruction that men have prepared with their own hands. Repent, for repentance is the first step on the way to holiness. Don't lose hope. I will speak to my Jesus for you. Courage. **You will yet see horrors on earth. Tehran and Istanbul will experience a heavy cross. Death will come and My poor children will weep and lament**. Return quickly. When you feel the weight of difficulties, call Jesus. You full joy is with Him and without Him you are nothing and can do nothing. This is the message I transmit to you today in the name of the Most Holy Trinity. Thank you for permitting me to reunite you here once more. I bless you in the name of The Father, and of The Son, and of The Holy Spirit. Amen. Be at Peace.

Egypt

May 24, 2005. Message 2527. Dear Sons and Daughters, fill yourselves with the love of God and let yourselves be led by the Holy Spirit. Flee from all that paralyzes true love. The times in which you live are difficult because the creature is considered more valuable than its Creator. Don't let the seed of evil overcome you. Belong only to The Lord. I am your mom and I suffer because of your suffering. Happen what may, God is always near you. A sleeping giant will arise in a region of Bahia and bring suffering for many people. Pray. Bend your knees in prayer in order to be able to bear the weight of the trials which must come. **News from Egypt will spread throughout the world, and many people will lose their faith.** Don't forget my appeals. Remain firm on the path I have pointed out. Accept the Gospel and the teachings of the true magisterium of the Church. Pay attention. Don't be deceived. This is the message I give you in the name of The Most Holy Trinity. Thank you for permitting me to reunite you here once more. I bless you in the name of The Father, and of The Son, and of The Holy Spirit. Amen. Be at peace.

April 20, 2006. Message 2670. Dear Sons and Daughters, The Lord is calling you. Answer His loving call joyfully and you will be saved. Know that the garden will no longer be a safe place, for the danger will come from the grounds of campo grande, near the rocks of Rio Negro. Bend your knees in prayer. Trust in the power of God and flee from all evil. Salta will be stricken and My poor children will carry a heavy cross. Be converted. Many things depend on your conversion. **The idolatry of Egypt will fall to the ground.** This is the message I give you today in the name of the Most Holy Trinity. Thank you for permitting me to bring you here once more. I bless you in the name of The Father, and of The Son, and of The Holy Spirit. Amen. Be at peace.

July 13, 2006. Message 2706. Dear Sons and Daughters, The Lord is the certainty of your victory. Seek your strength in Him and you never will experience the weight of defeat. Humanity has gone away from God and people are as blind leading the blind. Repent, and give witness by your lives that you belong to The Lord. **There will be a great slaughter in Egypt and My poor children will experience a heavy cross.** I am your Mom and I want to tell you that now is the time of the great return. Do not stand still. God is waiting for your yes. This is the message I transmit to you today in the name of The Most Holy Trinity. Thank you for permitting Me to reunite you here once more. I bless you in the name of The Father, and of The Son, and of The Holy Spirit. Amen. Be at peace.

The Blessed Virgin Mary And The Muslims

Blessed Mary Of Agreda

Blessed Mary of Agreda (17th century). "It was revealed to me that through the intercession of the Mother of God all heresies will disappear. The victory over heresies has been reserved by Christ for His blessed Mother. In the latter days, the Lord will in a special manner spread the renown of His Mother. Mary began salvation, and by her intercession it will be completed. Before the second coming of Christ, Mary, more than ever, must shine in mercy, might, and grace in order to bring unbelievers into the Catholic faith. **The power of Mary in the latter days will be very conspicuous. Mary will extend the reign of Christ over the heathens and the Mohammedans, and it will be a time of great joy when Mary in enthroned as Mistress and Queen of Hearts.**

An unusual chastisement of the human race will take place toward the end of the world." [18]

Brother Louis Rocco

Brother Louis Rocco (19th century). "Terrible wars will rage over Europe. God has long been patient with the corruption of morals; half of mankind He will destroy. Russia will witness many outrages. Great cities and towns alike will be destroyed in a bloody revolution that will cause the death of half the population. **In Istanbul (Constantinople) the Cross will replace the half-moon of Islamism, and Jerusalem will be the seat of a King. The southern Slavs will form a Great Catholic Empire and drive out of Europe the Turks (Mohammedans), who will withdraw to North Africa and subsequently embrace the Catholic faith."** [18]

St. Louis-Marie Grignion De Montfort

St. Louis-Marie Grignion De Montfort (18th century). "The power of Mary over all devils will be particularly outstanding in the last period of time. **She will extend the Kingdom of Christ over the idolaters and the Muslims, and there will be a glorious era when Mary is the Ruler and Queen of Hearts."** [18]

Chapter 9

Chastisements,
The Great Chastisement,
The Three Days Of Darkness

La Salette 1846

At La Salette on September 19, 1846 Our Lady gave Melanie a secret which she revealed later. In the November 21, 1878 written message revealing this secret Melanie wrote concerning part of the revealed secret: "... **The seasons will be altered,** the earth will produce nothing but bad fruit. The stars will lose their regular motion. **The moon will only reflect a faint reddish glow. Water and fire will give the earth's globe convulsions and terrible earthquakes which will swallow up mountains, cities, etc. ....**

Rome will lose the faith and become the seat of the Antichrist.

The demons of the air together with the Antichrist will perform great wonders on earth and in the atmosphere, and men will become more and more perverted. God will take care of his faithful servants and men of good will. **The Gospel will be preached everywhere,** and all peoples of all nations will get to know the truth....

The Church will be in eclipse, the world will be in dismay. But now Enoch and Eli will come, filled with the Spirit of God. They will preach with the Might of God, and men of good will will believe in God, and many souls will be comforted. They will make great steps forward through the virtue of the Holy Spirit and will condemn the devilish lapses of the Antichrist. **Woe to the inhabitants of the earth! There will be bloody wars and famines, plagues and infectious diseases.** It will rain with a fearful hail of animals. **There will be thunderstorms which will**

shake cities, earthquakes which will swallow up countries. Voices will be heard in the air. Men will beat their heads against walls, call for their death, and on another side death will be their torment. **Blood will flow on all sides.** Who will be the victor if God does not shorten the length of the test? At the blood, the tears and the prayers of the righteous, God will relent. Enoch and Eli will be put to death. **Pagan Rome will disappear. The fire of Heaven will fall** and consume three cities. **All the universe will be struck with terror** and many will let themselves be led astray because they have not worshipped the true Christ who lives among them. It is time; the sun is darkening; only faith will survive.

Now is the time; the abyss is opening. Here is the king of kings of darkness, **here is the Beast with his subjects, calling himself the savior of the world.** He will rise proudly into the air to go to Heaven. He will be smothered by the breath of the Archangel Saint Michael. He will fall, and **the earth, which will have been in a continuous series of evolutions for three days, will open up its fiery bowels;** and he will have plunged for eternity with all his followers into the everlasting chasms of hell. And **then water and fire will purge the earth and consume all the works of men's pride and all will be renewed. God will be served and glorified."** [7]

The Last Crisis

Marie-Julie Jahenny, the Breton stigmatist, born 1850, died 1941, announced that three quarters of the population of the globe will disappear in the last crisis; terrible earthquakes, epidemics of unknown diseases whose ravages would be frightful, terrible famines, inclement weather, cyclones, rising seas that would cause terrifying tidal waves.

August 17, 1905
The last crisis will be divided in three parts: the first long and painful when divine vengeance will be manifested, during which the most guilty will be destroyed. "This blow of justice will only irritate them."

The second will be shorter but more formidable, more sinister: "My Divine Son, seeing all these blows cannot bring back His people to pardon and mercy – lost souls – will strike again more fearfully...."

The third: "Everything must be lost from top to bottom. That, my dear children, is when **St. Michael, the Archangel, who is awaiting orders from Heaven, will descend with his armies to fight with my good children, the true and good children of victory.... Justice will pass everywhere. During this time you will not have the bread of the strong.**... No apostles, you will have only your faith as food, my Divine Son, as Sovereign Priest, to forgive you....

My dear children, all the souls living in His Divine Heart will run no danger; they will only have a faint knowledge of His anger.

They will be enclosed in this immense sea of prodigies and power, during these great blows of divine justice." [42]

We have been passing through a prolonged period of increasing chastisements: Notable among these were:

- **Hurricanes** Andrew August 24, 1992, Charley August 13, 2004, Katrina August 25, 2005, Rita September 20, 2005, the great hurricane/northeaster storm Sandy.
- **EF5 tornadoes** at Tuscaloosa Alabama Tornado April 27, 2011, Joplin Missouri May 22, 2011, Moore Oklahoma May 20, 2013, El Reno Oklahoma May 31, 2013, 16.2 miles long, 2.6 miles maximum width (widest on record) with winds of 295 mph. Unusual EF4 tornadoes for November in Illinois which on Nov 17, 2013 struck in New Minden with 166 mph winds and in Washington, with winds from 170 to 190 mph.
- **Volcanic eruption.** Mt. St. Helen's eruption on May, 18, 1980.
- **Great ice storm of January 5-10, 1998** affecting Canada, Vermont, Maine, New York State, and New Hampshire.
- **The Great Mississippi Floods of 1993 and 2011**, the so-called "500 year floods."
- **The greatest forest fires in the history of Arizona and New Mexico 2011**; forest fire in Arizona during May and June 2011, and in New Mexico during June and July 2011. Over 50 major forest fires burning in August 2013 in Western United States. Historic drought in California with forest fires in California in January 2014.

163

- **The Chernobyl nuclear accident on April 26, 1986** at the Chernobyl Nuclear Power Plant in the Ukraine, USSR.
- **9.0 and greater earthquakes with devastating tsunamis in the Indian Ocean December, 26, 2004 and Japan March 11, 2010.** The earthquake and mainly the subsequent tsunami on December 26, 2004 killed over 230,000 people. The tsunami produced by the March 11, 2010 earthquake produced a **nuclear disaster at the Fukushima nuclear facilities with 3 nuclear plants melting down.**
- **Terrorist attacks September 11, 2001** in New York and Washington, D.C.
- **Wars in the Middle East**, initially Iran and Iraq, then the Gulf War in 2000, then the invasion of Iraq and Afghanistan, then uprisings in Libya and Syria. The threat of nuclear War in Korea, and in the Middle East.
- **Financial collapse** in the United States in 2008 which has spread into Europe, and is still spreading in 2013.

Father Gerard McGinnity, Christine Gallagher's spiritual director, contacted *Signs and Wonders for Our Times* to have them place messages in their magazine Vol. 19, No. 3 / 4, Spring 2009, which was going to press. Among the messages that were received on March 29, 2009 by Christina Gallagher from Our Lady Queen of Peace were messages that:

- The birth pangs are over. The world is handed over to the anti-Christ.
- Civil war will break out in the United States and many will fight and kill each other. Nests of foreigners have already been placed in the United States. Christina was shown a scene of what will take place, the weapons being used and blood flowing. The horror was overpowering for her. Christina was then allowed to witness the explosion of a bomb which will be dropped on America. Its impact was horrific. She was shown an earthquake will follow some time later.
- The events in the U.S. will also filter throughout Europe and then throughout the world. A great suppression will come about.
- Pestilence will accompany the civil war and suppression.

Mosquitoes will carry all kinds of new diseases. Locusts such as have never been seen before will form a plague; it will seem as those themselves have an evil intent, almost as if they have an awareness that they are to wreak destruction....

An Earthquake Will Come And It Will Rise Along The Banks Of A Mighty River Where The Great Arch Bends

Jennifer – Words from Jesus. Message received 3/17/10 at 3:00 PM: "My child, pray for your country for it will not be spared. Pray for those who are not prepared to see their hour of judgment. **I have told you that an earthquake will come and it will rise along the banks of a mighty river where the great arch bends. Many will perish. Pray for those who live on the coastline of the Pacific for the transgressions of those there are greater than of the time of Sodom and Gomorrah.** Be attentive to My words and pray, pray, pray for I am Jesus and My mercy and justice will prevail."

The Chastisement Is Already Upon The World

On September 23, 1994 St. Joseph said to Janie Garza: "My little one, the chastisement is already upon the world. You can see its manifestation in the sinfulness of the world, the great apostasy, the schism that is destroying many priests and consecrated souls, the violence in the family, the bloody massacre of the innocent infants, the increase in false prophets that are misleading many, the destruction of the youth through drug abuse and unhealthy relationships, the deadly plague, the pestilence that sweeps throughout the world taking the lives of many, the increase in homosexuality, the broken marriages that end in divorce, the destruction in natural disasters, the corrupted world leaders who are bringing destruction upon their countries, and the blasphemies against God by those who hate God. These are some of the signs of the chastisement and the only refuge is the refuge that you will find in the Immaculate Heart of Mary." [8]

Financial Chastisement

On December 24, 1996 at 6:00 p.m., Christmas Eve, Our Blessed Mother told Sadie Jaramillo: "Catastrophic events await this United

States, events that will bring many to their knees in fear.... **The horsemen of the Apocalypse are sent forth in this time of plagues, famine, war and strife, and will bear the justice of God. For this sinful nation will be brought low to its knees. This nation will know captivity and economic collapse. Only those who have entered into the Ark of My Immaculate Heart, will know peace, protection and guidance.**

The last grain of sand has gone through the hourglass, and the time of all times to accomplish The Triumph of My Immaculate Heart and The Eucharistic Reign of Christ is here." [6]

Sadie Jaramillo received a message from Jesus on November 8, 1996. Jesus said to Sadie Jaramillo: "The hold of the enemy is such that this world cannot be touched but by a supernatural act of God.... The insatiable hunger for power, money, and man's own self-indulging vices have corrupted this society.

What happens now is prophecy fulfilled. The pockets of many now full will become empty. The floor of the financial market will crash and the repercussions will resound worldwide. The despair of many will cause their own self-destruction. The world has not seen anything like this to be. Why, do you have eyes, but yet are blind to the truth? Why do you have ears and fail to hear the truth?"

Prizes And Possessions Disappear In An Instant

Jesus told Sadie Jaramillo on January 5, 1997 at 7:00 p.m.: "My Father's Will for your life will be brought about because of your fidelity and perseverance. For what you consider your treasure, is what you should feel.

But contrary is true, and **many now face the trial of seeing their prizes and possessions disappear in an instant. It will not stand as their idols any longer, not their homes, nor their jobs, nor their money, nor their pleasure idols, nor their perverted ideas.**

None of it will stand in the fury of My Justice nor in the fury of the

control from the one who opposes Me, that he will show to those who live through his reign.

I am asking you to prepare by fasting and prayer, for My Divine Intervention will prevail over My vineyard, My harvest, My shepherd, My flock....

I do not exist in your measure of time, but I do say, your time is now. Prepare, for nothing will be the same. What exists today will cease to exist and control, total and final will be in force." [6]

Physical Chastisements

Blessed Elena Aiello (1895-1961)

Blessed Elena Aiello − Mystic, Stigmatic, Victim Soul, Prophet and Foundress of the Minim Tertiaries of the Passion of Our Lord Jesus Christ was declared Blessed on September 14, 2011 − Feast of the Exultation of the Holy Cross.

On Good Friday, April 16, 1954 the Madonna appeared and said to Blessed Elena Aiello, "Listen attentively, and reveal to all: 'My Heart is sad for so many sufferings in an impending world in ruin. The justice of Our Father is most offended. Men live in their obstinacy of sin. **The wrath of God is near. Soon the world will be afflicted with great calamities, bloody revolutions, frightful hurricanes, and the overflowing of streams and the seas.... If men do not return to God with prayers and penances, the world will be overturned in a new and more terrible war**. Arms most deadly will destroy peoples and nations! The dictators of the earth, specimens infernal, will demolish the churches and desecrate the Holy Eucharist, and will destroy things most dear. In this impious war, much will be destroyed of that which has been built by the hands of man.

Clouds with lightning flashes of fire in the sky and a tempest of fire shall fall upon the world. This terrible scourge, never before seen in

the history of humanity, will last seventy hours. Godless persons will be crushed and wiped out. Many will be lost because they remain in their obstinacy of sin. Then shall be seen the power of light over the power of darkness.

Be not silent, my daughter, because the hours of darkness, of abandonment, are near. **I am bending over the world, holding in suspension the justice of God. Otherwise these things would already have now come to pass.**

Prayers and penances are necessary because men must return to God and to my Immaculate Heart – the Mediatrix of men to God, and thus the world will be at least in part saved.

Cry out these things to all, like the very echo of my voice. Let this be known to all, because it will help save many souls, and prevent much destruction in the Church and in the world."

On Good Friday April 8, 1955 the Blessed Mother spoke to Blessed Elena Aiello: "My daughter, it is thy Mother speaking to thee, Listen attentively, and make known all that I tell thee, because men, in spite of repeated warnings, are not returning to God. They refuse grace, and are not listening to my voice. **If men do not amend their ways, a terrifying scourge of fire will come down from Heaven upon all the nations of the world, and men will be punished according to the debts contracted with Divine justice. There will be frightful moments for all, because Heaven will be joined with the earth, and all the un-Godly people will be destroyed, some nations will be purified, while others will disappear entirely."**

During 1959 the Madonna said to Blessed Elena Aiello: "The world will be once more afflicted with great calamity; with bloody revolutions; with great earthquakes; with famines; with epidemics; with fearful hurricanes; and with floods from rivers and seas. **But if men do not return to God, purifying fire will fall from the Heavens, like snowstorms, on all peoples, and a great part of humanity will be destroyed!**

No longer do men speak according to the true spirit of the Gospel. **The immorality of the times has reached a peak. But men do not listen to my motherly warnings, so the world must soon be purified.**

Russia will march upon all the nations of Europe, particularly Italy, and will raise her flag over the dome of St. Peter's. Italy will be severely tried by a great revolution, and Rome will be purified in blood for its many sins, especially those of impurity! The flock is about to be dispersed and the Pope must suffer greatly."

On August 22, 1960 the Madonna said to Blessed Elena Aiello: "The hour of the justice of God is close, and will be terrible! Tremendous scourges are impending over the world, and various nations are struck by epidemics, famines, great earthquakes, terrific hurricanes, with overflowing rivers and seas, which bring ruin and death. If the people do not recognize in these scourges (of nature) the warnings of Divine Mercy, and do not return to God with truly Christian living, another terrible war will come from the East to the West. Russia with her secret armies will battle America; will overrun Europe. The river Rhine will be overflowing with corpses and blood. Italy, also, will be harassed by a great revolution, and the Pope will suffer terribly.

Spread the devotion to my Immaculate Heart, in order that many souls maybe conquered by my love and that many sinners may return to my Maternal Heart. Do not fear, for I will accompany with my maternal protection my faithful ones, and all those who accept my urgent warnings, and they – especially by the recitations of my Rosary will be saved.

Satan goes furiously through this disordered world, and soon will show all his might. But, **because of my Immaculate Heart, the triumph of Light will not delay in its triumph over the power of darkness, and the world, finally, will have tranquility and peace."**

On Good Friday – 1961 the Sorrowful Madonna said to Blessed Elena Aiello: "People pay no attention to my motherly warnings, and thus the world is falling headlong evermore into an abyss of iniquity. Nations shall be convulsed by terrible disasters, causing destruction

and death.

Russia, spurred on by Satan, will seek to dominate the whole world and, by bloody revolutions, will propagate her false teachings throughout all the nations, especially in Italy. The Church will be persecuted and the Pope and the priests shall suffer much."

Blessed Elena Aiello said: "Oh, what a horrible vision I see! A great revolution is going on in Rome! They are entering the Vatican. The Pope is all alone; he is praying. They are holding the Pope. They take him by force. They knock him down to the floor. They are trying him.... They are kicking him....

Our Blessed Mother is drawing near. Like corpses those evil men fall down to the floor. Our Lady helps the Pope to his feet and, taking him by the arm, she covers him with Her mantle saying: 'Fear not! Flagstaffs (flying the Red flag over St. Peter's dome and elsewhere) collapse, and power is gone out of the clubs of those evil brutes. These atheists are ever shouting: 'We don't want God to rule over us; we want Satan to be our master!'

My daughter, Rome will not be saved, because the Italian rulers have forsaken the Divine Light and because only a few people really love the Church. **But the day is not far off when all the wicked shall perish, under the tremendous blows of Divine Justice."**

Mother Elena Patriarca Leonardi

Mother Elena Patriarca Leonardi was told by St. Padre Pio on February 4, 1947 that the Virgin would entrust her with a great Mission.

Mother Elena Patriarca Leonardi was, it appears, actually given the Third Part of The Secret of Fatima by Our Blessed Mother, although Our Lady didn't tell her it was the Third Part of The Secret. The

messages given to Mother Elena have both the Apostasy and the Great Chastisement for Mankind spelled out in some detail.

On March 26, 1978, Our Blessed Mother told Mother Elena Leonardi: "Because of the great sins of all kinds, a great punishment will befall mankind: flames and fire will fall from heaven; ocean waters will turn into vapor and their foam will rise up to overthrow humanity; a great war will break out, sowing death and hunger; diseases of all kinds. If penance is not done, and they do not pray, the punishments will be ghastly!..." [16]

In the message of March 26, 1978, the Virgin also told Mother Elena Leonardi: "The Vatican knows how urgent it is to make men pray, but it does not want to alarm the people. Nevertheless, the whole world is living a terrible reality, the true Apocalypse. These are the dark days.... Scandals, divorce, free abortion laws, have all accelerated the punishments." [16]

On February 12, 1979, Our Lady as the Mother of all Peoples said to Mother Elena Leonardi: "You, my daughter, must atone and make others atone for the sins which are committed: these evil mothers kill their own children in their wombs.... so many human lives thrown down the drains that cry for vengeance before God! My daughter, **many diseases sent from heaven will befall and hurt mankind.... God the Father has repeated many times that many nations will disappear off the face of the earth. Godless nations will be the scourge chosen by God Himself to punish the disrespectful and unscrupulous humanity. My daughter, a great punishment will befall mankind, a great war will break out, fire will fall from heaven, the ocean waters will be converted into vapor, and the foam will rise to sweep all humanity, wherever you look, there will be anguish, misery and ruin. Communism will triumph because of the godless rulers; many magistrates will perish; freemasonry in the churches, prelates without dignity.... My daughter, the time has run out; this is the Apocalyptic hour; if they do not return to my Heart, they will know only desolation...."** [16]

Darkness From Russia And China

Jennifer – Words From Jesus

5/2/06
8:00 AM
My child, it is an important time to take heed to all that I tell you. Know that the time in which you are in is quickly passing. **It is a time that mankind should have heeded to the warning of My Mother yet so many still turn away.** Many have become lukewarm and have distanced themselves so far from Me that the light of truth would bring them into their judgment.

My child I am showing you these *two countries* that will join together to control a great number, they are *Russia and China*. *Your country My child is in danger of falling into the hands of these two countries.* Many are friends with them and many are enemies with your nation of freedom.

My child your country will be inundated with great suffering, disease, storms and *a financial collapse of historic proportions*. I have told you to place things in which I desire of you away for I will multiply all so that you have a table of plenty

This is a nation that has so greatly offended Me for being the leader of killing My little ones, **yet mankind believes there is no repercussions for so willingly turning away for its Creator for I am Jesus.**

My child pray, pray at this time and *do novenas and fasting*. Offer your daily sufferings to Me for if you only knew the full depth of My love for I am Jesus and My mercy and justice will prevail.

2/15/07
3:00 PM
My child, My peace be with you. Come to Me dear child, come to Me for I desire for you to be with Me. **The hour is closing in for changes are coming forth. The lights of cities will be blackened and sirens of manmade warnings will ring out. The winds will shift coming from**

the East and in the midst of chaos and destruction the world will see its hour of judgment.

I have warned My people to **watch for darkness coming forth from Russia and China for this war is just beginning.** Mankind's only peace will come from his trust in Me and My Divine will for I am Jesus. Recite the St. Michael prayer each hour and be attentive, remain on guard for the days of change are coming forth.

My child pray for your friends in Rome, pray for the protection of the Holy Father for My son is soon to be surrounded by dangerous missiles. I come to you with My words so be confident in what I tell you out of great love. Now go forth for I am Jesus and be at peace for all will be done according to My will.

Other Visionaries And Locutionists

Shortly after March 1988, Christina Gallagher, County Mayo in Ireland, had a vision in which she saw a very large figure of Christ in the sky with hand outstretched, looking down on the earth and saying "Woe," and she then saw balls of fire in countless numbers falling from the sky, and people on a road, running in every direction, some falling, and all looking up fearfully. She found the vision very frightening." [30]

Sadie Jaramillo had a vision on April 8, 1997. Sadie said: "During the rosary I see flashes of light and **like balls of fire falling from the sky.** I also see a man running like he is trying to avoid being hit. I hear 'the time of conflagration is here.'" [6]

On April 19, 1994 Janie Garza received seven visions from Jesus. Janie said: "In the sixth vision I saw the sky and it became as if at night time only I knew it was still day time, about noon time. Yet, the day became like night. Then I saw the stars in the Heavens turn into balls of fire and they began to fall on the earth. The fire began burning the areas where it was falling. People had begun screaming in fear as the day had turned into night. People were running and trying to find safety but there was no safety. Although it was dark I was given the ability to see them." [26]

Jesus told Janie: "Only prayer can lessen the severity of these events.... It is not important that dates or times are revealed to you. **What you have seen is for you to plead for My Father's mercy through your prayers."** [26]

On September 29, 1995 Janie Garza was told by St. Michael: "Behold, beloved one of the Almighty God, and embrace what the Almighty has willed for you to see – this vision of evilness in the world, for this is what God sees every day. See the many souls that are infected with sin and who choose to remain in darkness. See the poison in their hearts and souls. Know, beloved daughter of the Most High God, that God is much offended by all the evil that exists in the hearts of many souls. **Behold! And see the wrath of the Almighty One if souls do not repent!"** [8]

Janie said: "I saw the world become dark and then the sky turned an orange color, and I saw balls of fire falling from the sky, destroying the areas where they hit. This caused great fear in me, and I begged St. Michael not to show me anymore, but he said that God wanted me to see all this, so that I would understand the evil which exists in many, many souls. I was sick and scared with pain, but St. Michael asked me to bless myself with the sign of the Cross. I immediately did this, and I felt God's peace. Praised be God and His goodness." [8]

Possibility Of A Third World War

Our Blessed Mother in October 1988 gave to Patricia of Ecuador a secret with three parts. Our Lady spoke several times about **the possibility of a Third World War, of natural disasters and man-made disasters.** Our Lady said: "Little children, know that all you do benefits the world. **Your prayers, penances, and fasts are helping to deter the determination of the Third World War.... Great catastrophes are coming upon humanity; the Third World War threatens the world. Natural catastrophes created by man are coming."** [22]

Our Blessed Mother told Patricia some details of the war that she was allowed to share with us: "The war is near. It will be started with false peace treaties, treaties in which we should not place our

trust. **Many countries would be involved, among them China, Romania, Russia, and the United States.** Initially Poland will be involved also, but when the Holy Father leaves Rome, going first to France and then to Poland, Poland would be protected." [22]

Our Blessed Mother stated to Patricia: "You know, my daughter, that **the third nuclear war is near. Pray, my children, for China, Russia, Czechoslovakia. Pray for the countries from the South. Catastrophes come there. Pray for Panama, Nicaragua, El Salvador. Repent, fast, make penance. The Third World War is near, natural catastrophes, earthquakes, floods such as humanity has never seen before, because of so much sin in the world....** Pray much for the countries of Latin America. Pray very much for the countries of Central America. Pray for the Soviet Union, Russia, United States, Czechoslovakia, and China." [22]

Josyp Terelya in Chapter 12 of the book *Witness, Russia in Flames,* **is reported to have had an apparition from Our Blessed Mother in which he "saw a map."** Josyp stated: "I saw a map and **parts of it were burning. There were fires erupting all over Russia. Surrounding countries were also involved. There were flames in various parts of the world. It was what could happen if mankind does not come back to her Son.** I saw entire landscapes. I saw a river. I recognized, the Amur. I don't know how I knew it was that river. I saw many islands there. **I saw tanks on the Soviet side – but not the Soviet type – and a city in flames. Siberia was on fire to the Ural Mountains.** I saw Moscow, and the people there had faces that were twisted and deformed. Moscow was sinking, and throughout the city were strange creatures running down the streets. Their faces were those of rats and their tails were long and fat with scaly skin and hairs sticking out like spikes. They were as big as a dog and whoever the creatures spat at would fall to the ground, as if by venom. **There was a tremendous fear that filled Moscow, and the city was falling into the earth. I saw hills, forests, cities, walls. The whole countryside was aflame. And all these explosions were taking place...."** [27]

Josyp said "prophecies are difficult to interpret, and they are not always set in concrete. Was it civil war, or solely war with a foreign power? All I understood was that this was war and saw one country

175

against whom this war was waged – China! *The tanks were Chinese.* **This war is inevitable....**" [27]

On September 18, 1992, Our Blessed Mother appeared to Josyp Terelya and said: "I have come because there are terrible events that will befall a godless humanity that does not want to receive my Son.... **But there is an event coming that will shake the entire world. A great war, the greatest that has ever been until now is imminent.** So many will not survive it; only those who accept Christ the King and obey God's commandments. All this has been written in the Holy Book in the Gospel of Christ. Everywhere are the servants of the Antichrist, the sons of Satan, who will come proclaiming peace and quiet, but **Satan is preparing a great war, such as has never been seen until now.** His power is invisible, this power will drive people to arm themselves." Personal Communication that was subsequently published in the book *In The Kingdom of The Spirit.*[28]

Our Blessed Mother in this apparition also told Josyp Terelya: "We are in those times, when the end is near.... In the end times Satan will be punished and all his forces will be destroyed. **The devil knows well his time is short**, the time to prepare for the great battle and his purpose is to destroy all mankind rather than seeing all men serve God.... **This is why the devil is into such a frenzy to drag all the nations of the world into a great War, in order that he might destroy God's creation.... This is why the invisible evil servants of the devil, the evil spirits, and also his visible evil forces who represent all the godless rulers of the earth, are being used by Satan to prepare the great war with only one purpose, to obliterate God's human creatures."** Personal Communication that was subsequently published in the book *In The Kingdom of The Spirit.*[28]

On April 19, 1994 Janie Garza received seven visions from Jesus. The first five visions were of wars, the fourth of war in the Church, the fifth of war in the Family.

Janie said of the first three visions of war:

"In the first vision I saw *Red China in total chaos.* There were loud noises that sounded like guns all over. People were lying in puddles of blood in the streets. Houses were destroyed. I could hear screams of people, and I could see men with weapons killing people. The vision was graphic in the sense of the numerous bodies that lay in the streets and that were burning in cars. Their body parts were dismembered from the fire and the weapons. The area was filled with smoke and fire.

In the second vision I found myself in *the Holy City of Jerusalem.* I could hear screams of men, women and children who were being killed by men. This city was also filled with fear. The buildings were destroyed, the churches were places of refuge for the people. This was a terrible place to be at this time. No safety, no safety only fear and death.

In the third vision I saw *South Africa in total chaos.* People were being killed by men with hate in their hearts. These men had weapons and were running all over the city killing whoever crossed their paths. Buildings were destroyed as well as houses. Cars and trucks were all over the streets, burning, and some had people burning in them. This seems to be a war for political power." [26]

God Will Send Two Punishments

Blessed Anna Maria Taigi (d. 1837) said: "God will send two punishments:

One will be in the form of wars, revolutions and other evils; it shall originate on earth.
The other will be sent from Heaven. There shall come over the whole earth an intense darkness lasting three days and three nights.

Two Events With Fire Falling From Heaven

There will be at least two events that cause fire to fall from heaven, each destroying a substantial part of mankind:

   1. the chastisement from man – nuclear war,

    2. the chastisement from God – the Comet with the Three Days of Darkness.

This will fulfill Blessed Anna-Maria Taigi's prophecy.

The First Punishment

This first punishment will most probably include a nuclear war.

With a nuclear world war fire will fall from heaven. Those who survive will experience hunger and famine. The Antichrist, who will survive the nuclear holocaust, will offer food to those who take the mark of the beast to buy and sell and who will worship him. Those who will not do this will be persecuted and killed.

A nuclear war could be brought on by the errors committed by the financial and political leaders, the non-believers, the followers of Satan, who worship the gods of power and money in their steadfast drive for a One World Government that ends up in Antichrist's hands.

The Second Punishment

After the nuclear war God will send the second punishment – the punishment from heaven: There is a possibility that one comet will just miss the Earth causing fire to fall from heaven, then later the Comet of Chastisement – the Comet of Darkness will strike the earth.
In the *Book of Revelation* chapter 8 we are told about a great mountain, burning with fire being cast into the sea, and a great star falling from the heavens burning like a torch falling on the rivers.

In the *Book of Revelation* chapter 9 we are told about a star falling from heaven upon the earth opening the bottomless pit with the smoke of the pit arising as smoke from a great furnace, with the sun and the air darkened by the smoke.

This Comet of Chastisement causes the period of darkness which we call the Three Days of Darkness during which prophecy tells us that the demons will roam the earth rounding up Satan's followers who will be cast into Hell with them, the Antichrist and the false prophet and Satan himself. Satan will be bound with the chain of the Rosary.

We then will enter into the Era of Peace.

Prophecies About A Comet And The Earth

Nuclear War Could Be In Progress At The Time The Comet Hits Earth

On April 2, 1976 there was a vision of the Heavenly Mother and Padre Pio to Mother Elena Leonardi in which Our Lady said: "My daughter.... Men live in the obstinacy of sin, but God's wrath is near, and **the world will be tormented by great calamities; bloody revolutions, strong earthquakes, famines, epidemics, and terrible hurricanes which will force the seas and rivers to overflow. The world will be entirely transformed by a terrible war! The most deadly weapons will destroy peoples and nations and those things which are most cherished.** In this sacrilegious struggle, much of which has been created by Man will be demolished due to both savage impulse and enraged resistance. **Finally, incandescent clouds will appear in the sky, and a flaming tempest will fall over the whole world. The terrible calamity never before seen in Man's history, will last for seventy hours; the impious will be pulverized, and many will be lost in the obstinacy of their sins.** Then, the power of light over the power of darkness will be seen. Do not be silent, my daughter, because the terrible forsaken hour is near! **Bending over the world, I have suspended Divine Justice. If this were not the case, these things would have already happened...."**[16]

There May Be Two Different Comets Involved In The Chastisement

The first of these comets would not strike the Earth, but just graze it causing fire to fall from heaven and the oceans to overflow their boundaries. Fragments landing in water could cause steam and mist. The Antichrist could possibly then come on the scene after this event only to perish in a short time when **the Comet of Chastisement, also called the Comet of Darkness strikes the Earth.**

A Comet That Skims Across
The Surface Of The Earth

Josyp Terelya, in interviews given in May and June 1993 to Signs and Wonders staff, stated: "There is a large comet that is approaching the earth. It will not hit the earth, but it will cause many cataclysms on the planet. Land today in America will be under water. Because of the tremendous flooding, crops won't grow, the animals then will have nothing to feed on, and **this will contribute to the great famine.** Sooner or later there will be a tremendous struggle for products. We will survive, but we will all witness major catastrophes. **Do not be afraid or worried; pray and the Holy Spirit will lead you."**

The Comet Of Chastisement, The Comet Of Darkness

Julka (Julia) of Yugoslavia during period 1960-1966 had a vision of darkness over the earth.

The Lord Jesus, Our Saviour, and his suffering Holy Mother, weep over the fate of sinful humanity, which is unwilling to be converted. **Our Lord Jesus Christ says: "A small Last Judgment is approaching!"**

Julka said: "The God-fearing Christians, Mary's true admirers, will be specially protected by their Heavenly Mother when the Great tribulation comes.

God will punish the sins of earth very severely." [33]

During The Great Trial A Comet Strikes Earth
With Resulting Darkness

Julka (Julia) of Yugoslavia in the period 1960 to 1966 had a vision in which she states: "I found myself in a garden, looking after the flowers. **Suddenly something so gigantic fell to the earth,** that the whole world shook and reared itself as though it was going to break in pieces. **All the air is in flames.** The whole atmosphere of the earth from the ground to the sky, was a gigantic sheet of flame...." [33 Vol.1 pg. 220]

Julka (Julia) of Yugoslavia in messages from 1974 through 1976 reported visions of **the comet of the Chastisement striking the earth. Julka named it the Comet of Darkness.**

On June 21, 1976, The Comet of Darkness, the Heavenly Mother said to Julka of Yugoslavia: "My dear children: Julia, in ecstasy, observed something strange. 'Dear Mother, what is this?' **The Comet of darkness.... I am afraid!" Julka the seeress said: "Something long and black came towards the Earth. It looked like a comet. Our dear Mother rushed past it to help us. Whilst She spoke, the comet stood still in space." [33]**

On October 21, 1974, in message *The Great Purification,* **Julka (Julia) of Yugoslavia revealed that "The Earth's crust began to contract like the surface of the ocean during a tremendous storm. The surface rose and sank, writhed and folded as if it would break apart. In the East a great fire fell on the Earth...." [33]**

Julka: In 1975 the Heavenly Father agreed: "The whole Earth will be covered by a great fire and will be infertile for some time for those who survive it." [33]

The Earth's Surface Rent Asunder
And Filled With Craters

Julka (Julia) of Yugoslavia (1975-1976: visions and messages). "Then the great calamity, together with all the demons, plunged to the

Earth. After this began an indescribable horror. The people struck and killed each other mercilessly. The air was filled with screams, lamentations and cries of help. The mountains were raised, fell over and disappeared into the abyss. It appeared as if they were smashed and thrown about by the demons....

After a certain amount of time, **Our Lord Jesus commanded the Great Trial to cease.** Thereupon the great darkness receded from the Earth and, along with all the demons, disappeared into the horrible abyss. **The Earth's surface was rent asunder and filled with craters. It was as if it had experienced a dreadful bombardment. Only here and there some small areas were preserved....** Our Lord said: "I have removed **the living earth from the dead earth.** To the living earth I have given the Grace of My Wisdom that it may live in My Spirit. God the Father and the Holy Spirit commanded the sun should shine with renewed strength upon the Earth. **The air became crystal clear and the Earth appeared new-born."** [33]

On June 20, 1976, the Lord Jesus appeared in front of the Tabernacle. He glanced at all present there and **commanded Julka, the seeress: "Come with Me!"** And they ascended. Several Angels joined them. After a while **the Lord said to Julia: "Look at the Earth!"** From that height it seemed as small as a full moon. When Julia looked carefully, she saw huge craters everywhere. Only a few areas remained without holes. The whole Earth was stained with blood. **Our Lord Jesus explained: "This is how the face of the Earth will look during the Catastrophe!"** [33]

Gladys Quiroga de Motta Of Argentina's Vision Of The Earth

Our Lady gave message #1,377, on March 21, 1988 to Gladys Quiroga de Motta, in San Nicholas, Argentina after Gladys had a vision. She said, I see the earth divided in two parts. One part represents two-thirds and the other one-third, in which I see the Blessed Virgin. She is with the Child and from her breast rays of light go towards the part that represents two-thirds of the earth. Immediately, she says to me: **'Gladys, you are seeing the world half destroyed.** These rays of light are sent from my heart that wants to save

Chastisements, The Great Chastisement, Three Days Of Darkness

as many hearts as it can.

My Heart is all powerful, but it can do nothing if hearts are unwilling. **The means to save souls are prayer and conversion.** Every soul must prepare so as not to be imprisoned eternally by darkness. Amen, Amen.'"
₄ page 293

Pedro Regis's Messages About A Great Comet And About Two Giants Colliding

January 15, 2009. Message 3109 from Our Lady of Peace, Anguera, Bahia, Brazil. Dear Sons and Daughters, humanity is heading for a bloody future.... **A great comet will come and cause much destruction.**

January 24, 2009. Message 3113 from Our Lady of Peace, Anguera, Bahia, Brazil. Dear Sons and Daughters, **a collision between two giants in the universe will provoke great damage on earth. Fire will fall from heaven and many regions of the earth will be stricken.**

Akita, Japan

The Good As Well As The Bad Will Perish During This Great Chastisement

On October 13, 1973, at Akita, Japan, an apparition which was twice approved by the Bishop, Bishop Ito, and twice approved by the Bishops of the Church in Japan, **the Holy Mother gave this message to Sister Agnes Sasagawa. Our Lady said,** "If men do not repent and better themselves, the Heavenly Father will inflict a great punishment on all humanity. It will definitely be a punishment greater than the Deluge, such as has never been seen before. **Fire will plunge from the sky and a large part of humanity will perish.... The good as well as the bad will perish, sparing neither priests nor the faithful. The survivors will find themselves plunged into such terrible hardships that they will envy the dead. The only arms which will remain for you will be the Rosary and the sign left by My Son (Eucharist)."** [21]

The Three Days Of Darkness

The Earth Going Out Of Orbit

At the end of the message of La Salette, given to Melanie Calvat, Sister Mary of the Cross, in an apparition of Our Weeping Blessed Mother on September 19, 1846, we are told: "Now is the time; the abyss is opening. Here is the King of Kings of darkness, here is the Beast with his subjects, calling himself the savior of the world. He will rise proudly into the air to go to Heaven. He will be smothered by the breath of the Archangel Saint Michael. He will fall, and the earth, which will have been in a continuous series of evolutions for three days, will open up its fiery bowels; and he will have plunged for eternity with all his followers into the everlasting chasms of hell. And then water and fire will purge the earth and consume all the works of men's pride and all will be renewed. God will be served and glorified." [7]

Our Blessed Mother, Guardian of the Faith, (during the period 1988 to 1990) told Patricia Talbott of Cuenca, Ecuador, "the earth would go out of its orbit for three days. At that time the Second Coming of Jesus will be near, the devil will take over the world. During those days, families should be in continuous prayer. Because of false prophets, who will falsify the Words of Christ, we have to be in the state of grace so that we can discern the good from evil. We have to have the flame of Jesus Christ in our soul. We should not open the door of our homes to anybody. We are simply to keep on praying. The Virgin said it would be better not even to look through the window because we will see the justice of God over the people. It will be so terrible, that we will not want to see it." [22]

Julka (Julia), Zagreb, Yugoslavia in the period of years from 1960 to 1966 had a vision. About this she stated: "A little more about the Great distress. To begin with, a strong wind will come from the south. It will seize upon the whole globe and cause dreadful storms. After this about ten claps of thunder at once will strike the earth with such force that it will shudder throughout. This is a sign that the Great Tribulation and the Black Darkness are beginning. These will last three days and three nights. On this account people should go into their houses, close them up well, darken the windows, bless themselves and the house with holy water, and light blessed candles. Outside such dreadful things will be happening, that those who venture to look out will die. All the devils will be let loose on earth, so that they can destroy their prey themselves.

The demons will howl upon the earth and call many, in order to destroy them. What? They will imitate the voices of relations and acquaintances, who have not reached a safer place. Once the horror commences, do not open your door to anyone at all!"[33]

Some People Will Fall Into A Deep Sleep

Julka of Yugoslavia said: "In many places several people will gather together in fear. From the same group, some will perish, others remain alive for **this Day and moment, and for that darkness many will have prepared the blessed candles, but they will not burn, if the people have not lived in accordance with My Commandment, others will even be unable to light them for fear. But, for those who believe, although they have but a stub of the blessed candle, it will burn for three days and nights without going out. Some people will fall into a deep sleep granted by Me, so as not to see what is happening on the earth. All the buildings on earth will collapse, and only here and there will remain a simple, modest, little house, in which the light of a candle will glimmer. In many places, the heaps of corpses will be so great, that no one will be able to make a passage through them on account of these bodies, there will not be anyone to bury them.**" [33] Vol. 1 pp. 223-224

The Followers Of Evil Will Be Annihilated

An Intense Darkness Lasting Three Days And Three Nights

Blessed Anna-Maria Taigi, (19th century): "**There shall come over the whole earth an intense darkness lasting three days and three nights.** Nothing can be seen, and the air will be laden with pestilence which will claim mainly, but not only, the enemies of religion. **It will be impossible to use any man-made lighting during this darkness,**

except blessed candles. He, who out of curiosity, opens his window to look out, or leaves his home, will fall dead on the spot. During these three days, people should remain in their homes, pray the Rosary and beg God for mercy.

All the enemies of the Church, whether known or unknown, will perish over the whole earth during that universal darkness, with the exception of a few whom God will soon convert. The air shall be infected by demons who will appear under all sorts of hideous forms."[18]

Marie-Julie Jahenny, born 1850, died 1941, announced the three days of darkness during which the infernal powers will be loosed and will execute all the enemies of God.

January 4, 1884. "I did everything in behalf of My people, says the Lord, I sent My Mother upon earth: very few believed in her word. I made My voice heard everywhere; I made choice for Myself victims upon whom I performed wonders and marvels: they have been despised and persecuted.

Here comes that I will call back to Myself those lightning rods and will destroy everything on earth. It will be laid in a coffin; but after purifying it in its blood, I will raise it again glorious, as I Myself came out of the tomb.

Desolation will be so great and chastisements so terrible as for many a one to dry out from being frightened and think the world is up.

There will be three days of physical darkness. **For three days nights and two days,** night will be continuous. **Blessed wax candles will be the only ones which could give out some light through that horrible darkness; just a single one will be sufficient for the three days, although in the houses of the wicked they will give no brightness.**

During those three days of darkness, the demons will appear under the most hideous forms. Through the air, you will hear the most horrible cursings. The lightnings will penetrate your homes, but will not put the candles out: neither wind nor storm will be able to extinguish them.

Clouds red like blood will run across the sky. The clatter of thunder will cause the earth to totter. Sinister lightnings will trace furrows through the clouds, during a season they are never used to take place. The earth will be shaken up down to its foundations. The sea will arise roaring waves overflowing the continent.

Blood will be shed in such a great abundance…. that the earth will turn out a vast graveyard. The corpses of the wicked and those of the just will litter the ground. Famine will be great. All will be overturned and three quarters of men will perish. The crisis will burst out all of a sudden. Chastisements will be common to the whole world and will follow one another without interruption.

When My people had fallen into indifference, I started threatening them. At present time, they deserve My Justice. I came upon the earth; they want to chase Me away, to take My Holy Tabernacle away from Me, to overthrow My Cross and refuse to acknowledge My power.

Yes, I will have mercy on the good people; but the other ones I will engulf them. The earth will open ajar and they will disappear forever."[39]
The Lord gave Marie-Julie Jahenny a prayer to be said during the chastisement:

"I hail, adore and embrace you, adorable Cross of my Saviour. Protect us, guard us, save us. Jesus loved you so much. After His example, I do love you. May your holy image appease my fears! Let me experience nothing but calm and confidence!"
(Cluzeau documents; January 17, 1922)[39]

Marie-Julie Jahenny stated that the three days of darkness "will be on a Thursday, Friday and Saturday. Days of the Most Holy Sacrament, of the Cross, and Our Lady...." three days less one night.

Our Lady on September 20, 1882 revealed to Marie-Julie Jahenny: "The earth will be covered in darkness, and hell will be loosed on earth. The thunder and lightning will cause those who have no faith or trust in my power to die of fear."

During these three days of terrifying darkness, no windows must be opened, because no one will be able to see the earth and the terrible color it will have in those days of punishment, without dying at once....

The sky will be on fire, the earth will split.... During these three days of darkness **let the blessed candle be lighted everywhere, no other light will shine....**

On March 24, 1881, Our Lady added: "Those who have served me well and invoked me, who have my blessed picture in their house, who carry my Rosary on them and say it often, I will keep intact all that belongs to them.... The heat from Heaven will be unbearably hot, even in the closed homes. **The whole sky will be on fire,** but the lightning will not penetrate into the houses where there will be the light of the blessed candle. This light will be the only thing that will protect you.

The candles of blessed wax alone will give light during this horrible darkness. One candle alone will be enough for the duration of this night of hell.... In the homes of the wicked and blasphemers these candles will give no light.

Everything will shake except the piece of furniture on which the blessed candle is burning. This will not shake. You will all gather around the crucifix and my blessed picture. This is what will keep away this terror.

During this darkness the devils and the wicked will take on the most hideous shapes.... red clouds like blood will move across the sky. The crash of the thunder will shake the earth and sinister lightning will streak the heavens out of season. The earth will be shaken to its foundations. The sea will rise, its roaring waves will spread over the continent."

October 17, 1883 Marie-Julie Jahenny received the message: "The wicked will commit all kinds of horrors. The Holy Hosts will he dispersed on the roads. They will be discovered in the mud. The priests as well as the faithful will pick them up and – will carry them on their breasts.

I understood that the angels would carry away many tabernacles from the churches to shield the Holy Sacrament." [42]

Flames In The Sky, Earthquakes, Tidal Waves

On May 9, 1973, Mother Elena Leonardi was told: "Listen well and listen to what I tell you: **For some days, darkness will cover the Earth. The sky will be clouded with flames. The earth will tremble. Torrential storms will be unchained. Men will perish. Nations will be stricken, and much blood will shed....**" [16]

December 28, 1975, Our Heavenly Mother told Mother Elena Leonardi that Divine Justice is prepared to act, that she is "the Lady of Sorrows because of the great cataclysm which will simultaneously convulse the earth. It will be terrible, frightful as if it were the end of the world! But the end of the world has not yet arrived, however, it is not far away.... This is a dangerous hour. **Five nations will be completely razed....** The rigors of God's Justice are awful! **Blood will be shed for mortal sins; disease, earthquakes, scourgings, flames from heaven, tidal waves, family – devastating thieves....**" [16]

On December 3, 1988, in Message 110, Our Lady told Pedro Regis, Dear Sons and Daughters,... **there will be three consecutive Days of darkness that not even science will know how to explain. All of you will suffer much in these days. I promise to all who are at my side that they will not lack light. I ask you to always keep candles blessed by a priest in your house.**...

The Wrath Of God

Messages About The Great Chastisement
Given To Pedro Regis, Brazil

March 16, 1993. Message 612 – Dear Sons and Daughters,... **If there is no conversion, the wrath of God will come upon you, so be converted, be converted, be converted. All the means of communication that work to destroy the plans of God will be laid**

waste by the wrath of God which will come as a great bolt of lightning and everything will be destroyed....

February 12, 2005. Message 2482 – Dear Sons and Daughters,... **The wrath of God will come. His name takes its origin from a plant from a long way off....**
Editor's note: (Rev 8:11, "The name of the star is called Wormwood; and a third of the waters became wormwood, and many men died from the waters, because they were made bitter." Wormwood is native to the Mediterranean region of Europe and Asia where it grows in dry, rocky waste places. This is a truly bitter plant.)

February 24, 2005. Message 2487 – Dear Sons and Daughters, the Supreme Judge will judge men and women for their crimes.... **When the wrath of God comes, men will fall to the earth in fear....**

February 3, 2007. Message 2794 – Dear Sons and Daughters,... **A giant will come and when men announce that it is near, humanity will live moments of great difficulties. The earth will go through an immense transformation....**

March 6, 2007. Message 2807 – Dear Sons and Daughters, bend your knees in prayer. **Humanity will carry a heavy cross when the earth loses its normal movement. There will be a change in the gravitational force of the earth which will attract a distant giant....** **The geography of the world will change. The day will come when the lives of men will no longer be the same....**

January 15, 2005. Message 2470 – Dear Sons and Daughters, **an immense ball of fire will come leaving a great desert. Screams and laments will be heard on all sides. It is the hour of The Lord....**

April 16, 2005. Message 2510 – Dear Sons and Daughters,... **People will see something like the sun visible in the sky for many hours. All eyes will see it....**

June 18, 2005. Message 2537 – Dear Sons and Daughters,... **This is the hour of The Lord. Mankind will see a great mystery. Night will become day....**

July 19, 2005. Message 2550 – Dear Sons and Daughters,… **Behold, humanity will see fire in the sky. Light that does not illuminate and tears of suffering**…. **China and Russia: heavy rocks for humanity.**

April 6, 2006. Message 2664 – Dear Sons and Daughters,… **There will be lights in the heavens and people will marvel.**…

January 30, 2007. Message 2792 – Dear Sons and Daughters,… **A light never seen by men will appear. It will be visible to human eyes and will contribute to great changes on earth.**…

The Transformation Of The Earth

The Force Of Nature Will Provoke
Phenomena Never Seen Before

October 31, 2009. Message 3234 – from Our Lady of Peace, Anguera, Bahia, Brazil. Dear Sons and Daughters,… **Humanity is living is a time of great tensions and heading towards a great abyss. The force of nature will provoke phenomena never seen before. Objects will be thrown from the earth by a force that no one can explain. Forces will arise from the depths of the earth that leave men preoccupied, but I want to tell you that God will not abandon His people. Pray. You will yet see things that human eyes have never seen.**

Great Mountains (Asteroids, Comets) Will Fall

May 21, 2005. Message 2525 – Dear Sons and Daughters,… **Something enormous will fall, and when it hits the water it will cause great destruction. Regions on the earth will suffer, but whoever is with The Lord will receive comfort and peace.**…

September 3, 2005. Message 2570 – Dear Sons and Daughters,… **A great mountain will fall to the ground.**…

February 14, 2006. Message 2641 – Dear Sons and Daughters, **a giant mountain will travel the Pacific at high speed, causing great**

destruction in many regions....

January 11, 2007. Message 2784 – Dear Sons and Daughters, **a giant mountain will fall. A city at the end of the world will live moments of great affliction....** **A great chastisement will fall upon humanity without delay....**

Great Earthquakes, Mountains Fall, Volcanoes Will Burst With Great Force

February 19, 2005. Message 2485 – Dear Sons and Daughters,... **There will be signs in the sun, moon, and stars. Nature will be transformed and men and women will be confused. China will go through great tests. There will be an earthquake causing the death of millions of innocents....**

March 18, 2006. Message 2655 – Dear Sons and Daughters,... **A great sorrow for mankind will come from the lithosphere** (translator; crust of the earth). **The earth will be shaken and mountains will fall. The sorrow will be great.**

June 27, 2006. Message 2699 – Dear Sons and Daughters,... **A groan will be heard from the depths of the earth. The earth has been wounded by men, and the future consequences will be catastrophic....**

May 29, 2008. Message 3003 – from Our Lady of Peace, Anguera, Bahia, Brazil. Dear Sons and Daughters,... Humanity will confront a great sorrow. **Energy accumulated in the interior of the earth will provoke great explosions and there will be great earthquakes. Destruction will come from the depths** which will bring men to drink the bitter cup of suffering. Courage.

December 29, 2009. Message 3259 – from Our Lady of Peace, Anguera, Bahia, Brazil. Dear Sons and Daughters,... **The crust of the earth will split in many regions of the earth. Energy coming from the interior of the earth will bring suffering to many of My poor children.**

July 1, 2006. Message 2701 – Dear Sons and Daughters,... Humanity will drink the bitter chalice of suffering. **The continental plates will be shaken by a great earthquake, such as has never been seen since the time of Adam.**

July 8, 2006. Message 2704 – Dear Sons and Daughters, **days will come when the earth shakes and the mountains move. Volcanoes will burst with great force and many will experience great sufferings.**

The Earth Will Incline When The Great Object Comes Nearer, The Earth Will Shake, Continents Will Disappear.

July 15, 2006. Message 2707 – Dear Sons and Daughters,... **Know that humanity will live moments of great tribulations. There will be a great change in the angle of the orbit of the earth which will affect the lives of humans and animals. It will cause great pain.**

January 18, 2007. Message 2787 – Pay attention to the signs of God. **The day will come when the earth loses its natural movement; the sun will become dark and nothing will be like it was before.**...

May 3, 2007. Message 2832 – Dear Sons and Daughters,... **Humanity will carry a heavy cross. The earth will incline when the great object comes nearer. Time will be lost. People will be confused by what The Lord will permit.**

Anguera BA. Brazil. Dear Sons and Daughters,... **The earth will shake and immense rivers of fire will rise from the depths. Sleeping giants will awake and there will be great suffering for many nations. The axis of the earth will change and My poor children will live moments of great tribulations.**...

January 25, 2009. Message 3114 – from Our Lady of Peace, Batatan/Maragogipe, Bahia, Brazil. Dear Sons and Daughters,... **My poor children will weep and lament. Continents will disappear. The desert will no longer be desert.**...

193

October 6, 2009. Message 3223 – from Our Lady of Peace, Anguera, Bahia, Brazil. Dear Sons and Daughters,... **Continents will disappear and people will contemplate things that are not visible to the human eye now. These will be sorrowful times for you.**

The Poles Will Move

June 20, 2006. Message 2596 – Dear Sons and Daughters, **the poles will move and the earth will go through great transformations. All living beings will suffer....**

October 25, 2006. Message 2751 – Dear Sons and Daughters, **a sudden movement of the poles will bring suffering to the land of the rising sun and its neighbors....**

January 26, 2007. Message 2790 – Dear Sons and Daughters,... **The moving of the poles will change life on earth and my poor children will live moments of anguish. The day will come when the sophisticated means of communication will fail. Men will be deaf and blind....**

June 22, 2006. Message 2597 – given in Maceio. Dear Sons and Daughters,... these are the times of the great tribulations.... Humanity will pass through great trials. **The earth will be shaken and mountains will fall apart. Continents will move, and cities will be dragged into the sea....**

July 29, 2006. Message 2713 – Dear Sons and Daughters,... **Great sufferings for My poor children will come from water and fire. There will be gaps in the magnetic field of the earth, and this will cause disequilibria in the life of humans and animals.**

September 8, 2006. Message 2730 – Dear Sons and Daughters, **the earth will go through great transformations, such as will leave wise men confused. They won't be able to explain it. Thus The Lord will fulfill His promises.**

194

In The End God Will Reign With His Peace

December 25, 2007. Message 2934 – from Our Lady of Peace. Dear Sons and Daughters,... **The day will come when the earth will be completely transformed. The geography will no longer be the same. Seeing these great changes, people will realize that alone they will never win, and so, will confide in Jesus. Peace will reign in hearts, and the nations at war will be reconciled. Violence will become extinct, and God will reign with His peace.**...

Mitigation

The Times Will Be Shortened

On November 23, 1976, Our Lord Jesus Christ told Julka (Julia), Yugoslavia: "The True Roman Catholic Faith is being put to a great test because of My Most Holy Mother and My Words from Her mouth. It will be even more difficult when the hour comes which I have decided upon for Earth.

Then the face of the Earth will be renewed and all Sanctuaries will become holy. These are My chosen Places in every country, on every Continent, wherever I Myself appear or My Mother, or My Servants of Heaven.

In the young Church of My Little Flock My Teaching is being confirmed. My pious faithful who will survive the Great Tribulation will visit such Places and Shrines wherever they will be. My pious servants, priests whom I shall let live on Earth, will carefully explore all Areas and Places where My Holy Words and those of My Mother, have been preached. **All this must be because of the far too heavy sins of the world; but I shall shorten everything and sincere, Christian hearts will inhabit the Earth, My Spirit will be above them.** We Ourselves shall approach Earth, and Earth will come close to Us – thus speaks the Most Holy Trinity." [33]

195

The Great Chastisement At The Time Of The Garabandal And Akita Messages Was Conditional

At Garabandal We Were Told It Was Conditional

According to the messages at Garabandal The (Great) Chastisement could be avoided.

June 19, 1962 Maria Dolores Mazon (Mary Loli) and Jacinta Gonzalez said: "The Virgin told us: That we do not expect the Chastisement. That without expecting it, it will come, since the world has not changed.

And she has already told us twice; and we do not pay attention to her, since the world is getting worse. And it should change very much. And it has not changed at all.

Prepare yourself. Confess, because the Chastisement will come soon. And the world continues the same....

I tell you this: That the world continues the same. How unfortunate that it does not change! **Soon will come a very great Chastisement, if it does not change.**"19Page 193 *She Went In Haste To The Mountain. Book Two*

On March 25, 1965 Mary Loli wrote: "I also tell you this, that **in order to avoid the Chastisement, we have to make many sacrifices and penances, to pray the family rosary every day; this is what Our Most Holy Mother requests of us. Also, that we should love one another, as Our Lord loves us.** We have to love; the whites must love the blacks; and the blacks, the whites, since we are all brothers."19 Page 159 *She Went In Haste to The Mountain, Book Three*

Conchita of Garabandal said: "The chastisement, if we do not change, will be horrible."19 Page 159 *She went In Haste To The Mountain. Book Three*

At Akita In 1973 We Were Told That The Great Chastisement Was Conditional

On October 13, 1973, at Akita, Japan, an apparition approved by the

Church, the Holy Mother gave this message to Sister Agnes Sasagawa: **"If men do not repent and better themselves, the Heavenly Father will inflict a great punishment on all humanity.** It will definitely be a punishment greater than the Deluge, such as has never been seen before, Fire will plunge from the sky and a large part of humanity will perish....

The good as well as the bad will perish, sparing neither priests nor the faithful. The survivors will find themselves plunged into such terrible hardships that they will envy the dead. The only arms which will remain for you will be the Rosary and the sign left by My Son (Eucharist)." [21]

Signs, Secrets And Prophecies – Road To The Triumph

Chapter 10

The Beloved Remnant

Those Who Acknowledge Our Blessed Mother As Leader And Triumphant Queen

The True Remnant

The true remnant will remain faithful and are those with whom Jesus will bring about the realization of His Reign.

On August 1, 1995 Jesus said to Sadie Jaramillo: "All is being fulfilled even as I give My words to you. Yes, **violent changes in the climate, these are My signs!** And sooner than most believe or realize, All, All, All will be fulfilled. I emphasize, for in that way, you understand.…

My children have been running too far ahead of Me up to now! But the pace of My faithful remnant has slowed, and must fully understand it can only be the divine will of God that is fulfilled!

In all things comes the appointed time. My words to you speak of the time as now, it is; but things and events will happen according to the will of God.

I give this message to console your sorrow, to receive your love and prayers, to encourage you to do all that I say. You have been formed and molded, as many of the true remnant have been. **Who is the true remnant? Those who cast their wills and desires aside and desire only holiness and God; who acknowledge My mother as leader and Triumphant Queen, and respond to Her simple, yet powerful** requests...." [6]

On June 8, 1995 Jesus said to Sadie Jaramillo: "All those who have entered into the protection of My mercy, who have worked towards the coming of the Father's kingdom, who have entered into the heart of My Mother; you have reserved for yourselves a special place in heaven, for you are the beloved remnant.

In this image, I am. From this image I will pour torrents of grace and mercy. For now torrents of sorrow will be poured forth from the hand of My Father's justice. You have refused Me mankind. You have rejected My instruments. You have persecuted the brothers of My Heart for the truth they proclaim!

You will now reach for the one who opposes Me. But, you will find, too late, you were held by the deceiver. Too late, you will acknowledge the truth.

I speak and those who walk in My love, My Father's will, under the influence and power of the Spirit, are the beloved remnant. They hear, they see, they believe. They have taken the hand of My Beloved Mother and have allowed Her to lead and guide.

Come, My children, rejoice with Me, your Savior and Christ, for soon We will dwell together in the midst of peace and love, God's love, and His divine will.

I pour torrents of graces on those who believe, on those who trust...." [6]

The Triumph Of My Immaculate Heart Exists In The Hearts And Souls Of My Faithful Remnant

The Remnant Protected As Sealed By Our Blessed Mother

Mary said to Sadie Jaramillo on January 4, 1994: "Through your consecration you are sealed as Mine. As the Woman Clothed with the Sun leading My remnant through the battle, I am protecting those sealed as Mine...." [6]

The Spirit Of God Is Leading, Moving, Guiding, The Remnant

God the Father said to Sadie Jaramillo on October 31, 1994: "But the true remnant that is persevering, rejoice! I have heard your cries! Heaven has received your prayers! Yes! Through the hands of My Daughter of the Magnificat, I have seen the brightness and flame of your hearts! They are worthy of My son.

All of you, you know who you are – for I have shown you, I have led you – have not to worry or fear! Stay close to your spiritual leader and teacher, My Spirit! My Holy Spirit. The Spirit of God is leading, moving, guiding My Daughter's army.

The finality and totality of the rebellious one's defeat has already been won! It is for you, all My children, to go forth and be not afraid...." [6]

All That Was Given Was To Prepare The Remnant For The Great Tribulation

Mary told Sadie Jaramillo on July 28, 1995: "The division in many of the prayer groups has been foretold, 'even the elect, if possible, will be deceived.' What makes it possible for deception? Pride, the evil one's tool from the beginning.

My children will have to walk by faith and know all that has been given was to prepare the remnant for the great tribulation, through which you are going to go, the final bloody hour. Pray now, child, for the souls that will be lost in many devastating events...." [6]

The Remnant Church Will Be Built From Those Who Follow Only The Truth

November 8, 1993 Jesus said to Sadie Jaramillo: "For soon I lay on this nation and others the blows of My justice! My people, harken to the pleas of your God and My Mother! **The remnant church will be built from those who will follow only the truth. They will be few...."** [6]

Be Prepared To Live In Eucharistic Communities

On October 19, 1993 Jesus said to Sadie Jaramillo: "I come in the name of the great I Am, Your Lord and Savior Jesus the Christ, whose name is praised! I tell you My child, **the great schism spoken about is upon My children. My sheep will scatter and be hard-pressed to find a church that still has one of My consecrated sons true to his consecration, true to the faith handed down through the ages.**

You (traditional believers and followers of Our Lady) will be ostracized and held in ridicule by most. They will no longer hold back many of their abominations. For this reason, My Father's hand will fall and His justice will be mercy for My children My flock.

Your deliverance is near, but a little while and I will be with you. You will gather and know, My remnant flock, there will be a few of My priests who will gather My sheep. Behold they strike and My sheep scatter. But there is no snatching from My hand what My Father has given to Me.

Those who stand against Me will be lost in the slaughter. For it is not the strongest, or mightiest, or the wealthiest, or the most well-known who will stand. No, **it is the ones chosen by God, My Father – those who do His Will who will stand. They will know His protection. Look to My holy word and know this is true.**

My small flock, be prepared, you do not know all that is about to fall on mankind, fall on what remains of My Church. The blows of My hand will move the very bowels of the earth! Woe to mankind! You cannot stand in the slime of your filth any longer.

My innocents annihilated before any chance of life! The perversion of man's wanton desires! My religious have become the cesspools of iniquity! No, it will not be without their just reward:

Sadie was told, "He created all things good, and good there are, but

202

only a few. **For you, My little flock, will walk and be led, and you will see a thousand fall on one side and ten thousand on your other, yet on you will be My protection!**

You will be prepared to live in Eucharistic communities. For you will see your country in ruins: economic ruin: civil unrest, threats of attack by foreign nations and natural disasters. It will be very difficult for those who believe they can stay behind.

Be warned, prayerful and alert. Pray. My peace to My children, in the name of My Father, in the name of My Son, in the name of My Spirit, holy and just." [6]

The Remnant Will Go Into The Underground Church

On October 13, 1995 in her message to Sadie Jaramillo Mary said: "You tell one and all: On this anniversary of the great miracle of Fatima, I knew even then what was to come, and **I have come in these waning years of the fullness of time, that My voice would be heard as the voices from the Churches became stilled (voices of the priests). That My voice would direct all to the saving power and love of My Son Jesus. That My voice would call all to conversion, repentance and reparation.**

Many have not believed, many have grown tired, many have grown indifferent amid the cares of the world. Many refuse to recognize the times which have arrived. But as My voice called forth a few, very few responded. Responded by their total commitment to My desires, instructions and implorings.

And these are the mouths that give voice to My words. That all would recognize these as the times spoken of to many, many of My visionaries at My apparition sites. Now comes the fullness of this time and many of My children will believe and return to the truth. For I come now to lead many of My remnant through this final bloody hour.

Through this final hour many will be forced to go underground as

the enemy rages against all that is of Christ. For he is the antichrist in the world and ready to unleash the fullness of his fury against humanity and in particular the Church. These are the signs to which I point, and these are the times of which you will speak....

I am the voice that calls all to be anchored in the sea of My Eucharistic Son. I am the voice given power and authority to form the heel that will destroy Satan and all his works...."

On August 13, 1997 Jesus told Sadie Jaramillo: "My Glory reigns in the hearts of the small remnant of My Mother's army. My glory reigns in those who unreservedly serve Me....

The day draws ever nearer that the abolishment of My sacrifice will come, and those who know Me will know the True Church will exist as it did in the catacombs. Many will know persecution, some even death. For these souls you pray; for these souls of My ministers you pray." [6]

On February 10, 1998 Jesus said to Sadie Jaramillo: "As you, the True Church go underground, as you become more and more persecuted, keep your eyes and your heart looking towards the East! As the way you will worship during this time (persecution) is not the same as you have had up to now. (To worship openly).

Again, keep your eyes and hearts eagerly anticipating My coming! From the East I will come! Yes! As sure as the flash of lightening!

Much will come ever so swiftly, but you are following Her (The Virgin Mary), who has come to lead the remnant into the battle! It has already been won! Do not fear!" [6]

The Illumination: The Moment Which Will Lead The Remnant To Begin Harvesting In God's Vineyard

On February 19, 1995 Sadie Jaramillo was told by Mary: "My little sorrowful rose, I request you to take down my words. I, your victorious Queen of the World, your Mother and the Mother of all

humanity, sing the praises of Jesus, My Son, for I dwell in the midst of the Most Holy Trinity.

I come to implore you to remain united with me in prayer. The angels of the Lord from on high have been dispatched. They are sent to cover God's holy people with peace, by their protection over them. **For the greatest moment of divine mercy will bring many to the foot of my Son's glorious Cross. It will also be a time of chaos and confusion. I clarify to you, to prepare for a shortage of food items upon the arrival of this moment. And then, for the control of famine which will follow.**

It is the illumination of man's heart and soul. The heavens will crack with God's thunder. It will be the most awesome, holy fulfillment of Calvary; a moment to choose the path to eternal life, or to be led to eternal damnation.

The moment which will lead my remnant to begin harvesting in God's vineyard. You will tire, but you will work ceaselessly. Know that, as our chosen one, every word taken down in dictation has been a prayer for the soul of someone lost. And everything which has been required of you will be brought to fulfillment.

Because my remnant have sacrificed and offered acts of reparation, the Father's holy anger has many, many times over, been appeased. But this time of all times has come. My children have entered into the ark of my Immaculate Heart. With me are the angels and saints, to bring in the Triumph of the Two Hearts!

So that from pole to pole the cry may resound: Our Father in heaven, praise to thee for the Triumph of the Immaculate Heart of Mary and the Sacred Heart of Your Son, Jesus. May Your Holy Spirit lead us and fill us with Your holy gifts. Abba, Amen. Christ the king reign! Glorious is the Queen of the Most Holy Rosary's triumph.

All who have participated in preparing this glorious moment, I bless you from my holy throne on high in the name of my Father and yours, my Son, Jesus, and the Power of My Spouse, the Holy Spirit." [6]

Be Not Fearful My Remnant

On May 5, 1995 Our Lord Jesus revealed to Sadie Jaramillo: "Remember child, soon My Vicar will be taken, and all will need to know the truth of the way. You will need to teach the true way. I am He who gives life by My Body and Blood! I am He who strengthens, for greater are you if I am in you than he who is in the world. My Body and Blood are real food to strengthen and nourish you for the time ahead. You will be strong for I am strong and I will support you in all you do.

The days of silence and preparation are coming to an end. No more the exile. No more the banishing of My faithful ministers. Soon the harvest will be of multitudes. For this harvest, **My remnant has toiled in suffering, pain, poverty, and dejection. But come now and reap what has been sown!**

I will renew your strength, and you will be a laborer. Day will blend into day, for the work will not cease, but I will nourish you. I will seek and I will find! And all who do not embrace Me now, will embrace Me from that moment, that I bring into the light what lies hidden and bound by darkness....." [6]

May 14, 1996 Our Lord Jesus told Sadie Jaramillo: "As I once spoke to Jonah to go forth and proclaim the number of days left to Nineveh, to call to their ears and hearts the sins that would draw down the anger of God's justice, so too in these days I have sent many as Jonah to proclaim the same message.

But, the difference between the people of Nineveh and humanity, is that they, the people of Nineveh, heard, received and repented. They prayed as one and fasted as one and put on sackcloth. They wailed and lamented for their sins and I, in compassion and response to prayer, did not do what I had proclaimed.

But oh mankind you are so dull of heart. My many Jonahs have gone forth to proclaim the same, and, as I, the Master was once rejected, ridiculed and persecuted, you have done the same to these I send you.

In these 20 and 2 days the sins of Nineveh will come to light as the soul of every man, woman, child of reason, sit in the seat of judgment. What you have done in darkness will be shown in the light. What you have plotted as evil will be revealed to the minutest detail.

And I will be the King of compassion, embracing you with My mercy. You will come and I will wash you whiter than snow. And, as at Calvary, I will give you My Mother to be your Mother and through the ministering of the remnant flock you will be brought into the one true fold.

But prepare, oh children of Mine, for the enemies of Christ, and the antichrist, will rage even more. Through the confusion and mayhem, you will walk. **Many will be gathered in pockets of peoples with the protection of God upon you.**

My Vicar will be martyred and the abomination of Daniel's prophecy will come to pass. What you now see in the churches is the prelude...." [6]

On January 30, 1998 Mary told Sadie Jaramillo: "Be not fearful, my remnant. You are led by the Woman who has stepped on the head of the serpent! **Continue to pray for My priest sons, you and those praying with you. Many priests will come back to the harbor of Truth, who would be totally lost otherwise." ** [6]

Chapter 11

The Rosary, Consecration, And Family Prayer

Pedro Regis

Messages About The Holy Rosary, And Consecration To Mary's Immaculate Heart

Unceasing Rosaries So Mankind May Encounter Peace

August 30, 1988. Message 76 – Dear Sons and Daughters. **In Fatima, when I appeared to the three little shepherds, I asked for unceasing rosaries so mankind may encounter peace. Today I return, appearing in various places in the world to make the same request. Within this year will happen great events which I foretold in Fatima….**

Consecration To Mary's Immaculate Heart
Pray The Holy Rosary Mary's Preferred Prayer

May 13, 1989. Message 169 – Dear Sons and Daughters. I am your heavenly commander. I am the Queen of Peace. As you remember today my first apparition in the poor Cova de Iria, in 1917, you are living the events that I then foretold. **All that I foretold in Fatima to My daughter, Sister Lucy, is happening today. The struggle between me, the woman clothed with the sun, and my adversary, the red dragon, is now coming to its decisive phase. So I still appear today in a most extraordinary manner, to reassure you that I am always present in your midst. You are now living the moments in which the red dragon, that is, marxist atheism, has spread over the whole world causing more and more damage in poor souls. He has truly seduced**

and thrown down a third of the stars in the sky. These stars in the firmament of the church are the pastors. They are you, my poor beloved children. The moment has come when I desire to manifest myself to the whole church through you, for the time of the triumph of my Immaculate Heart has come. As a loving mother, I give the consecration to My Heart as a vaccine to preserve you from the epidemics of atheism that contaminate so many of my children, taking them to a true spiritual death. I also ask you to pray the Holy Rosary. The Rosary is my preferred prayer, and so in my numerous appearances I always invite you to pray it. I am always at the side of all those who pray, and ask it with urgent motherly preoccupation. From this humble place, I encourage and bless all of you in the name of The Father, and of The Son, and of The Holy Spirit. Amen. Be at peace.

We Will Find Our Refuge And Peace
Only In Mary's Immaculate Heart

October 13, 1990. Message 341 – Dear Sons and Daughters, what I foretold in Fatima is about to happen, and so the time of the great triumph of My Immaculate Heart has come. Today, remember with joy my apparition in the Cova de Iria, and the great miracle of the sun realized by me to witness my presence and to show you that these are my times, times of great purification. Don' be trapped by sin. Give yourselves to me. You will find your refuge and peace only in My Immaculate Heart. So all of you should remain in My Immaculate Heart. This is the message that I transmit to you today in the name of The Most Holy Trinity. Thank you for permitting me to bring you here once more. I bless you in the name of the Father, and of the son, and of the Holy Spirit. Amen. Be at peace.

Our Lady Asks Us To Pray The Holy Rosary Every Day

October 13, 1992. Message 559 – Dear Sons and Daughters, I am the Mother and Queen of Brazil. I ask all of you to pray with fervor that God the Father pour out His Grace and Mercy on all brazilians, and in a special way on those withdrawn from His Grace. I desire that the presence of Jesus in your life be not for just one moment, but eternal.

Today I renew the invitation I made in Fatima and ask you to pray the Holy Rosary every day, for this is the only way the world will attain peace. Pray, pray. Especially pray in a heartfelt way so you can feel the presence of God in your life. And I repeat, pray also for your Brazil. This is the message that I transmit to you today in the name of The Most Holy Trinity. Thank you for permitting me to reunite you here one more time. I bless you in the name of the Father, and of the Son, and of the Holy Spirit. Amen. Be at peace.

Mary Invites Us To Pray The Holy Rosary And To Consecrate Ourselves Every Day To Her Heart

May 13, 1996. Message 1110 – Dear Sons and Daughters, I am the Mother of the poorest. **I come from heaven to lead you to Him Who is your all. Today remember My appearance in Fatima in the poor Cova da Iria and open your hearts to the appeal I made in that place. Once again I invite you to pray the Holy Rosary and be like Jesus in everything. I have come from heaven to direct you and reclaim what belongs to God.** Know that all of you are precious to Me, and so I want you in My Immaculate Heart. Be courageous! **Consecrate yourselves every day to My Heart and you will find peace!** I am sad because of your sins. I don't want to judge you, for only God is your judge, but I want to warn you, because I love you and want to see you happy already here on earth, and later with Me in heaven. This is the message that I transmit to you in the name of The Most Holy Trinity. Thank you for permitting Me to reunite you here once more. I bless you in the name of The Father, and of The Son, and of The Holy Spirit. Amen. Be at peace.

Our Weapon Of Defense Is The Holy Rosary Consecration To Mary's Immaculate Heart For Her Special Protection

May 13, 2000. Message 1738 – Dear Sons and Daughters, I am the Mother of God the Son and your Mother. I am happy that you are here. I ask you to be always of The Lord and that whatever you do in this life be for the glory of God and the salvation of souls. God sent Me to show you the way to Heaven. I encourage you to joyfully respond to the call of The Lord. I am your Mom. How does a mother feel to see her child in the darkness of sin? Understand that I care for each one of you. I am your Mother and love doesn't obligate, but I call you with docility because you are free, but I want to tell you that the most important thing is to do the will of God. Hurry up. Your time is short. Go firmly in prayer, strong in faith. Behave as true sons and daughters. Your testimony of faith should be your true identity as christians. So many years since I have come to the world, but men and women don't want to receive My appeals. What do you think of your final destination? Tell everyone that I don't come from Heaven as a joke. Be men and women of prayer. **You are living in the time of the great combat. Your weapon of defense is the Holy Rosary. Pray it with love and you will be saved. If humanity had received the appeal I made in Fatima, humanity would be spiritually cured. If in the past many did not open themselves to My appeals, you can do so.** You can be My faithful ones. For the spiritual security of each one of you, **I offer you My Immaculate Heart. Consecrate yourselves to Me and you will always have My special protection.** Forward. Courage. This is the message that I transmit to you in the name of The Most Holy Trinity. Thank you for permitting Me to reunite you here once more. I bless you in the name of The Father, and of The Son, and of The Holy Spirit. Amen. Be at peace.

Family Prayer And Prayer Groups

Medjugorje

April 25, 1996
"Dear children! Today I invite you again to put prayer in the first place in your families. Little children, when God is in the first place, then you will, in all that you do, seek the will of God. In this way your daily conversion will become easier. Little children, seek with humility that which is not in order in your hearts, and you shall understand what you have to do. **Conversion will become a daily duty that you will do with joy.** Little children, I am with you, I bless you all and I invite you to become my witnesses by prayer and personal conversion. Thank you for having responded to my call."

Renew Prayer In Your Families And Form Prayer Groups

September 25, 2000
"Dear children! Today I call you to open yourselves to prayer. May prayer become joy for you. **Renew prayer in your families and form prayer groups. In this way, you will experience joy in prayer and togetherness. All those who pray and are members of prayer groups are open to God's will in their hearts and joyfully witness God's lo**ve. I am with you, I carry all of you in my heart and I bless you with my motherly blessing. Thank you for having responded to my call."

I Desire To Call You To A Renewal Of Family Prayer

May 20, 2011
"Dear children, today more than ever I desire to call you to prayer. Dear children, satan wants to destroy today's families, therefore I desire to call you to a renewal of family prayer. Pray, dear children, in your families with your children, do not permit access to satan. Thank you, dear children, for also today responding to my call."

The Holy Rosary

Christina Gallagher, Ireland

Pray The Rosary From Your Heart

On February 4, 1988 the Mother of God said to Christina Gallagher: **"To all the people who find it difficult to accept my messages and those of my Son; pray the Rosary from your heart, all three mysteries, for nine days. Offer up these prayers to my Son's Heart, and to the Holy Spirit for enlightenment. If you do that, you will understand...."**

On May 22, 1988, Our Lady said to Christina: "I would like you to pray the Rosary to me, from your heart. Offer each Hail Mary as a beautiful white rose, or precious jewel, and the Lord's Prayer as a

very fine red rose or special jewel, to clothe me in. But you must know that you cannot have precious jewels that wilt not sparkle, or beautiful roses, that are only ready to be thrown away. My child, if you do not pray the Rosary from your heart, with love and joy, the roses or the jewels you offer to clothe me in will be lost forever: Pray the Rosary with love and joy and it will last for all eternity. Please my child, do not disappoint me, let it be a garment that will sparkle, pray my beautiful Rosary."[46]

Arm Yourself With My Rosary

On August 17, 1988, Christina received the message: "My child, the calamity has started. The influence of the Prince of Darkness is all around you. Arm yourself with My Rosary. My Church will be shaken, even its very foundation. My children who want to be saved must repent. Repent, I say, to all my children. Arm yourselves with my Rosary. Let it never be out of your hearts. My chosen children, you are now like lambs among wolves. Stand firm, hove no fear for the Hand of the Mighty One is with you."[8]

On September 24, 1988 Jesus requested Christina pray the Rosary to Him: "Pray the Rosary to My Heart for souls who are in great darkness. Offer all your pain to My Merciful Heart...."[8]

On November 13, 1990 Our Lady said to Christina during a long message: "My children, the laws of God are despised. Those who deny the laws of Christ, deny Christ. ... It is you little ones who will help me bring about the triumph of My Immaculate Heart....

My children. I plead with you, arm yourselves with My Rosary, live the Ten Commandments God has given you. Each day pray for the Vicar of My Son, Jesus, he begins Calvary with me. My children, I invite you, each morning, make the sign of the Cross with Holy Water. Beg Jesus through His Mercy that you be protected from the darkness that overflows around you. The battle of principalities rages."[8]

214

Messages To Janie Garza

The Family That Includes The Rosary As Part Of Their Daily Prayer Will Receive Graces And Blessings In Every Aspect Of Their Life

In his message of November 12, 1993 to Janie Garza St. Joseph said: "Every family member must learn prayer of the heart, where the family abandons themselves totally to God. They must trust God and seek His mercy in their prayers. The family that includes the Rosary as part of their daily prayer, this family will receive graces and blessings in every aspect of their life. Through praying the family Rosary, conversion will begin to blossom in the hearts of the family members who are walking in darkness. Through praying the Rosary, God will send His peace and light. Hearts will be healed and love will be born in the hearts of the family. The Rosary is a prayer in which God invites us, through the Holy Spirit, to live the life and mystery of Jesus through the eyes of His Mother, Mary.

I St. Joseph, ask you, my little one, to share this message. **All families must pray the Rosary, trusting Most Holy Mary to guide them gently to her Son, Jesus, as they pray the Holy Rosary.... She will be present to all who recite the Holy Rosary....**"[8]

Satan Knows That The Rosary Is A Powerful Weapon Against All His Evil Forces

On January 11, 1995 St. Joseph tells Janie that the Rosary disarms Satan. St. Joseph said: "You must know that prayer helps you to overcome any obstacles which Satan puts in your path. Know that this is Satan's time, when he is most busy trying to destroy as many souls as he can. God allowed him this time; he is allowed to test God's children.

Do not allow him to put fear or doubt in your heart. You have in your possession a powerful weapon, which is your Rosary. Satan knows that the Rosary is a powerful weapon against all his evil

215

forces. He knows that through praying the Rosary he can be disarmed. He flees from any home where the Rosary is prayed continuously. This is why families everywhere must be found with the Rosary in their hands, as they gather to pray as a family.... God's children will never comprehend the profound effect that the Rosary has on those praying it, as well as the souls that the Rosary is being prayed for.... Continue to pray the Rosary with your family and pay no attention to the distractions. Know that it is Satan trying to keep you from praying."[8]

On February 27, 1995 St. Joseph said to Janie: "Reflect on the Passion of Jesus each day and do not allow one day to go by without praying together as a family, especially your family Rosary. Allow no distraction or interruptions to keep you from praying together as a family."[8]

Messages to Josefina-Maria

Arm Yourselves With The Rosary

On November 10, 1993 Jesus told Josefina-Maria: "Do not be afraid My people. Those of you who are devoted to Our Two Hearts have nil to fear. But I say, woe to those who do not recognize the time of My Visitation! I will overpower you with My strength My people. I will not abandon you when the Great Tribulation arrives.

Again I say to you My people, prayer is your strength. The Rosary is your great weapon to fight against the fires of hell. The Enemy is lurking in your midst waiting to devour as many souls as possible. Arm yourselves with the Rosary. Do not be afraid; do not be troubled and be at peace. My followers will not be harmed. Be at peace. Take refuge under the protection of Our Two Hearts. Be at peace. Peace, shalom My peace. Jesus, your Lord."[50]

You Must Pray The Rosary

Mary Jesus told Josefina-Maria: "Pray the Rosary constantly. I am always with the Rosary beads in my hands when you see me my child because you must pray the Rosary. Even if you are unable to do other prayers the Rosary is a must! My children the world is in a grave state. Please try to help us. Peace! I love you. Thank you for responding to my call. Mary your Mother who loves you dearly."[50]

The Rosary Is God's Gift To You, A Gift Of Love

Our Lady on April 8, 1993 told Josefina-Maria: "Do not be troubled my child. The pains of this world are much, and I know you suffer my children. Know that I love you all, and My Immaculate Heart is your shield.

My people do not wish to pray the Rosary or even know about it. This pains My Immaculate Heart. The Rosary my children, is God's gift to you; a gift of love; another very important means of prayer. People find it so repetitious and meaningless. Repetition with love my children, is a small price to pay for the salvation of your souls.

Oh my loved ones, pray with your hearts. Pray in the silence of your hearts. Pray without making a big show of it. Pray for peace. Pray for love to come back into the hearts of my children. Thank you for responding to my call of love. Mother Mary, Queen of the Rosary."[50]

The Power Of The Rosary Throughout History

Battle of Lepanto, Greece, October 7, 1571

On October 7, 1571, a sea battle was fought on the Bay of Lepanto, which lies beyond the Isthmus of Corinth connecting the Peloponnesus with mainland Greece. **This sea battle decided the fate of Christendom, which was threatened by consolidated Islamic power under Suleiman the Magnificent.**

In 638, Caliph Oman, Mohammed's successor, rode into Jerusalem and took control of the Holy Land.

In 712 Spain fell to Islamic rule.

Muslim armies crossed the Pyrennes and reached as far north as Poitiers, France before being stopped in 732 by Charles Martel.

The Turks were a nomadic tribe that embraced Islam. They spread their newly found religion throughout the Middle East, and began a campaign against Western Europe.

In the Mediterranean region the Turks consolidated Islamic power under Suleiman the Magnificent, who was virtually undefeated in battle. He considered himself the undisputed Sultan of East and West. His grandfather had vowed to stable his horse beneath the dome of St. Peter's in Rome and to wind the Pope's head with a turban.

A Christian outpost on the Island of Malta stood in his way. The Knights of St. John had retreated to Malta in 1565 after being driven from Rhodes by the Turks. From Malta these Knights harassed the Turkish fleets.

Suleiman the Magnificient attacked Malta where the badly outnumbered Knights of St. John firmly stood their ground. At the end of the seige, three-quarters of the Turks perished and only 600 Knights remained alive.

Suleiman went back to Constantinople to rebuild his armada make plans to reclaim his honor and prestige.

Germany and France made conciliatory noises to Constantinople. Only two nations, Venice and Spain were even vaguely interested in forming a buttress for Christendom.

Venice, on the Adriatic had waged an ineffective defensive war against the Turks. Spain, led by Philip, II, the King of Spain, the Netherlands, England, Master of Italy, and Lord of parts of the Western Hemisphere, and of the Philippines responded cautiously to Pope Pius V's efforts to rally the Christian princes, since his armies were committed elsewhere to defend Spanish possessions.

A new Sultan of the Turks, Selim the Sot, came to power. He decided as "owner of all men's necks" it was now appropriate to officially include all European necks.

Pope Pius V, seeing the threat of European capitulation to Islam was real, on March 7, 1571, at that time the Feast day of St. Dominic, signed his name to a document calling for the establishment of a Holy League against the Turks. He entrusted the Christian cause into the hands of Our Lady.

Philip II of Spain agreed to send ships, troops, and his half-brother, 26 year old Don Juan of Austria to command the fleet. Don Juan had distinguished himself in fighting the Moors in southern Spain. **The Venetians agreed to rebuild the small fleet of the Holy See.**

Prayer was recognized as the strongest defense for Christendom and the Holy League. Philip II traveled to the shrine of Our Lady of Guadalupe in Extremadura, Spain. **The Christian fleet, set sail in the middle of September and prayed the Rosary every day.**

On October 6, 1571 the ships assembled, Dominican and Jesuit priests passed from deck to deck, hearing confessions and offering Mass. In Rome Pope Pius V ordered prayers to be said in all convents and monasteries of the city. Don Juan led the fleet from his flagship the Real, which sailed under the blue banner of Our Lady of Guadalupe. On the evening of October 6, Pope Pius V led the prayer of the Holy Rosary at the Dominican convent in Rome.

On the morning of October 7, 1571 the superior naval forces of the Turks sailed in traditional Islamic crescent formation from their harbor at Navkapos (Lepanto in Italian). The flagship of the Sultan carries a tooth of the prophet Mohammed encased in a crystal ball to aid their forces in battle.

Don Juan seeing a crimson banner billow on the Turkish flagship with Arabic words of the prophet set in gold, in response **unfurled a banner of blue damask with the figure of Christ crucified embroided in gold thread surmounting the allied emblems.**

With great speed the opposing ships clashed. The Holy League lost about 8,000 lives and 17 of the 100 galley ships were sunk. 15,000 Christian galley slaves on the Turkish ships were freed. The Sultan's 300 ship armada lost 260 ships and about 30,000 men.

In the sea battle Don Juan maneuvered his ship to personally confront Ali Pasha, the commander of the Turkish fleet. The Turkish admiral was beheaded by a cannon ball. "This was the turning point in the battle and by sunset the Turkish fleet was in total disarray."

"During the evening on the day of battle, Pope Pius V was in the midst of discussions in his study in the Vatican when he suddenly broke away from his companions and crossed to the window. He paused and with a radiant smile, turned to announce that a great victory had been won that day for the Holy League. This was more than 2 weeks before the official courier from Venice arrived in Rome."

Pope Pius V decreed that October 7 would be a feast day thereafter to be celebrated as the Feast of Our Lady of Victories in honor of the triumph accorded all Christendom at Lepanto.

Gregory XIII instituted the Feast of the Holy Rosary in 1573. This was extended to the universal Church by Clement XI. Benedict XIII added it to the Breviary with the explanation that the Turks were defeated "on the very day on which the Confraternities of the Most Holy Rosary throughout the world were offering up their rosaries as they had been asked to do by Pope St. Pius V."

Pope Leo XIII wrote no less than 12 encyclicals on devotion to the Rosary and **dedicated the entire month of October to Our Lady of the Holy Rosary.**

The Venetians commissioned the building of a chapel to Our Lady of the Rosary. They inscribed the legend for all to see: **NEITHER VALOR, NOR ARMS, NOR LEADERS BUT OUR LADY OF THE ROSARY GAVE VICTORY."**

Battle of Vienna, Austria 1683
And Our Lady of Czestochowa

The sea battle at Lepanto in 1571 had broken the domination of the Turks on the sea and Ottoman sea power had been effectively contained in the Eastern Mediterranean.

About 100 years later Europe was faced with land invasion. The Star and Crescent of the Turkish Empire ruled the Danube river and flew over Budapest (Hungary), and was on the march toward Vienna when the Papal legate arrived in Warsaw to request the urgent aid from Poland. A vast Turkish army poised to lay siege to Vienna. King John III Sobieski had been victorious over them three times. The Germans and the Austrians had been unable to defeat the Turkish invaders.

The Turks approached Vienna. On July 13 they surrounded Vienna and began the siege.

When the news reached King John III, he raised his heart to heaven and prayed, "Blessed Virgin of Czestochowa allow me two miracles: that those in Vienna shall resist the siege until September and those of us outside reach there in time to save them."

King John III went to Jasna Gora to pray before the Black Madonna. After four days of prayer, as he was preparing to leave, a priest handed him a picture of the Madonna suspended from a gold chain. The King gratefully accepted it, slipped it over his head and began his march to Vienna with between 26,000 and 27,000 armed Polish troops.

The Turks had nearly as many tents pitched around Vienna as the King had fighting men. There were about 115,000 Turkish fighting men. The Polish King received about 51,000 reinforcements from Austria and Germany.

At 3:15 in the morning of September 12, 1683, the Feast of the Holy Name of Mary, King John III arose, prayed, put on the picture of

Our Lady of Czestochowa, and launched the attack. The Polish men, it is said, had the words, "Mary help us" on their lips as they met the Turks in fierce combat.

Surprisingly the battle was over early in the day. After the victory, King John III declared, "I came, I saw, and GOD conquered."

Battles Of Tremesvar, Hungary And Of Corfu, 1716

In Leo XIII's Encyclical, Supremi Apotolatus, September 1, 1883, he wrote, "Similarly, important successes were in the past century gained over the Turks at Tremesvar, Hungary and at Corfu; and in both cases these engagements coincided with feast of the Blessed Virgin and the conclusion of public devotions of the Rosary. And this led our predecessor, Clement XI, in his gratitude to decree that the Blessed Mother of God should every year be especially honored in the Rosary by the whole Church."

Austria, May 18, 1955

On May 13, 1955, the anniversary of the first apparition of Our Lady of Fatima, Soviet Russia agreed to the independence of Austria and shortly thereafter withdrew its troops completely. On Sunday, May 15, 1955 the agreement was signed.

For seven years the people of Vienna faithfully prayed daily from 3pm to 8pm, one Rosary after the other.

Therese Neumann, the famous German stigmatist, before her death on September 18, 1962, said, "Definitely, definitely, it was the prayers and many Rosaries of the Austrian people that purchased their freedom from Russian domination."

Brazil, 1964

In Brazil with 215 million people in the 1960s, a Communist-leaning president who was on the verge of fomenting a thoroughly Red

revolution, was ousted in a victory solidly attributed to Our Lady of the Rosary, and in the process of the victory, not a life was lost. The devoted women of Brazil had rallied behind Our Lady of the Rosary to stop a takeover of their country.

The first major encounter was at Belo Horizonte when 20,000 women with rosaries in hand broke up a Communist rally. The women in Sao Paulo arranged a demonstration called the March of the Family of God toward Freedom. 600,000 participated, marching through downtown Sao Paulo praying the Rosary and singing religious hymns for 3 hours. It became to President Goulart that he did not have the popular support necessary to affect a revolution in Brazil and he fled the country.

Philippines February 22-25, 1986

EDSA II January 18-20, 2001

Catholic Filipinos' prayers were answered as former president Estrada was dumped in favor of Gloria Arroyo as new President.

Averting certain disaster, millions of Filipino Catholics, led by Cardinal Jamie Sin gave thanks for the peaceful coup that ousted former president Estrada in favor of the new President Gloria Macapagal-Arroyo. **Cardinal Sin likened it to the "Rosary Revolution" of 1986 in which prayer overcame a strong military takeover of President Corazon Aquino's administration.**

In 1985 Cardinal Sin had consecrated the entire Filipino nation to the Immaculate Heart of Mary in the Marian Bimillennium Year of COR (Heart) – Conversion, Offering, and Reparation to God. This turned out to be a fitting precursor to the first EDSA miracle the following year.

EDSA I Feb. 22-25, 1986

In February 1986, the dictatorial Ferdinand Marcos called a snap presidential election in order to crush the building opposition.

Signs, Secrets And Prophecies – Road To The Triumph

Corazon Aquino, the widow and reluctant political replacement of slain opposition leader Ninoy Aquino won by an overwhelming margin.
Marcos was not through. It was reported that by ballot box stuffing, other illegal activities, and a total control of the media, he had himself declared the winner.

A dissatisfied segment of the military launched an unexpected coup attempt to which Marcos responded by sending tanks down the streets of the city.

Manila Archbishop Jaime Cardinal Sin, called on the public to protect the military rebels from being attacked by Marcos's military.

Up to two million people took to the streets of Manila flocking to the area outside the main military camps in Manila in support of these military rebels.

As a full convoy of tanks and other armament manned by hard-core militant soldiers came against millions of civilians, many of whom were virtually lying down in the streets in front of the tanks, Marcos gave the order to fire on the people.

Cardinal Sin, the Archbishop of Manila, told Wayne Weible, as reported in *Medjugorje the Mission*: "What I am telling you now was told to me by many of these same soldiers who were ready to fire on the people. The tanks were trying to penetrate the crowd. And the people were praying and showing their rosaries. That is when, according to these soldiers, the Marines who were riding on top of the tanks, the so-called Loyalists (to Marcos), they saw up in the clouds the form of the cross. The many sisters had tried to stop them, but they (the soldiers) told me they had already decided to obey instruction and push through. It is now just a question of ten minutes or so. You push the trigger and there you are – everybody will be dead.

Then, a beautiful lady appeared to them. I don't know if she appeared in the sky or was standing down on the ground. So beautiful she was, and **her eyes were sparkling. And the beautiful lady spoke to them like this: 'Dear soldiers, stop! Do not proceed! Do not harm my children!' And when they heard that, the soldiers put down**

224

everything. They came down from the tanks and they joined the people. So, that was the end of the Loyalists.

I don't know who these soldiers are. All I know is that they came here crying to me. They did not tell me that it was the Virgin. They told me only that it was beautiful sister. But you know, I have seen all the sisters in Manila, and there are no beautiful ones. So it must have been the Virgin!"

Wayne Weible asked: **"Cardinal, do you really believe it was Our Lady that the people and the soldiers saw?"**

Cardinal Sin replied: "Yes, My heart was telling me, this was Mary. And since they obeyed this woman who appeared to them and did not follow orders and fire on the people, then Marcos had nobody anymore. So, he had to flee. That was the end of him."

On February 25, 1986, after a standoff that began four days earlier, Marcos fled the Philippines and went into exile, with the help of the US government.

(EDSA: is an acronym derived from **Epifanio de los Santos Avenue**, the major thoroughfare connecting five cities in Metropolitan Manila along which the majority of the demonstrations took place.)
EDSA I: Is also known as The Yellow Revolution, The People Power Revolution.
EDSA II: The 2001 EDSA Revolution, was called by the local media **EDSA II.**

Chapter 12

The Events That Will Bring

True World Peace

1.The Final Marian Dogma
2.Our Lady Of America
3.Consecration Of Russia To The Immaculate Heart
   By The Pope Joined With All The Bishops

1. The Final Marian Dogma

Dogma

By dogma in the strict sense is understood a truth immediately (formally) revealed by God ("Divine Revelation") which has been proposed by the Teaching Authority of the Church to be believed as such. Dogma is the object of the Divine Faith by reason of its Divine Revelation. It is the object of Catholic Faith on account of the infallible doctrinal definition by the Church. Dogma reflects not only the full authority of the Church received from Christ but also the Church's tradition, liturgical practice and the faith of the people ("Sensus Fidelium"). The promulgation by the Church may be made in an extraordinary manner through a solemn decision of faith made by the Pope or a General Council or through the ordinary and general teaching power of the Church ("Magisterium Ordinarium et Universale"). Dogmas are lights on our path of faith. They have binding character, and intellect and heart to a deeper understanding of God's mystery.[56] To learn more about the subject of "dogma" read the *Catechism of the Catholic Church* ("CCC" 88-89).[32]

The Four Marian Dogmas

1.   **Mary is Truly the Mother of God**: The Council of Ephesus (431) declared, "If anyone does not confess that the Emmanuel (Christ) in truth is God and that on this account the Holy Virgin is the Mother of God — since according to the flesh she brought forth the Word of God made flesh — let him be anathema." This normative decision was further explicated by the Council of Chalcedon (451) which says with regard to Mary's divine motherhood: "...begotten from the Father before the ages as regards His Godhead, and in the last days, the same, because of us and because of our salvation begotten from the Virgin Mary, the *Theotokos, as* regards his manhood; one and the same Christ, Son, Lord, only-begotten..."[51]

2.   **Mary's Perpetual Virginity**, before, during and after the Birth of Jesus Christ: Lateran Synod of the year 649 declared this dogma. The expression perpetual virginity, ever-virgin, or simply 'Mary the Virgin' refers primarily to the conception and birth of Jesus. From the first formulations of faith, especially in baptismal formulas or professions of faith, the Church professed that Jesus Christ was conceived without human seed by the power of the Holy Spirit only. Vatican II reiterated the teaching about Mary, the Ever-Virgin, by stating that Christ's birth did not diminish Mary's virginal integrity but sanctified it. The *Catechism of the Catholic Church* ponders the deeper meaning of the virgin bride and perpetual virginity It also maintains that Jesus Christ was Mary's only child. The so-called "brothers and sisters" are close relations. [51]

3.   **Mary's Immaculate Conception:** On December 8, 1854, Pope Pius IX, having consulted the entire episcopate, and speaking Ex Cathedra, declared the doctrine of the Immaculate Conception to be a Dogma of the Faith. The solemn definition of Mary's Immaculate Conception is like Divine Motherhood and Perpetual Virginity part of the Christological doctrine, but it was proclaimed as independent dogma. The dogma of the Immaculate Conception states "that the most Blessed

Virgin Mary, from the first moment of her conception, by a singular grace and privilege from Almighty God and in view of the merits of Jesus Christ, was kept free of every stain of original sin." [51]

4.   **The Bodily Assumption of Mary, Body and Soul, into Heaven**: On November 1, 1950, Pope Pius XII promulgated the Apostolic Constitution "Munificentissimus Deus." "The Dogma states that "Mary, Immaculate Mother of God ever Virgin, after finishing the course of her life on earth was taken up in body and soul to heavenly glory." The definition of the dogma does not say how the transition from Mary's earthly state to her heavenly state happened. Did Mary die? Was she assumed to Heaven without prior separation of soul and body? The question remains open for discussion. However, the opinion that Mary passed through death as her Son did, has the stronger support in tradition. [51]

Proposed Fifth And Final Marian Dogma
Mary, Co-Redemptrix, Mediatrix And Advocate

Co-Redemptrix

When the Church invokes Mary under the title, "Co-Redemptrix," she means that Mary uniquely participated in the redemption of the human family by Jesus Christ, Our Lord and Saviour. **It is important to note that the prefix "co" in the title Co-Redemptrix does not mean "equal to" but rather "with," coming from the Latin word cum.** The Marian title Co-Redemptrix never places Mary on a level of equality with her Divine Son, Jesus Christ. Rather it refers to Mary's unique human participation which is completely secondary and subordinate to the redeeming role of Jesus, who alone is true God and true Man.

At the foot of the cross of our Saviour (Jn.19:26), Mary's intense sufferings, united with those of her Son, as Saint Pope John Paul II tells us, were, "also a contribution to the Redemption of us all" (Salvifici Doloris, n.25). Because of this intimate sharing in the redemption accomplished by the Lord, the Mother of the Redeemer is uniquely and rightly referred to by Pope John Paul II and the Church as the "Co-Redemptrix."[32]

It is precisely by her free consent to collaborate in God's saving plan that she becomes the Co-Redemptrix. Mary at the Annunciation gave her free and full consent to conceive this child Jesus Christ, Our Lord and Saviour. The prophecy of Simeon to Mary, "and a sword will pierce through your own soul also" (Luke 2:25), affirms Mary's unique participation in the work of redemption, as it warns her that she will undergo an unspeakable pain that will pierce her soul, for the salvation of mankind. John 19:25 tells us of Jesus' Mother at the very foot of the cross, persevering with her Son in his worst hour of agony, and therein suffering the death of her Son. [32]

Jesus Christ as true God and true man redeems the human family, while Mary as Co-Redemptrix participates with the Redeemer in His one perfect Sacrifice in a completely subordinate and dependent way. The key word here is "participation" in that which is exclusively true of Jesus Christ. The title "Co-Redemptrix" never puts Mary on a level of equality with our Lord; rather, it refers to Mary's unique and intimate participation with her Divine Son in the work of redemption. Mary's sufferings are efficacious towards the redemption of man because they are wholly rooted in the redemptive graces of Christ and are perfectly united to His redeeming will. [32]

Mediatrix

As Mediatrix, the Mother of Jesus does not "rival" Christ's mediation but rather participates in the one mediation of Jesus Christ. Jesus is the infinite "reservoir" of all grace, which is distributed to us through Mary. Catholics hold that Jesus is the one and only mediator between man and God.

Advocate

The Catechism of the Catholic Church, Second Edition in 969 states, "This motherhood of Mary in the order of grace continues uninterruptedly from the consent which she loyally gave at the Annunciation and which she sustained without wavering beneath the cross, until the eternal fulfilment of all the elect. Taken up by heaven she did not lay aside this saving office but by her manifold intercession continues to bring us the gifts of eternal salvation.... Therefore the Blessed Virgin is invoked in the Church under the titles of Advocate, Helper, Benefactress, and Mediatrix." (LG 62)

Hail, Holy Queen Prayer

Hail, Holy Queen, Mother of Mercy, our life, our sweetness, and our hope!

To thee do we cry, poor banished children of Eve.

To thee do we send up our sighs, mourning and weeping in this valley of tears.

Turn then, most gracious **advocate**, thine eyes of mercy toward us and after this our exile show unto us the blessed fruit of thy womb, Jesus.

O clement, O loving, O sweet Virgin Mary.

Pray for us, O Holy Mother of God that we may be made worthy of the promises of Christ.

Amen

What The Proclamation Of This Marian Dogma Will Accomplish

This final dogma was preserved by the Lord for this time. The other dogmas had to come first. Once this dogma has been proclaimed, the Lady of All Nations will give peace, true peace to the world.

When the dogma is proclaimed Our Lady will help all her children to triumph over evil, to reestablish unity, love and true peace among families, among priests, among all peoples. God wants to send true peace to the world through the proclamation of the dogma.

When the dogma is proclaimed the Catholic Church will be renewed and strengthened, Faith will be renewed in many fallen away priests and religious, the commandments of God will be accepted by many.

The world needs the dogma to preserve it from degeneration, disaster and war.

Our Lady Of All Nations

During the period from April 29, 1951 through May 31, 1955, from the Thirty-Second Apparition through the Fifty-First apparition **Our Lady of All Nations gave in messages to Ida Peerdeman, of Amsterdam, the Netherlands, the theological basis for this final Marian Dogma.**

Ida Peerdeman

Ida Peerdeman, the youngest of five children was born in Alkmaar, Holland, on August 13, 1905.

When Ida was twelve, on Saturday, October 13, the day of the miracle of the sun at Fatima, a "Lady in White," in dazzling light, seemingly the Virgin Mary, appeared to her while she was walking home from the parish church. On each of the following two Saturdays this happened again.

Many years later, on March 25, 1945, The Feast of the Annunciation, while Ida Peerdeman, her three sisters, a family friend, and a priest were sitting around a stove, Ida saw an immense light appear and her surroundings seemed to fade away in an infinite depth. A heavenly figure, a woman dressed in white, came forth from the light and began to speak to Ida and showed her a rosary. Ida immediately recognized her as this same "Lady in White."

Thus began a series of approved apparitions through May 31, 1955 of Mary, under the title, *The Lady of All Nations*.

Our Lady Of All Nations Prayer

On February 11, 1951, the Lady gives a prayer, which has to be spread over the whole world together with her image. The prayer is directed to the Lord Jesus Christ, asking for the coming of the Holy Spirit, now, in this time. **As our Advocate, she promises Grace, Redemption and Peace to all people who say this prayer.**

On February 11, 1951, during her twenty-seventh vision, **Our Lady gave Ida Peerdeman the following prayer:**

LORD JESUS CHRIST, SON OF THE FATHER,

SEND FORTH NOW THY SPIRIT OVER ALL THE EARTH.

LET THE HOLY GHOST LIVE IN THE HEARTS OF ALL

NATIONS,

THAT THEY MAY BE PRESERVED

FROM MORAL DECLINE, DISASTERS, AND WAR.

MAY THE LADY OF ALL NATIONS, WHO ONCE WAS MARY,

BE OUR ADVOCATE.

AMEN.

This is the prayer as given by Our Blessed Mother, the Lady of All Nations to Ida. The language was changed in 2006 by the Congregation for the Doctrine of the Faith (CDF) in the Vatican. The Vatican changed the words the Blessed Mother had asked from "who once was Mary" to "the Blessed Virgin Mary."

The prayer and the picture are also the preparation for and the representation of a new dogma, the final and greatest Marian dogma: Mary Co-Redemptrix, Mediatrix and Advocate. *The Lady foretells that much controversy and struggle will arise over this dogma,* *but when this dogma is proclaimed, a new era of peace will start for humanity.*

The Lady draws special attention to the way she appears and asks to make an image of it. She stands on the globe because she comes for the whole world. As the Lady, she stands in sacrifice before the Cross, clothed with the sun that is Christ; her body translucent as of the Spirit. Out of her hands are coming three rays, the rays of Grace, Redemption and Peace that she may bestow upon the nations. She promises to give grace for soul and body – according to the Son's will to all who pray before the image and call upon Mary, the Lady of All Nations. She asks to send the prayer also to the nations where faith has declined, who are being kept away from the Son. She shows the visionary images of the church that she wants to be built in Amsterdam, as the place where she wants to bring the nations together. Amsterdam has been chosen, so she says, because it is the city of the Eucharistic Miracle. [55]

The New And Last Marian Dogma

Thirty-Second Apparition, April 29, 1951

"I stand here as the Co-Redemptrix and Advocate. Everything should be concentrated on that. Repeat this after me: **The new dogma will be [referred to as] the dogma of the Co-Redemptrix. Notice I lay the special emphasis on Co.** I have said that this will arouse much controversy. Once again I tell you that the Church, Rome, will carry it through and silence all objections. The Church Rome, will incur opposition and overcome it. Rome will become stronger and mightier in proportion to the resistance she puts up in the struggle.

"**My purpose and my commission to you is none other than to urge the Church, the theologians, to wage this battle. For the Father, the Son, and the Holy Spirit wills to send the Lady, chosen to bear the Redeemer into this world, as Co-Redemptrix and Advocate.** I have said, This time is Our Time. By this I mean the following: The world is caught up in degeneration and superficiality. It is at a loss. Therefore, **the Father sends me to be the Advocate to implore the Holy Spirit to come. For the world is not saved by force, the world will be saved by**

the Spirit. It is only ideas that rule the world. Know your responsibility then, Church of Rome. Get your ideas across; bring Christ back into the world once more...

"In the sufferings both spiritual and bodily, the Lady, the Mother has shared. She has always gone on before. As soon as the Father had elected Her, She was the Co-Redemptrix with the Redeemer, who came into the world as the Man-God. Tell that to your theologians.

"I know well the struggle will be hard and bitter (and then the Lady smiles to herself and seems to gaze into the far distance) but the outcome is already assured...

"...**The world is degenerating, so much so, that it was necessary for the Father and the Son to send me into the world among all the peoples, in order to be their Advocate and save them.** Tell your theologians this. And then I see the Lady leave and again I hear Her say, 'This time is Our Time.'"

Thirty-Third Apparition, May 31, 1951

"...**it is the wish of the Father and the Son to send me into the world in these times as "Co-Redemptrix, Mediatrix and Advocate." This will constitute a new and last Marian dogma. This picture will go before it.** This dogma will be much disputed; and yet it will prevail!"

Forty-Second Apparition, June 15, 1952

"...**The Lady, who once was Mary. Only at the departure of the Lord Jesus Christ did Co-Redemption have its beginning. Only when the Lord Jesus Christ went away, did she become the Mediatrix and Advocate.**"

Forty-Third Apparition, October 5, 1952

"**Never has Miriam or Mary in the Community, the Church been officially called Co-Redemptrix. Never has she officially been called Mediatrix. Never has she officially been called Advocate. These three thoughts are not only closely connected, they form one whole.**

Therefore this will be the keystone of Marian history; it will become the dogma of the Co-Redemptrix, Mediatrix and Advocate.

"I do not reproach the theologians if I say: why can you not come to an agreement about this dogma? Once more I shall explain it and make it clearer still: **The Father sent the Lord Jesus Christ as the Redeemer of All Nations. The Lord Jesus Christ was this from the beginning. He became this in the Sacrifice and in His going to the Father.**

"**Miriam or Mary became the Handmaid of the Lord, chosen by the Father and the Holy Spirit. From the beginning she was, in virtue of this choice, the Co-Redemptrix, Mediatrix and Advocate. Only at the departure of the God–Man, the Lord Jesus Christ, she became the Co-Redemptrix, Mediatrix and Advocate. When leaving, in one final act, the Lord Jesus Christ gave Miriam or Mary to the nations, gave her as the Lady of All Nations.**

"**He spoke the words, Woman, behold thy son; son behold thy Mother. One act! And by this, Miriam or Mary received this new title.**

"How is it that this new title, *The Lady of All Nations* only now enters the world? It **is because the Lord reserved it for this time. The other dogmas had to come first; just as her life on earth had to precede the Lady of All Nations. All previous dogmas comprised the mortal life and the leaving of this life by the Lady. For the theologians this simple explanation should suffice.** It was necessary to give this explanation once more."

Forty-Seventh Apparition, October 11, 1953

"**The Lady of All Nations has the power to bring the world peace. Yet she has to be asked for it under this title.** The Lady of All Nations will assist the Church of Rome..."

Forty-Ninth Apparition, April 4, 1954

"Listen well: **from the outset the Handmaid of the Lord was chosen to be Co-Redemptrix**. Tell your theologians they can find it all in their books!... **I am not bringing a new doctrine. I am now bringing old ideas...**

"**Because the Lady is Co-Redemptrix, she is also Mediatrix and Advocate not only because she is the Mother of the Lord Jesus Christ, but – and mark this well – because she is the Immaculate Conception**... Do fight and ask for this dogma: it is the crowning of Your Lady..."

Fiftieth Apparition, May 31, 1954

"...**When the dogma, the last dogma in Marian history, has been proclaimed, the Lady of All Nations will give peace, true peace to the world.**"

Fifty-First Apparition, May 31, 1955

"...Satan is not banished yet. **The Lady of All Nations is now permitted to come in order to banish Satan. She comes to announce the Holy Spirit. The Holy Spirit will only now descend over this earth**...

"Know well that the Holy Spirit is nearer than ever. **The Holy Spirit will come now only, if you pray for His coming. He has always been ready; now, however, the time has come**...

"**Once the dogma has been pronounced, the Lady of All Nations will give her blessing**..."

Local Bishop Declared Apparitions Of Our Lady Of All Nations Authentic

The Declaration By Bishop Joseph Punt

Regarding The Supernatural Authenticity Of The Apparitions Of The Lady Of All Nations

Joseph Marianus Punt
Bisschop von Haarlem

May 31, 2002

In Response to Inquiries Concerning the Lady of All Nations Apparitions

As Bishop of Haarlem/Amsterdam, I have been requested to make a statement regarding the authenticity of the apparitions of Mary as the Lady of All Nations in Amsterdam during the years of 1945 - 1959. Many members of the faithful and bishops have emphasized the urgency for clarification. I also have been personally aware that this development of devotion, which has spanned over 50 years, call for this.

As it is known, my predecessor, Msgr. H. Bomers and myself had previously given permission for public veneration in 1996. As to the supernatural character of the apparitions and contents of the messages, we did not give our judgment, but declared that "everyone is free to make a judgment for himself or herself according to their conscience." Having had a generally positive attitude towards authenticity, we decided to await further development and to "discern the spirit" further (cf. 1 *Thes* 5: 19-21).

Over the period of six subsequent years, I observed that the devotion had taken its place in the spiritual life of millions all over the world, and that it possesses the support of many bishops. Many experiences of conversion and reconciliation, as well as healings and special protection also have been reported to me. In full recognition of the responsibility of the Holy See, it is primarily the task of the local bishop to speak out in conscience regarding the authenticity of private revelations that take place or have taken place within his diocese.

Therefore I have asked once again for the advice of theologians and psychologists concerning the outcomes of previous investigations, and the questions and objections deriving from them. Their recommendations state that no theological or psychological impediments for a declaration of supernatural authenticity can be found therein. I have also requested the judgment of a number of brother bishops concerning the fruits and development of the devotion, who within their own dioceses have experienced a strong devotion of Mary as the Mother and Lady of All Nations. In light and virtue of all these recommendations, testimonies, and developments, and in pondering all this in prayer and theological reflection, I have come to the conclusion that the apparitions of the Lady of All Nations in Amsterdam consist of a supernatural origin.

Naturally, the influence of the human element still exists. Authentic images and visions are always transmitted to us, in the words of Joseph Cardinal Ratzinger, Prefect of the Congregation of the Doctrine of Faith, "through the filter of our senses, which carry out a work of translation..." and "...are influenced by the potentialities and limitations of the perceiving subject' (Cardinal Ratzinger, *Theological Commentary In Preparation for the Release of the Third Part of the Secret of Fatima, L 'Osservatore Romano, June 28, 2000).*

Unlike Holy Scripture, private revelations are never binding upon the conscience of the faithful. They are a help in understanding the signs of the times and to help live more fully the Gospel (cf. *Lk* 12:56, *Catechism of the Catholic Church,* n, *67.* And the signs of our times are dramatic. The devotion to the Lady of All Nations can help us, in my sincere conviction, in guiding us on the right path during the present serious drama of our times, the path to a new and special outpouring of the Holy Spirit, Who alone can heal the great wounds of our times.

To follow the further development of this devotion and to come to an even deeper insight into its meaning, I have installed a commission whose task it will be to continue to document all initiatives, experiences, and testimonies stemming from the devotion in order to help insure and preserve correct ecclesial and theological progress of devotion.
I hope this has provided sufficient information and clarification.

(signed) + Bishop Joseph Marianus Punt

Messages Given To Janie Garza About This Proposed Final Marian Dogma

Trust Also In My Motherly Intercession As Mary, Co-Redemptrix, Mediatrix and Advocate

September 8, 2000

Dear Children:

"Today you honor your heavenly Mother as you gather to celebrate my birthday. I am deeply touched, little children by your love and devotion. I

239

desire to thank each one of you as a family for all your prayers and sacrifices. Little children, I invite you as a family to continue to pray your rosary. Praying together is so important and powerful. You break the attacks of my adversary when you pray as a family. I know, little children that many of you are suffering more than ever. Have courage and know that I am at your side. Abandon all your family concerns to my Immaculate Heart. Do not allow the smallest worry to be a distraction to you. Remain peaceful during trials and sufferings. God who knows all your needs will carry you through every thing.

Little children, live a life of prayer and peace without fear. Allow your family prayer to transform your life. Do not allow yourselves to be distracted by the diabolical forces of my adversary. Keep your focus on prayer. Do not fear these troubled times, but grow stronger in your family prayer. Little children, I am with you and I carry each one of you in the bosom of my Immaculate Heart. Share in my joy and continue to draw closer to my Immaculate Heart. Little children, you are living in special times of grace. Embrace these times with prayer and joy. Know, little children that you are sharing and carrying the victory of my Immaculate Heart through all your prayers and sacrifices. Continue to live heaven on earth by praying and converting. Bring the kingdom of God to every heart with love and peace in your heart. Trust in the light and power of the Holy Spirit in everything you do.

Trust also in my motherly intercession as Mary, Co-Redemptrix, Mediatrix and Advocate. I am with you as a family and I give you my motherly blessing."

Only By The Proclamation Of The Dogma Of Mary, Co-Redemptrix, Mediatrix And Advocate, Can True Peace Come To Your Country And All The World.

November 10, 2000

Janie: While I was in prayer, Our Lady came as the Lady of All Nations. These are her words.

240

Our Lady: "My angel, today, **I come to visit you under the title of,** *The Lady of All Nations, Mother of All Peoples*. I have come to share my heart with you. You have been so absorbed by prayer, pleading mercy for your country…

I, the Lady of All Nations, call my children back to the love and mercy of my Son, Jesus. I invite all my children to turn to their heavenly mother and to pray, pray, pray. **My angel, you now understand why the proclamation of the dogma is so important.** There is so little peace in your country. Many are being distracted by the noise and the darkness that surrounds them. **Only by the proclamation of the dogma of Mary, Co-Redemptrix, Mediatrix and Advocate, can true peace come to your country and all the world**.

My angel, **what I say to you concerning your country is also applied to the whole world, but your country is suffering much.** Pray your Rosary with your family. Offer Holy Mass and Adoration for the spiritual and physical safety of your country.

Do not fear these times, my angel, but pray, pray, pray for the conversion of your country and poor sinners around the world. Peace, my angel, peace."

When The Dogma Is Proclaimed

November 11, 2000

Janie: Our Lady of All Nations came this morning while I was praying.

Our Lady: "Today, again, **I come to visit you as the Lady of All Nations, Mother of All Peoples**. I come once more to share my heart with you, my humble little angel….

I beg all my children who believe in the dogma of Mary, Co-Redemptrix, Mediatrix and Advocate, to keep vigil with their heavenly mother and pray for the dogma.

241

As the Lady of All Nations, I come to help all my children, to give them new faith, to seek them out and to bring them back to my Son, Jesus. **When the dogma is proclaimed, I will help all my children to triumph over evil, to reestablish unity, love and true peace among families, among priests, among all peoples.**

When the dogma is proclaimed there will be much conversion of hardened sinners, health of mind, body and of spirit, holy marriages and good children. There will be such a renewal of faith, and the Holy Spirit will be working and touching every heart. All of this will happen. My angel, I share all this with you to encourage you to keep your focus on the proclamation of the dogma...."

Hope For The World Lies Within The Proclamation Of Mary Co-Redemptrix, Mediatrix And Advocate

September 15, 2002

Our Lady comes through an interior locution. Mary said, "...My angel, do not be afraid of what I am sharing with you concerning a world that is destroying itself.

There is hope for the world. This hope lies within the proclamation of Mary Co-Redemptrix, Mediatrix and Advocate. God sent His only beloved Son for the salvation of humanity. This was a great act of mercy. God once more wants to bestow another great act of mercy upon a world that is walking in darkness. **God wants to send true peace to the world through the proclamation of the dogma.**

The world needs the dogma especially in this troubled time when the spirit of war is rampant in many hearts. **Pray for the dogma, asking the Lady of All Nations to intercede for a troubled world. The Lady of All Nations will help.** Call upon her intercession. Pray for the Holy Father and petition him for the dogma. Pray and fast, my angel, for these intentions, please pray and fast."

Janie then writes, I understand that **the dogma is the remedy for this world**.

The Dogma Will Be A Miracle For
The Renewal Of Faith For Many

January 6, 2003

"...When the Dogma of Mary, Co-Redemptrix, Mediatrix and Advocate is proclaimed, a new divine radiance will cover the world. The Catholic Church will be renewed and strengthened. Faith will be renewed in many fallen away priests and religious. The commandments of God will again be accepted by many. The Church will have its authority. The sacraments will be accepted once more by many especially the true Presence in the Blessed Sacrament. Confession and all the sacramental and pious means to salvation will be renewed in many hearts.** My Angel, this is why I ask so much of you and others. **The Dogma will be a miracle for the renewal of faith for many.** Peace, My Angel, peace. (In a vision, I saw myself praying for many priests in the Church)."

The Dogma Is The Miracle That The World Needs
To Bring True Peace To The World

August 27, 2003

Mary said: "... Convey to all my children that I am their Heavenly Mother full of love for her children and that I stand with each one of them, praying for them, protecting them in this difficult time. Convey to all my children that I take them all under my special gracious protection as we battle together the attacks of my adversary, who at this time is waging war on all my children and throughout the world. My Angel I love you. Never forget how dear you are to the Two Hearts. **Continue to offer all your suffering for the proclamation of the dogma of Mary**

243

Co-Redemptrix, Mediatrix and Advocate, for this is the miracle that the world needs to bring true peace to the world. Embrace my Son Vicar through your prayers. He is suffering, he is suffering.

My Angel, convey to all my children to make every effort to pray for all that I ask of them. Convey to them to pray specially when they do not feel like praying. I will turn all their prayers into special graces of Redemption for all of my un-converted children, beginning with their loved ones. Peace, my Angel, peace."

[Editor's Note: Some believe that the event that occurs in the Church that coincides with the Great Miracle prophesied at Garabandal is the Proclamation of the Fifth and Final Marian Dogma. Once the Miracle at Garabandal occurs, Our Lord said that Russia will be totally converted....]

The Triumph Of The Immaculate Heart Of Mary Will Come Through The Proclamation Of The Dogma Of Mary Co-Redemptrix, Mediatrix And Advocate

January 1, 2005

"My angel, I come to speak to you with a sad heart, for **I know how much you are suffering for the proclamation of the Dogma of Mary Co-Redemptrix, Mediatrix and Advocate. Do not entertain any doubts regarding the Dogma. Do not listen to the lies of my adversary, but listen to the words of your Heavenly Mother. There will be a Dogma of Mary Co-Redemptrix, Mediatrix and Advocate. The world needs it to preserve it from degeneration, disaster and war. The Lady of All Nations will have her crowning in the end—the victory is ours.** For now, pray, sacrifice, doing penance in expiation for poor sinners and **to assure the Triumph of the Immaculate Heart of Mary that will come through the proclamation of the Dogma of Mary Co-Redemptrix, Mediatrix and Advocate.** Peace my Angel, peace. I am with you in a special way and I am securing your path that leads to Heaven."[60]

Papal Teachings About Mary
As Advocate And Mediatrix

"Papal teachings of the last two centuries have recognized and officially taught the scriptural and patristic role of Advocate by the Mother of Jesus as well as countless saints have validated her titles.

"**Pope Pius VII**, "…While the prayers of those in heaven have, it is true, some claim on God's watchful eye, Mary's prayers place their assurance in a mother's right. For that reason, when she approaches her divine Son's throne, **as Advocate she begs**, as Handmaid she prays, but as Mother she commands."

"**Pope St. Pius X composed a papal prayer** for the fiftieth anniversary of the papal definition of the Immaculate Conception: "**O Blessed Mother, our Queen and Advocate**…gather together our prayers and we beseech you present them before God's throne…that we may reach the portal of salvation.[53]

Pope Pius XI, "…trusting in her intercession with Christ our Lord, who though sole Mediator between God and man, **wished however to make His Mother advocate for sinners and the dispenser and Mediatrix of Grace**…."[54]

"God alone gives grace according to the measure which, in His infinite wisdom, He foresees. But**, though that grace comes from God, it is given through Mary, our Advocate and Mediatrix, since motherly affection on the one hand finds response in filial devotion on the other…God gives grace; Mary obtains and distributes it.**"[34]

"We must of necessity wish that the youth of today, exposed as they are to many dangers, should make devotion to Mary the predominant thought of their whole life. **By persevering prayer let us make Mary our daily Mediatrix, our true Advocate. In this way we may hope that she herself, assumed into heavenly glory, will be our advocate before divine goodness and mercy at the hour of our passing.**"[37]

Pope Pius XII, "**Our Advocate, placed between God and the sinner, takes it upon herself to invoke clemency of the Judge so as to temper**

245

His justice, touch the heart of the sinner and overcome his obstinacy."[38]

The Relationship Of Our Lady Of All Nations To Akita, Japan

The events that took place at Akita address the Blessed Virgin Mary as Co-Redemptrix. The events at Akita focus on a weeping statue of Mary located in the convent. The message of Mary as Co-Redemptrix, Mediatrix, and Advocate comes through the image.

The statue is a reproduction of Our Lady of All Nations as she appeared in Amsterdam, when she announced a forthcoming dogmatic proclamation of Mary as Co-Redemptrix, Mediatrix, and Advocate.

The right hand of the statue bears a stigmata in the shape of a cross which bled.

The statue sweat fluid and wept blood. The sweat and blood evoke images of Our Lord during His Passion. The Mother of Christ as Co-Redemptrix shares in her Son's suffering.

Father Jacqes, a French missionary in Japan for thirty years, was the superior to the Sisters at Akita. He said, "If there is a particular conclusion to be drawn from the blood shed by Our Lady at Akita, it is that her mission as Co-Redemptrix has never ended, that it continues to this very day."

The statue wept 101 times, 98 of which Father Yasuda, Sister Agnes' spiritual director witnessed.

On September 29, 1981 Sister Agnes during Adoration of the Blessed Sacrament felt the presence of her angel at her side. An opened Bible appeared before her eyes. The passage was Genesis 3:15. The angel explained, **"There is a meaning to the figure 101.** It signifies that sin came into the world by a woman and it is also by a woman that salvation came to the world. **The zero between the two signifies the Eternal God** who is from all eternity until eternity. **The first one represents Eve and the last, the Virgin Mary.**"

On April 22, 1984, the Most Reverend John Shojiro Ito, Bishop of Niigata, issued a pastoral letter declaring the events of Akita to be supernatural.

In June 1988, Joseph Cardinal Ratzinger (Pope Emeritus Benedict XVI), Prefect for the Congregation for the Doctrine of the Faith, gave his judgment on the Akita events and messages as reliable and worthy of belief.

2. Our Lady Of America

A movement has commenced for a definite response by the United States Catholic Bishops in response to private revelations which long ago received official Church recognition as having occurred in the United States. The revelations included apparitions of Our Lord and St. Joseph as well as St. Gabriel and St. Michael, as well as apparitions of The Blessed Virgin Mary as *Our Lady of America*" to Sister Mary Ephrem (Mildred Neuzil), of the Precious Blood Sisters (1933-1979).

Sister Mary Ephrem, deceased on January 10, 2000, said she was asked by The Blessed Virgin Mary to draw a picture according to the vision of Our Lady of America and have a statue constructed accordingly and placed after a solemn procession into the National Shrine of the Immaculate Conception, in Washington, D.C..

The Blessed Virgin Mary wishes to be honored in the National Shrine of the Immaculate Conception at Washington D.C. as *Our Lady of America.* Our Lady says that if this is done, the United States of America would turn back toward morality and the shrine would become a place of "wonders."

Signs and Wonders for Our Times Magazine since 1991 has written many articles about this very important apparition.

Our Lady Wishes To Be Honored In The Basilica Of The National Shrine Of The Immaculate Conception In Washington D.C. As Our Lady Of America, The Immaculate Virgin

On November 15, 1956, Our Lady of America requested that a statue be made according to her likeness and that it be solemnly carried in procession and placed in the Basilica of the National Shrine of the Immaculate Conception in Washington D.C. She wishes to be honored there in a special way as *"Our Lady of America, the Immaculate Virgin."*

The Blessed Virgin Mary has promised that her statue as Our Lady of America once placed in the National Shrine of the Immaculate Conception would be a safeguard for our country, and her picture or statue honored in all homes, a safeguard for the family. She also promised that the medal would be a safeguard against evil for those who wear it with great faith and devotion.

According to Sister Mary Ephrem, **Our Lady often emphasized her desire that the Shrine of the Immaculate Conception in Washington, D.C., be made a place of special pilgrimage and that she be honored there under this image and this title** *"Our Lady of America, the Immaculate Virgin."*

Sr. Mary Ephrem (Mildred Neuzil)

It was on the eve of the feast of the North American martyrs, September 25, 1956, that Our Lady appeared to Sr. Mary Ephrem.

In 1938, Sister began to have what seem like mystical spiritual experiences. As these visits took on the nature of a specific program of devotion to Mary which Sister was asked to propagate, she then turned to Monsignor Paul F. Leibold. **Monsignor Leibold, later Archbishop of the Cincinnati, Ohio Archdiocese, would be her spiritual director from many years until 1972,** when he suddenly died due to an aneurysm.

Archbishop Leibold Became So Convinced Of The Authenticity Of This Message

Archbishop Leibold had become so convinced of the authenticity of this message that he approved Sister's writings and placed his imprimatur on the design of the medal. Our Lady had asked Sister to have struck a medal that would bear the image of *Our Lady of America* on the front and the symbol of the Christian Family and the Blessed Trinity on the back.

Our Lady Of America (In The Singular) Focuses Primarily On The United States Of America

In the course of approving the writings of Sister Mary Ephrem, Monsignor Paul F. Leibold considered the Blessed Virgin Mary under the title, **"Our Lady of America"** (basically referring to the United States of America), as **distinct from her title, "Empress of The Americas" (referring to Our Lady of Guadalupe),** as declared by Pope Pius XII in 1945, as having patronage over all the American nations.

Our Lady of America (in the singular) focuses primarily on the United States of America as revealed in 1956.

Our Lady promised that greater miracles than those granted at Lourdes and Fatima would be granted here in America, the United States in particular, if we do as she desires. Sister Mary Ephrem stated that Our Lady called herself *Our Lady of America* in response to the love and desire that reached out for this special title in the hearts of her children in America.

The Mandate Given By Heaven To The United States Is To Lead The World To Peace

"It is the United States that is to lead the world to peace, the peace of Christ, the peace that He brought with Him from heaven"

249

Sister Mary Ephrem quoted The Virgin as saying. *"Dear children, unless the United States accepts and carries out faithfully the mandate given to it by heaven to lead the world to peace, there will come upon it and all nations a great havoc of war and incredible suffering. If, however, the United States is faithful to this mandate from heaven and yet fails in the pursuit of peace because the rest of the world will not accept or cooperate, then the United States will not be burdened with the punishment about to fall."*

3. Consecration Of Russia (By Name) To The Immaculate Heart Of Mary By The Pope In Union With All The Bishops Of The World As Requested By Our Lady At Fatima

On June 13, 1929 in the convent at Tuy, Spain had a vision of the Blessed Trinity and Mary as the Virgin of Fatima. Mary was holding the Immaculate Heart in her hand and told Sister Lucy, "The moment has come in which God asks the Holy Father in union with all the bishops of the world to make the consecration of Russia to my Immaculate Heart, promising to save it by this means."

On July 7, 1952 Pope Pius XII specifically consecrated Russia to the Immaculate Heart of Mary, but did not ask any of the world's Catholic bishops to join him in this.

November 21, 1964 Pope Paul VI renewed Pope Pius XII consecration of Russia to the Immaculate Heart, but without the world' Catholic bishops joining him in the consecration.

On March 25, 1984 Saint Pope John Paul II performed a consecration of the world to Mary's Immaculate Heart after writing all the Catholic bishops of the world asking to join him in this consecration. Russia was not mentioned by name and the Pope lacked the necessary support from the world's bishops.

On March 25, 1984 Saint Pope John Paul II departed from his prepared text and asked Our Lady of Fatima to "enlighten especially the peoples of which you yourself are awaiting our consecration and confiding." L'Osservatore Romano on March 26, 1984 included these words in its official report.

In the summer of 1987 in a brief interview outside her convent while voting in an election confirmed to journalist Enrico Romero that the consecration had not been done.

Pope Francis in 2014 again consecrated the World, but not Russia by name as Our Lady had requested.

Many private revelations from Our Lady have said as to how and why this consecration has not been done fully according to her wishes.[62]

Messages from Our Lady to Father Gobbi on March 25, 1984, May 13, 1987 and May 13, 1990 reveal this Consecration had not been done as our Lady had requested at Fatima. They did however produce some good fruit. In the year dedicated to Our Lady by Saint John Paul II (1987-1988) in the Soviet Union communism began to be toppled.

The system was dismantled and new freedoms and structures arose, but Russia again was a named nation and was still not purified.

On March 25, 1984 Saint Pope John Paul II attempted the consecration in a solemn manner after writing to all the bishops of the world. He did not name Russia in this consecration. Our Lady had requested many times that in this consecration Russia be named. Also she wanted all the bishops to do this in union with the Pope.

Our Lady in message 287, that same day, said through Fr. Gobbi that unfortunately the invitation was not welcomed by all the bishops and that particular circumstances had not yet permitted the explicit consecration of Russia which she had requested many times. She promised because of this attempt she would intervene to shorten greatly the hours of the purification and to lessen the gravity of the trial. She said that this consecration will be made to her when the bloody events are well on the way to actuality.

Our Lady revealed through Fr. Gobbi on two other occasions that this request that Russia be consecrated to her by the Pope with all the bishops had not been done. Our Lady revealed this through Fr. Gobbi in messages 351 on May 13, 1987 and 425 on May 13, 1990.

The Testimony Of Roman Stigmatist Antonio Ruffini About When This Consecration Of Russia Will Be Done

The Roman stigmatist, Antonio Ruffini in the early 1990s was asked in his home, "Is John Paul II the Pope who is going to do the Consecration of Russia?" Antonio Ruffini answered, "No, it's not John Paul. It will not be his immediate successor either, but the one after that. He is the one who will consecrate Russia"

Pope Pius XII had authorized the blessing of a chapel on the spot where Antonio Ruffini had received the stigmata.[61]

Russia In 2014 Was On The Move With Actions That Could Lead To World War III

The people of Russia were liberated but not converted. Russia is once again a country by name and not just a part of the Soviet Union. Russia is still a threat to the world and could well precipitate World War III through her territorial expansion.

In March of 2014 Russia, again on the move, invaded the Ukraine and annexed the Crimea over the protests of the Ukraine and the nations making up NATO. This again threatened world peace.

If Russia continues to annex nations to restore the Soviet Union which had fallen after the March 25, 1984 Consecration of the World to the Immaculate Heart of Mary by St. John Paul II in union with the bishops of the world and the Marian year dedicated to Our Lady in 1987-1988, then there could be a great war, with fire falling from heaven, the oceans being vaporized, Italy invaded with the red flag of Russia raised over the dome of St. Peter's Basilica. We must pray and fast like never before!

When the Pope consecrates Russia in union with all the bishops of the world to Our Lady's Immaculate Heart Russia then will be converted bringing about the triumph of her Immaculate Heart. This needs to be done as soon as possible to prevent a World War III, a war that this time would be nuclear!

Result Of Papal And Bishops Action Or Inaction

If Russia Is Not Consecrated By Name As Our Lady Requested

Blessed Elena Aiello in 1959 received the message from the Madonna that **Russia will march upon all the nations of Europe, particularly Italy, and will raise her flag over the dome of St. Peter's.... The flock is about to be dispersed and the Pope must suffer greatly.**

Mother Elena Leonardi was told on February 12, 1979 by Our Lady as Mother of All Peoples that godless nations will be the scourge chosen by God Himself to punish the disrespectful and unscrupulous humanity. A great punishment will befall all mankind, a great war will break out, fire will fall from heaven, the ocean waters will be converted to vapor, and the foam will rise up to sweep all humanity...**Communism will triumph because of godless rulers**.

When This Consecration Is Done As Our Lady Requested

While recuperating from the wounds suffered in the attempted assassination in 1981, St. John Paul II told his friend Bishop Paul M. Hnilica, SJ, "Paul, in these three months I have come to understand that the only solution to all the problems of the world, deliverance from war, the deliverance from atheism, and from the defection from God is the conversion of Russia.[52]

When Russia is consecrated by name, as requested, to Our Lady's Immaculate Heart by the Pope joined by all the bishops of the world,

253

Russia will be converted, and a certain period of peace be granted to the world.

Chapter 13

The Era Of Peace

The remnant will enter into the promised Era of Peace after the Three Days of Darkness, at the end of the great chastisement, when three quarters of humanity has been destroyed. The earth will be permanently transformed. Satan will be bound and cast into hell. His diabolical power will be destroyed and the gates of the abyss shut so that he cannot get out to harm the world.

The exact duration of this coming Era of Peace is a still a mystery.

The messages from La Salette, (Leece), talks about 25 years of peace.

The message given to Julka of Yugoslavia mentions the length as 30-34 years.

Maria Valtorta was told by Jesus that this would be s short period of peace.

In the Book of Revelation the phrase a thousand years is mentioned. The Church follows the concept of St. Augustine that the thousand years is not actually a thousand years as we ordinarily would understand it, but either as an equivalent for the whole duration of this world, employing the number of perfection to mark the fullness of time, or as a thousand put for totality. St. Augustine said, "if a hundred is sometimes used for totality ... how much greater reason is a thousand put for totality since it is the cube, while the other is only the square." The duration could thus be less than, equal to, or greater than a thousand years.

"This new era corresponds to a particular encounter of love, of light and of life between paradise and earth. ... This is the heavenly Jerusalem, which comes down from heaven upon earth, to transform it completely and thus shape the new heavens and the new earth."

In this Era of Peace **"the hearts of men will be transformed by the powerful force of the Holy Spirit, who will pour Himself out upon them through the miracle of his Second Pentecost."** We will have the glorious Eucharistic Reign of Christ which coincides "with the perfect accomplishment of the will of God on the part of every one of His creatures, in such a way that, as in heaven, so it will also be on this earth." At last there will have arrived that which Jesus taught us to ask for from the Heavenly Father, "Your will be done on earth as it is in heaven."

A New Paradise, A New Earth

The earth will be a new paradise and God will reign in the heart of His people. The chosen ones of God will no longer experience suffering and all will live in conformity with the will of God. There will be no pain, no poverty, and no violence. Babies will no longer die in infancy. All will live happily for a long time. Peace will reign among men and between nations. **There will be no wars and all will embrace love. Men and women full of spirituality will run the world**.

With the transformation of the earth to a new earth, there will be no pollution, rivers and lakes will appear, there will be great abundance in the poorest regions of the earth, the earth will be impregnated with much life, the ocean will be beautiful and abundant with life.

Joy will reign in the hearts of those chosen by God and there will be only one flock and one shepherd.

This will be the definitive Triumph of the Immaculate Heart of Mary.

In this Era of Peace humanity will get back most, if not all, of the preternatural gifts that were lost when Adam sinned. Adam lost the preternatural gifts that God had given to him, and thus through original sin also lost them for us.

Preternatural gifts are favors granted by God above and beyond the powers or capacities of the nature that receives them but not beyond those of all created nature. Such gifts perfect nature but do not carry it beyond the limits of created nature. They include three great privileges to

256

which human beings have no title – **infused knowledge, absence of concupiscence**, and **bodily immortality**. Adam and Eve possessed these gifts before the Fall.

These were the preternatural gifts that Adam lost:
1. Immortality – You don't die.
2. Impassibility – Don't feel pain or harm.
3. Freedom from concupiscence (sexual desire), ignorance, and sin.
4. Lordship over the earth.

The supernatural events, of the **Warning**, the **Miracle** and the **Great Sign**, the schism in the Church with the False Prophet as Antipope, the reign of Antichrist, the abomination of desolation prophesied by Daniel and the Great Chastisement will occur before we enter into the Era of Peace. This Era of Peace will include the Eucharistic Reign of Jesus and the Era when we will live in the Divine Will with the Second Coming of Jesus in glory.

Sadie Jaramillo on November 13, 1995 was told by Jesus: "Through the impending events, My hand is on you and all who are Mine and My Mother's. This triumph of Her Heart is the peace that will see you through and lead you into the Era of Peace!..." [6]

Jesus told Sr. Natalia of Hungary, b 1901, "The right hand of my Father will annihilate all those sinners who, despite the warnings and the period of grace and the tireless effort of the Church, will not convert." [24]

Sr. Natalia states: "I saw God's Holy Spirit – as a devastating fire – inundate the world. This fire did not bring peace, nor mercy, but devastating punishment. Wherever the flame of the Holy Spirit swept through, the evil spirits by the thousands fell back to hell." In this vision of Sr. Natalia: "The Holy Virgin took off from her shoulder the mantle of peace and suddenly covered the world with it. All those parts of the world covered with the mantle escaped the punishment and shone in the blue color of peace. But where the mantle did not cover the surface, the red color of anger could be seen radiating as embers." **Sr. Natalia said: "I understood that we can escape from the just punishment of God only if we seek refuge under**

the mantle of our Blessed Virgin Mother, and supplicate mercy through her." [24]

After The Three Days Of Darkness

Blessed Anna Maria Taigi (d. 1837) said: "After the three days of darkness, St. Peter and St. Paul, having come down from Heaven, will preach in the whole world and designate a new Pope.... Christianity will then spread throughout the world....

Whole nations will come back to the Church and **the face of the earth will be renewed.** *Russia, England*, and *China* **will come back to the Church."** [18]

Julka (Julia), of Yugoslavia said of her vision of the three days of darkness: "But after the darkness the earth remained waste. The beautiful warm sun rose to shine upon the earth and all living things upon it, but only here and there was any human being still alive. Nature created by God, remained empty – without human beings. The Lord Jesus counseled the visionary, and left her in the little flock.

All My creatures who survive the great tribulation, will see Me. No one will then be able to say that I do not exist, because **I shall be near the earth;** and **all the creatures of the earth will hear My voice. They will see Me present then, and, for the second time, at the Final Judgment."** [33]

The Era Of Peace As Revealed To Sister Natalia Of Hungary

Sr. Natalia of Hungary was told by Jesus that the Church, cleansed and renewed by the great sufferings, will dress again in humility and simpleness, and will be poor as at her beginning.... They will live by the spirit of the Sermon on the Mount. Sr. Natalia said that she saw that when the glorious peace arrives and love reigns, there will be only "one fold and one shepherd." [24]

Jesus told Sr. Natalia: "I brought peace when I was born, but the world has not yet enjoyed it. **The world is entitled to that peace.** Men are the children of God. God breathes His own souls into them. God cannot let Himself be put to shame, and that is why **the children of God are entitled to enjoy the peace that I promised."** [24]

Sr. Natalia was told by Jesus about the cleansing of the world, "the coming age of paradise, when humanity will live as if without sin. This will be a new world and a new age. This will be the age when mankind will get back what it lost in paradise*. When My Immaculate mother will step on the neck of the serpent, the gates of hell will be closed. The host of angels will be part of this fight. **I have sealed with My seal My own that they shall not be lost in this fight.**" [24]
*Adam lost the preternatural gifts which God had given to him.

The Era Of Peace As Revealed To Janie Garza

On April 19, 1994 Janie Garza received from Jesus a vision of the New Jerusalem. Janie said: "In the seventh vision I saw new life. I saw a garden full of life. The trees were beautiful and very green. I saw flowers of all kinds. I saw beautiful springs of water in different areas of the garden. *This is the most beautiful garden I have ever seen, and I knew it was like no garden on this earth. Then I heard Jesus speak Scripture to me. Jesus said: 'This is the New Jerusalem.* This is the new house of the people of My Father. **Here there will be no more weeping,** no more calling for help. **Babies will no longer die in infancy and all people will live out their life span. Those who live to be a hundred will be considered young and to die before that time will be a sign that My Father had punished them.**

Like trees, people will live long lives. They will build their homes and get to live in them. Their homes will not be used by someone else. The work they do will be successful and their children will not meet with disaster.'" [26] **(cf. Isaiah 65:19-21)**

On September 5, 1996 Janie Garza had a vision of the new earth. Janie said: "St. Michael showed me a vision of the world as it is in these evil times. Then he **showed me a vision of the new earth. It was beautiful. There was no pollution, and the earth was impregnated**

with much life. The ocean was so beautiful and abundant with sea life. There was no poverty, no suffering, no violence, only true peace from Heaven. This was a vision of hope for all of God's children who keep their focus on God in these evil times." [8]

The Short Duration Of The Period Of Peace

La Salette And The Short Duration Of The Period Of Peace

At La Salette, in the message to Melanie Calvat, we are told that the period of peace will be twenty-five years: "The righteous will suffer greatly. Their prayers, their penances, and their tears will rise up to Heaven. And all of God's people will beg for forgiveness and mercy, and will plead for my help and intercession. **And then Jesus Christ, in an act of His justice and His great mercy, will command His Angels to have all His enemies put to death. Suddenly, the persecutors of the Church of Jesus Christ and all those given over to sin will perish and the earth will become desert-like.** And then peace will be made, and man will be reconciled with God. **Jesus Christ will be served, worshiped and glorified.** *Charity will flourish everywhere. The new kings will be the right arm of the holy Church, which will be strong, humble, pious in its poor but fervent imitation of the virtues of Jesus Christ. The Gospel will be preached everywhere and mankind will make great progress in its faith, for there will be unity among the workers of Jesus Christ and man will live in fear of God.*

"This peace among men will be short-lived. Twenty-five years of plentiful harvests will make them forget that the sins of men are the cause of all the troubles on this earth." [7]

Julka Of Yugoslavia (Period 1960-1966) Message On The Duration Of The Era Of Peace

Jesus said to Julka: "As you have seen, so it will be. I shall come quickly and in splendour. **All My creatures who survive the Great tribulation, will see Me. No one will then be able to say that I do not exist,** because I shall be near the earth; and all the creatures of the earth will hear My Voice. **They will see Me present then, and, for the second time, at the Final Judgment.**

This will be the Little Flock and I shall hover over it. In those days there will be one Shepherd and one Faith, that of the Roman Catholic Church, which I established when I walked visibly on earth. After the distresses, which I am now permitting to come upon My obstinate people on earth, there will arise a fair and pure Race and the earth will abound with My Gifts. My Sons and My daughters will keep My Commandments. **Thus everything will live and grow with My Blessing for thirty years."**

Our Lord said also: "If I should protract the years of the Little Flock, it will live at the most for 34 years in peace; 30 years is the destined time." [5]

The Era Of Peace As Revealed By Jesus To Maria Valtorta

Maria Valtorta was born in Caserta in 1897. She died on October 12, 1961. In 1924 her family finally settled in Viareggio, a Mediterranean port near Pisa.

By 1934 Maria was permanently bed-ridden, seriously disabled as the final outcome of a violent assault fourteen years earlier. Her spiritual life grew powerful and in late 1942 her spiritual director asked her to write her autobiography. **In 1943 she began to receive private revelations from Heaven. Her spiritual director told her to put everything down in writing. By late 1950, the revelations to her were mostly finished.** *The Poem of the Man-God*, **4228 pages in five books is her writing of private revelation that is probably the most well known.**

In Maria's writings published in the book *The End Times As Revealed To Maria Valtorta* **Jesus tells her about the short Era of Peace.**

This era of peace following the three days of darkness during which the antichrist, the false prophet and their unrepentant followers are cast into hell has a termination with Satan, who, raging at the sight of mankind worshipping Christ, goes wild for the last battle.

Maria Valtorta was told by Jesus on September 16, 1943 that the period after the Antichrist is a period of truce. Jesus told her that during this time, after having shown you with the blood-shedding trial what kind of gifts Satan can give, I will try to draw all of you to Me by showering you with My gifts.

"Oh! My gifts! They will be your delight! You will not experience hunger, slaughters, disasters. *Your bodies and more your souls will be fed by My hand, Earth will seem to spring from a second creation, wholly renewed in the sentiments of peace and goodwill among the nations, and of peace between Heaven and Earth, because I will have My Spirit flood over you the supernatural sight of God's decrees.*

It will be the Kingdom of the Spirit, the Kingdom of God, which you ask for in the 'Our Father'—and you do not know what you are asking for because you never think about it. *Where do you expect the Kingdom of God to come about but in your hearts? That is where My Kingdom on Earth must begin. A great Kingdom, but still limited.*

The Kingdom without limits, neither of land, nor of time, will come after. It is the eternal Kingdom which will turn all of you into eternal dwellers of the Heavens, because, naturally, *I am speaking to those who are My subjects and not to reprobates who already have their ghastly king: Satan.*

On October 29, 1943 Jesus said to Maria Valtorta, "My Church, before the hour of the world comes to an end, will have its glittering triumph. Nothing differs in the Mystical Body's life from that which was in Christ's life. There will be the hosanna on the eve of Passion, the hosanna when the nations, seized by the fascination of the Divinity, bend the knee before the Lord. Then the Passion of My church militant will come, and finally the glory of eternal Resurrection in Heaven.

Oh bliss of that day when the conspiracies, retaliations, struggles of this earth, of Satan, of the flesh will be over forever! **My Church will then be made up of real Christians, in that time, in the next-to-last day. Few as in the beginning, but holy as in the beginning. The Church**

will end in holiness as it began in holiness. Liars, betrayers, idolaters will stay outside, those who on the last day will imitate Judas and sell their souls to Satan, harming Christ's Mystical Body. In them the Beast will have its replacements for its last war....

On January 23, 1944 Jesus told Maria that **Israel will again be joined to Rome, there will no longer be two branches of God's people**...there shall be only one tree-trunk known *as of Christ*, because it will be alive in Me.

The last time of three years and six months shall be more awful than what mankind ever experienced. **Satan shall be inflamed with utmost spite, because even the split between the two branches of God's people will be over, and with it the cause of so many material, moral and spiritual evils.**

Jesus told Maria the meaning of Daniel's prophecy that "There shall be 1290 days (of this oppression). Blessed is he that waits, and comes unto 1335 days.

"This means that during the three years and six months coming before the end, a short time will be laid aside in the end for the faithful to gather to listen to the last Words, resounding in their spirits, as an invitation to Heaven, *while Michael with his angels crushes Satan and his demons.* **'Blessed is he that waits, and comes unto 1335 days' means: '*Blessed is he that shall persevere unto the end*' because he shall be saved.**

Jesus told Maria Valtorta in the message of October 29, 1943 that **at the last hour three quarters of My church will disown Me, and I will have to cut them off** from the tree-trunk as dead branches infected by an unclean leprosy.

Jesus told Maria Valtorta in the message of November 12, 1943 that the Satanic period will be three times more ferocious than the period of the Antichrist. But it will be short....

The Thousand Years
In The Book Of Revelation

Saint Augustine

St. Augustine, in City of God, Book XX, Chapter 7 tells us 1000 is a number of perfection, 10^3 meaning totality, marking the fullness of time.

The Number 1,000 Is Used To Mean Totality,
Marking The Fullness of Time

In *City of God*, **Book XX, Chapter 7, St. Augustine writes: "Now the thousand years may be understood in two ways,** so far as occurs to me: **either** because these things happen in the sixth thousand of years or sixth millennium (the latter part of which is now passing), as if during the sixth day, which is to be followed by a Sabbath which has no evening, the endless rest of the saints, so that, speaking of a part under the name of the whole, he calls the last part of the millennium – the part, that is, which had yet to expire before the end of the world – a thousand years; **or he used the thousand years as an equivalent for the whole duration of this world, employing the number of perfection to mark the fullness of time.** For a thousand is the cube of ten. For ten times ten makes a hundred, that is; the square on a plane superficies. But to give this superficies height, and make it a cube, the hundred is again multiplied by ten, which gives a thousand. **Besides, if a hundred is sometimes used for totality,** as when the Lord said by way of promise to him that left all and followed Him "He shall receive in this world an hundredfold;" of which the apostle gives, as it were, an explanation when he says, "As having nothing, yet possessing all things," – for even of old it had been said, The whole world is the wealth of a believer, – **with how much greater reason is a thousand put for totality since it is the cube, while the other is only the square?**

The Era Of Peace In Messages Received By Pedro Regis, Brazil From May 18, 2005 Through November 26, 2012

Transformation Of The Earth

No More Anxiety, No More Pain

May 18, 2005. Message 2524 – Dear Sons and Daughters, **humanity will be purified by suffering and when all the tribulations pass, man will return to serving only The Lord.** *Everything on earth will be transformed and the chosen people will live happily.* **No more will there be anxiety on earth because there will be no more pain. Men and women will walk without fear because evil will be no more. The earth will be a paradise and everybody will experience endless joy.**

God Will Make Rivers Flow In The Desert

August 5, 2006. Message 2716 – Dear Sons and Daughters,... **After all the tribulation, The Lord will transform the earth, and peace will reign among men.** *God will make rivers flow in the desert and there will be a great abundance in the poorest regions of the earth.* **The prodigies of The Lord will be grandiose. Men and women will understand the call of The Lord and all will serve Him with love and fidelity. Happiness will reign among men for a long time.**

There Will Be No Wars

September 5, 2006. Message 2729 – **After all the tribulation The Lord will transform the earth and the teachings of my Jesus will be accepted by men and women. Everybody will understand the message of salvation offered by My Jesus and all will unite. By the mercy of The Lord humanity will attain peace. There will be no wars and all will embrace love.** All that I have announced to you will happen, but in the end will come the victory of God with the definitive triumph of My Immaculate Heart.

Peace Will Reign Between Nations

September 26, 2006. Message 2738 – Dear Sons and Daughters,... **After all the tribulation** *The Lord will transform the earth.* **Humanity will see the powerful hand of God in action. Mankind will live happily and peace will reign between nations.**

Rivers And Lakes Will Appear

February 3, 2007. Message 2794 – Dear Sons and Daughters,... **A giant will come and when men announce that it is near, humanity will live moments of great difficulties.** *The earth will go through an immense transformation.* Know that all this must happen, but in the end the faithful will win. **God will transform the earth and those who are just will live happily. Rivers and lakes will appear. There will be riches and abundance.**

Men And Women Full Of Spirituality
Will Run The World

February 21, 2007. Message 2802 – Dear Sons and Daughters,... **After all the tribulation The Lord will send His angels and they will lead men to a new form of life.** *Humanity will experience peace and men and women full of spirituality will run the world. Those who are faithful will see the marvels of God.*

No More Tribulations In The Life
Of The Just

July 24, 2007. Message 2866 – Dear Sons and Daughters, **the day will come when there will be no more tribulations in the life of the just. The Lord will act with His strong arm to help you. He will dry your tears, and** *when all tribulations have passed, you will see the transformation of the earth....* **When all seems lost The Lord will come to help you.**

All Will Live In Conformity With The Will Of The Lord

July 28, 2007. Message 2869 – Dear Sons and Daughters,... **Know that The Lord will transform the earth and people will live happily. There will be no more suffering and all will live in conformity with the will of The Lord. After all the tribulation you shall contemplate a new earth.**

After A Great Tribulation The Lord Will Transform The Earth

August 15, 2011. Message 3525. Message of Our Lady, Pontalina/GO at Santo Antonio Parish. Dear children,... "The day is coming when mankind will have a chance to repent. God will show a great sign and mankind will have no explanation. **After a great tribulation, the Lord will transform the Earth and you will see the powerful Hand of God at work.** Repent and return. My Lord awaits you with open arms. What you have to do, do not put off until tomorrow."

Mankind Will Live In A New Time Of Peace

August 14, 2007. Message 2876 – from Our Lady. Dear Sons and Daughters, **an Angel of The Lord will blow his trumpet and the whole world will be shaken.** *This will be the beginning of a new time; the time awaited by the just.* **Humanity will experience a long time of peace. The just will see the fulfillment of promises of The Lord. The victory of The Lord will be your victory.**

August 21, 2012. Message 3697 – from Our Lady Queen of Peace Campo do Brito/SE. Dear children,... **"My Jesus has prepared for you something that human eyes have never seen.** *The Earth will experience a great transformation*, **and mankind will live in a new time of peace. Be happy, for your names are already written in heaven."**

267

New Heavens And New Earth

New Heavens And New Earths Will Arise

May 28, 2005. **Message 2528 – Dear Sons and Daughters, I want to tell you that the day will come when men and women will live in full happiness, for The Lord will reign in all hearts.** *You will walk in an earthly paradise, and there will be no more suffering.* **Know that The Lord has prepared for His own that which human eyes have never seen. Don't lose heart.** *When all the tribulations have passed, new heavens and new earths will* **arise. There will be an extraordinary sign in the heavens. Men will seek an answer, but will not find it, for the secret comes from God.**

The Chosen Ones Of God Will See A New Heavens And A New Earth

January 11, 2011. Message 3424 – Message from Our Lady of Peace, Anguera, Bahia, Brazil. Dear Sons and Daughters, trust in the power of God and all will come out well for you. Whoever is with The Lord will experience the Grace of victory. **His holy and powerful name is the vessel that will take you to paradise, even passing through the storms of this world.** There is no victory without the cross. I will speak to my Jesus for you. Open your hearts and tomorrow will be better. **When all seems lost, a great victory of God for you will appear. The earth will be transformed and men will see the powerful hand of God in action. The signs of death present in the world will no longer exist.** *This will be the definitive triumph of my Immaculate Heart. The chosen ones of God will see a new heavens and a new earth.* Courage. Your greatest riches are the talents The Lord offers to you. Use them for the good of your brothers. Forward without fear.

The Hearts Of The Just Will Be Full Of Joy

June 4, 2012. Message 3633 – from Our Lady Queen of Peace. Dear children,... **"The day will come when you will see peace reign upon the Earth and promises made by the Lord to men and women of faith will be fulfilled. Then there will be no motive for sadness; the** hearts of the just will be full of joy. Thus you will see a new Heaven and a new Earth. Be happy, for your names are already written in Heaven."

The Earth Will Be A New Paradise

God Will Reign In The Heart Of His People

March 27, 2007. Message 2817 – Dear Sons and Daughters,... **The Lord will act and men and women will return to His heart full of joy. The happiness of mankind will be immense when it contemplates the transformation of the world. Human eyes will see that which mankind has never perceived.** *The earth will be a new paradise and God will reign in the heart of His people.*

The Creator Will Restore The Earth

January 19, 2010. Message 3268 – from Our Lady, Queen of Peace, Anguera, Bahia, Brazil, transmitted. Dear Sons and Daughters,... **You live in a time of great tribulations. Humanity will drink the bitter cup of suffering, but God will not abandon you.** *He will dry your tears and the world will be transformed into a new paradise.* **The Creator will restore the earth and you will see what human eyes have never seen.**

Death Will No Longer Exist

The Lord Will Reign In All Hearts

March 13, 2007. Message 2810, given in Campinas, St. Paul. Dear Sons and Daughters,... **When all the tribulations have passed The Lord will act with His strong arm.** *The earth will be totally transformed and the just will experience immense joy.* **There will be no more pain. Death will no longer exist and The Lord will reign in all hearts.**

Jesus Will Reign And Everybody Will Be Happy

March 17, 2007. Message 2812 – Dear Sons and Daughters,... **Humanity will be transformed and mankind will live happily. Everything will be different. Your joy will be grandiose.** *God will send His angels to direct you, and you will always go in towards the All-powerful. There will be no death nor sorrow.* **Humanity will be at peace. Jesus will reign and everybody will be happy.**

There Will Be No More Anguish Or Death

September 11, 2007. Message 2888 – from Our Lady. Dear Sons and Daughters,... **The earth will be transformed and people will see the powerful hand of God in action. That which the great prophets foretold will happen. Then there will be no more anguish or death.**

November 24, 2007. Message 2921 – from Our Lady of Peace. Dear Sons and Daughters,... **After all the tribulation, My Jesus will send His angels. The earth will be transformed and all that you contemplate today will be different.** *The just will inherit a transformed earth in which there will be neither death nor pain. All will be happy and peace will reign forever.*

The Lord Has Reserved For The Just That
Which Human Eyes Have Not Seen

August 11, 2005. Message 2560 – Dear Sons and Daughters, the time will come when men and women live in prefect communion with God. **After all the tribulations have passed, peace will reign on earth. Know that The Lord has reserved for the just that which human eyes have not seen. The angels of The Lord will pass, and woe to those who have corrupted the earth. Woe to those who have defied The Creator and seduced my poor children into error.**

February 24, 2008. Message 2961 – from Our Lady of Peace, Paulo Afonso, Bahia. Dear Sons and Daughters, **there will still be great trials and you will confront great storms, but don't back out. Stay firmly with the Church of My Jesus. The triumph of the Church will be grand and my Jesus will reward the men and women of faith.** *Those* *who remain faithful to the end will experience something they never experienced in this life. The just will see what human eyes have never seen.*

March 6, 2010. Message 3289 – from Our Lady, Queen of Peace, Anguera, Bahia, Brazil. Dear Sons and Daughters,… **You live in a time of great tribulations,… After all the tribulation, the transformation of the world will come, God will work a great miracle, and you will see that which human eyes have never seen, It will be a time of joy for God's chosen ones.**

There Will Be Only One Flock And One Shepherd

March 25, 2007. Message 2816, transmitted in Maceió. Dear Sons and Daughters,… **The day will come when men and women must serve only The Lord.** *Then there will be only one flock and only one Pastor.* **No one will be separate for The Lord only will reign. Men and women will contemplate the marvels of God and will not stumble again, for God Himself will guide them.** *Humanity will be in perfect union with the Creator. Peace will reign among nations.* **There will be no more wars and the weapon of men will be confidence in their God. Rejoice, for your names are already written in heaven.**

August 11, 2007. Message 2875 – Dear Sons and Daughters,… **After all the tribulation, the faithful people will experience great peace.** *The earth will be transformed and there will be only one flock and only one pastor. It will be the moment of definitive triumph of My Immaculate Heart.* **Know, all of you, what The Lord has reserved for His own, that which human eyes have never seen.**

July 11, 2010. Message 3344 – from Our Lady of Peace, given in Araxa/MG, Brazil. Dear Sons and Daughters, I am your Mom and I come from heaven to lead you to my Son Jesus. Rejoice, for your names are already written in heaven. Don't be discouraged. Don't back out. **After all the tribulations the Lord will wipe away your tears. All darkness will be gone and the light of God will shine in the hearts of men and women of faith.** *Joy will reign in the hearts of those chosen by God and there will be only one flock and one shepherd. The victory* *of God over the forces of evil will come with the final triumph of my Immaculate Heart.*

The Nations At War Will Be Reconciled

December 25, 2007. Message 2934 – from Our Lady of Peace. Dear Sons and Daughters,... *The day will come when the earth will be completely transformed.* **The geography will no longer be the same. Seeing these great changes, people will realize that alone they will never win, and so, will confide in Jesus. Peace will reign in hearts, and the nations at war will be reconciled. Violence will become extinct, and God will reign with His peace.**

The Triumph Of Mary's Immaculate Heart

The Church Will Again Be As
When Jesus Confided It To Peter

March 6, 2008. Message 2965 – from Our Lady of Peace, given in Luzania, Goias, Brazil. Dear Sons and Daughters,... **After all the tribulation that will come to the Church, The Lord will make His victory felt. He will dry the tears of the faithful and all will live happily. The Church will be at peace. The enemies will be destroyed by the force and power of My Jesus. The Church will again be as when Jesus confided it to Peter, and my children will experience the definitive triumph of my Immaculate Heart.**

There Will Be No Pain. Death Will No Longer Exist.

February 9, 2010. Message 3277 – from Our Lady, Queen of peace, Valparaiso/GO. BR.. Dear Sons and Daughters, ... **Know that a great miracle of God will happen in favor of those who are devoted to me. In the great tribulation, my chosen ones will not experience suffering.** *They will be chosen by God and will inherit a new world. There will be no pain. Death will no longer exist and all will live happily. This will be the time of the definitive triumph of my Immaculate Heart.*

272

You Will See A New Earth

October 22, 2011. Message 3558 of Our Lady. Dear children,… "Do not be discouraged in the face of your problems. When everything seems lost, the Lord will come to you. He will dry your tears, and you will see a transformation of humanity. **After the great final tribulation, you will see a new Earth. That will be the time of the definitive triumph of my Immaculate Heart. Humanity will find peace and men and women of faith will live in happiness. Do not be discouraged. Tomorrow will be joyful for the elect of God. Go forward without fear.** Separate yourselves from sin and serve the Lord with joy. I will plead with my Jesus for you. Courage."

The Triumph Of The Lord Will Happen

February 2, 2011. Message 3443 – from Our Lady of Peace, Goiânia, GO. Brazil. Dear Sons and Daughters,… "Joyful days are coming for the chosen people of God. God will send a sign to people who have gone away from God. It will be a chance for all those who decide in favor of God. **The triumph of the Lord will happen and those who are chosen will contemplate that which human eyes have never contemplated. It will be the time of the definitive triumph of My Immaculate Heart. Forward without fear.**"

The Just Will Live Happily

December 12, 2011. Message 3584 of Our Lady. Dear children,… "You still have long years ahead of you on Earth. Seek strength in Jesus. **The day is coming when God will transform the Earth. Your 'yes' with the help of God will bring peace to the earth forever. It will be the time of the definitive triumph of my Immaculate Heart. And the just will live happily. Be happy for you are precious in the eyes of God. Do not hold back.** *When everything seems lost, a new time of peace and happiness will come for humanity. Go forward without fear.*"

All Men Will Walk In The Truth And Love The Truth

September 6, 2012. Message 3704 from Our Lady of Peace, GraoMogol/MG. **Dear children,...** **"My Lord will transform the Earth and all men will walk in the truth and love the truth. It will be a time of grace for humanity. Everything will occur with the definitive Triumph of my Immaculate Heart."**

Humanity Will Again Have Peace

November 26, 2012. Message 3742 – from Our Lady of Peace, Nucleo Bandeirantes/DF. **Dear children,...** **"When everything seems lost, the Lord will dry your tears and humanity will again have peace. The Earth will pass through a great transformation. That will be the time of the definitive triumph of my Immaculate Heart."**

Our Lady Told Father Gobbi That The Triumph Of The Immaculate Heart Of Mary[2]

- **Is won in the souls and the lives of her faithful children. Message #116**
- Consists in the greatest triumph of the merciful love of Jesus, which will change the whole world and bring us to a new era of love, of holiness and of peace. **Message #392**
- Return of humanity, like a prodigal son, into the arms of the Heavenly Father. **Message #523**
- The triumph coincides with the triumph of divine mercy upon the world. **Message #536**
- The miracle of the second Pentecost will come with the triumph of my Immaculate Heart in the world. **Message #546**
- The new heart of the new Church will be born with the triumph. **Message #547**
- With the triumph enter into the New Era of Peace: for the Church, for humanity, for all of you. **Message #549**
- Then the miracle of divine mercy, in the power of the Holy Spirit, will renew the face of the earth. **Message #554**

- The Coming Together Of All The Christian Confessions In The Catholic Church. **Message #565**
- You will see my Son Jesus returning on the clouds in the splendor of His Divine Glory. **Message #576**
- You will be completely liberated from every form of practical atheism. **Message #577**
- Will come about in the greatest triumph of Jesus: who will bring into the world His glorious reign of love, of justice and peace, and will make all things new. **Message #604**

Bibliography

1. *Our Lady Of All Nations,* Queenship Publishing Company, P.O. Box 42028 Santa Barbara CA 93140-2028.
2. *To The Priests Our Lady's Beloved Sons,* The Marian Movement of Priests, Rev. Albert G. Roux, P.O. Box 8, St. Francis, Maine 04774-0008. Tel. 207 -398-3375 / Fax: 207-398-3352.
3. *The Great Sign Volume II.* Messages to Sadie Jaramillo. St. Dominic Media, P.O. Box 345, Herndon, VA 20172-0345.
4. *Messages Of Our Lady At San Nicolas,* Faith Publishing Company, P.O. Box 237, Milford, Ohio 45150, 1991.
5. From *Jesus Calls Us,* Volume 1, pages 218-227.
6. The Great Sign (Volume I). Messages to Sadie Jaramillo. St. Dominic Media, P.O. Box 345, Herndon, VA 20172-0345.
7. *Sister Mary of the Cross Shepherdess of La Salette,* by Fr. Paul Gouin. The 101 Foundation, P.O. Box 151, Asbury, New Jersey 08804, pages 61-69. Pamphlet published at Leece, November 15, 1879 with Imprimatur by Bishop Zola who had been a confessor of Melanie.
8. *Heaven's Messages For The Family, Vol. 2,* 1999. Messages to Janie Garza. St. Dominic Media, P.O. Box 345, Herndon, VA 20172-0345.
9. *Dreams, Visions & Prophecies of Don Bosco,* Don Bosco Publications, New Rochelle, New York. Re Two Columns pages 105-108 May 30, 1862.
10. *The Secret Archives of the Vatican,* by Maria Luisa Ambrosini with Mary Willis, Barnes & Noble Books, New York, 1969.
11. *The Mystery of Freemasonry Unveiled,* by the Cardinal of Chile. Christian Book Club of America, P.O. Box 900566, CA 93590, First Printing Circa 1928, Fifth Printing 1992.
12. *En Route to Global Occupation,* by Gary H. Kah, Huntington House Publishers, P.O. Box 53788, Lafayette, Louisiana 70505, 1992.
13. *New World Order: The Ancient Plan of Secret Societies,* by William T. Still, Huntington House Publishers, P.O. Box 53788, Lafayette, Louisiana 70505, 1990.
14. *Towards World Government, New World Order,* by Deirdre Manifold.

15. *Grand Orient Freemasonry Unmasked as the Secret Power behind Communism*, by Mgr. George E. Dillon, D.D. Lectures Delivered in Edinburg in October, 1884. Republished 1950. Christian Book Club, P.O. Box 900566, Palmdale, CA 93590.
16. *Mary's Triumph, Years of Revelation*, Via dei Gracchi, 29 B. Roma, Italia.
17. *Eucharistic Experiences,* Messages to Ida Peerdeman, July 17, 1958 to March 25, 1984. Queenship Publishers.
18. *Catholic Prophecy, The Coming Chastisement*, by Yves Dupont, 1973. TAN Books and Publishers, Inc., P.O. BOX 424, Rockford, IL 61105.
19. *She Went In Haste To The Mountain, Books One, Two, Three.* Eusebio Garcia De Pesquera O.F.M. Translated from the Spanish by Gerard Suel& Otto Miller. 1981 by St. Joseph Publications, 17700 Lorain Avenue, Cleveland, Ohio 44111.
20. *Divine Mercy In My Soul. Diary.* Saint Sister M. Faustina Kowalska. Marian Helpers, Stockbridge, MA 01263.
21. *Akita: Mother of God as CoRedemptrix. Modern Miracles of the Holy Eucharist*, by Francis Matsuo Fukushima. Visions and Messages to Sr. Agnes Sasagawa, Akita, Japan. Queenship Publishing, P.O. Box 42028 Santa Barbara, CA 93140-2028.
22. *I Am the Guardian Of The Faith, Reported Apparitions of the Mother of God in Ecuador*, by Sr. Isabel Bettwy, 1991. Franciscan University Press, Steubenville, OH 43952.
23. *The Keys of This Blood*, 1990, by Fr. Malachi Martin, Simon & Shuster, Inc. (Touchstone).
24. *The Victorious Queen of the World*, 1992, Two Hearts Books and Publishers, P.O. Box 844, Mountain View, CA 94042.
25. Nelly Hurtado, from Internet – e-mail.
26. *Heaven's Messages For The Family, Vol. 1*, 1998. Messages to Janie Garza. St. Dominic Media, P.O. Box 345, Herndon, VA 20172-0345.
27. *Josyp Terelya Witness to Apparitions and Persecution in the USSR, An Autobiography Josyp Terelya with Michael H. Brown*, Faith Publishing Company.
28. *In The Kingdom of the Spirit.* Abba House.
29. *Conversations in Heaven.* Eileen George. Meet The Father Ministry, Millbury, Massachusetts.

30. *Please Come Back To Me And My Son*, by R. Vincent. Ireland's Eye Publications, Lynn Industrial Estate, Mullinger, Co, Westmeath, Ireland.

31. *Apparitions In Betania, Venezuela*, Sister Margaret Catherine Sims, CSJ, 1992, Marian Messengers, P.O. Box 647, Framingham, MA 01704-0647.

32. *The Thunder of Justice, by Ted and Maureen Flynn*. MaxKol, 1993. Revised & Updated 2010. MaxKol Communications, Inc. P.O. Box 345, Herndon, Virginia 20172, www.sign.org, Phone: (703) 707-0799.

33. *Jesus Calls Us, Vol. 1, 2, 3: Vol. 2*, 1983. Haupt Cristi - Verlag, Munchen-Oberschleissheim Vol. 3, 1988, Vol. 1, 1990 In Wahrheit Und Treue, Postfach 279, 8401 Winterthur (Switzerland). All 3 Volumes distributed by Center of Mary Queen of Light, Route 1, Box 904, Turner, ME 04282 USA.

34. Pope Pius XI. Papal Allocution to French Pilgrims present for the reading of decree "de tuto" (Canonization of Blessed Antida Thouret, 15 August 1933. *L'Osservatore Romano,* 16 August 1933; cf. Dante, Paradiso, Canto 33, 14, 15..

35. *A Catechism of Modernism*, The Rev. J.B. Lemius, O.M.I, TAN Books and Publishers, Rockford, Illinois, 1981.

36. *The Sorrow, The Sacrifice and The Triumph* by Thomas W. Petrisco.   Visions and Messages—Christina Gallagher.   A Touchstone Book, Published by Simon & Schuster, New York.

37. Pope Pius XI. Papal Allocution to French Pilgrims present for the reading of decree "de tuto" (Canonization of Blessed Antida Thouret, 15 August 1933.

38. Pope Pius XII, Papal Allocution at the Canonization of Blessed Louis Marie Grignion de Montfort, 21 July 1947, AAS 39, 408.

39. *Prophecies of La Fraudais of Marie-Julie JAHENNY,* April 10. 1977, by Editions Resiac, 53150 Montsurs France.

40. *AA-1025, The Memoirs of an Anti-Apostle,* MarieCarre,TAN Books and Publishers, Inc., P.O. Box 424, Rockford, Illinois, 61105, 1991.

41. *Humanum Genus*, Encyclical Letter of His Holiness Pope Leo XIII on Freemasonry, April 20, 1884. TAN Books and Publishers, Inc., P.O. Box 424, Rockford, Illinois, 61105, 1978.

42. *Marie-Julie Jahenny, The Breton Stigmatist*, Marquis de la Franguerie MMR Publishing, P.O. Box 45348, Omaha, Nebraska

68145.

43. *Fatima in Lucia's Own Words, Sister Lucia's Memoirs*, Edited by Fr. Louis Kondor, SVD. Translated by Dominican Nuns of Perpetual Rosary. Distributed by The Ravengate Press, Box 49, Still Water, Massachusetts 01467.

44. *The Reign of Antichrist*. Rev. R. Gerald Culleton. TAN Books and Publishers, Rockford, Il 61105.

45. *Beyond the Millennium,* by John Bird, 1998, Queenship Publishing Company, P.O. Box 42028 Santa Barbara, CA 93140-2028.

46. *Out Of The Ecstasy & Onto The Cross.Biography of Christina Gallagher*, 1996. Written by Rev'd Dr. Gerard McGinnity and Christina Gallagher. Published in the United States by Helpers of Our Lady Queen of Peace, P.O. Box 295 Allison Park, PA 15101, Tel: 412 492 9905.

47. *The Islamic Antichrist* by Joel Richardson, World Net Daily.

48. *The End Times As Revealed To Maria Valtorta*, Valtorta Publishing, 21 Austin Drive, Rochester, NY 14625. Telephone: (716) 385-9836.

49. *Signs and Wonders for Our Times*, Vol. 17 No. 3-4 2006.

50. *A Pilgrimage To The Heart Of Man Thtough My Mercy, In The Age Of The Two Hearts.* MaxKol Communications, Inc. 1994. St. Dominic Media, P.O. Box 345, Herndon, VA 20172-0345.

51. University of Dayton's Website. Based upon explanations authored by Fr. Johann G. Roten, S. M.

52. Fatima Family Messenger, July – September, 1992

53. Pope St. Pius X. *Virgine Sanctissima, Papal Prayer on the Fiftieth Anniversary of the Definition of the Immaculate Conception,* 8 September 1903; A.A. 1, p.97.

54. Pope Pius XI. Encyclical Letter, *Miserentissimus Redemptor*, 8 May 1928, AAS 20, 185.

55. *The Lady of All Nations*, 2002 The Lady of All Nations Foundation.

    a. From *Mary, Co-Redemptrix, Mediatrix, Advocate*, Chapter 3, by Dr. Mark I. Miravale, S.T.D., Franciscan University, Steubenville, Ohio.

56. Fundamentals of Catholic Dogma by Dr. Ludwig Ott, TAN 1974.

Index

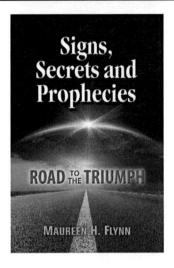

Signs, Secrets and Prophecies – Road to the Triumph
By Maureen H. Flynn

This is the latest book by Maureen Flynn, author of *The Global Warning – An Illumination of the Conscience of Mankind* and co-author of the bestseller *The Thunder of Justice.*

Throughout these pages are messages from contemporary visions and locutions from Heaven in our times:

- What is the future of the Church and mankind on the Road to the Triumph?
- Learn about the role of ecclesiastical masonry in the Church. Is this the real evil in the Church?
- What are the events related to the Warning, i.e., the Illumination of Conscience — will all see the state of their soul?
- Learn about the events of the Great Chastisement and the Three Days of Darkness.
- What are the three ecclesiastical events that will bring true world peace?
- What are the spiritual weapons that Heaven has given for our protection in these times?
- What is the glorious future of the Remnant?
- What is the Triumph of the Immaculate Heart of Mary?
- When will the Era of Peace occur?

Reverend Joseph M. Esper, author of several books including *Catholicism in Crisis: Satan's Assault on the Church and the Coming Triumph of the Immaculate Heart* and *Spiritual Dangers of the 21ˢᵗ Century,* said in his foreword that this book serves as a well-organized and thorough presentation of many of heavenly messages having a direct bearing on our own times.

List Price $24.95   Member Price $19.95
plus $6.95 S&H

The Secret Power of the Rosary

"A gold mine of info – jump-start your prayer life!"
Maureen Flynn, editor of Signs and Wonders Magazine

THE
SECRET POWER
OF THE
ROSARY

111 Daily Meditations for Peace and Healing of Families and Nations

BARBARA KLOSS

Many problems in the world start on a spiritual level and manifest in the physical. To fix them you need the right weapons. The ROSARY is one of the most powerful spiritual weapons!

Maureen Flynn, editor of Signs and Wonders Magazine

Polish mystic Barbara Kloss received messages on the mysteries of the Rosary per Our Lady of Fatima's call. But from the beginning, Barbara's First Saturday messages were dictated by an inward voice which she heard and wrote down. In the last five years of her life, paralyzed by rheumatism, she dictated these messages to a friend or to her nurse. This book is the result.

From *The Secret Power of the Rosary:*

In regard to the Rosary...the more you know it - the more you love it, and the more you love it - the more you know it.

Its power is immense, its action manifold, its domain unending, but the vast majority pf people , even those who love it and say it, do not know its chief and essential meaning which is the disablement of the demons.

It is necessary by means of the Rosary, to expose this mystery of all their activity in everything. Hence, particularly and universally, is known its efficacious action in:
- healing of the sick
- consoling the sorrowful
- helping the afflicted
- rescue and defense in times of danger
- subduing of evil
- return of sinners
- sanctifying of hearts
- purifying of thoughts
- drawing near to God Himself

$16.95 plus $6.95 S&H

ORDER ONLINE OR CALL:
1-888-478-PRAY (7729)   www.sign.org   signsorders@gmail.com

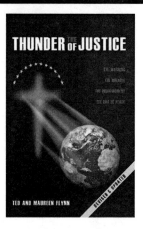

Heaven's Messages for the Family

Heaven's Messages for The Family Volume II –
How to become the family God wants you to be

"The future of humanity passes by way of the family."
— Pope John Paul II

Families are under attack by the forces of evil. The rise in divorce, spousal violence and child abuse – all point to a situation which makes supernatural intervention appropriate and credible.

Mrs. Janie Garza of Austin, Texas, wife, mother and mystic was chosen by the Lord to be a vessel of simple and holy messages for the family of today. She has been receiving messages and visions since February 15, 1989, up to the present time.

Read and learn about:

- What the main spiritual attacks are against the family today.
- The spiritual tools given by Heaven to combat the attacks against the family.
- What the roles of the husband, wife and children are according to God's divine order.
- What you can do to protect your marriage and family members.
- The seven visions about the state of the world and families.

$14.95 plus $6.95 S&H

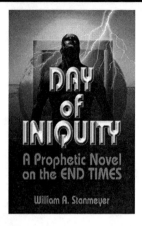

The Great Sign Volume II

This book is a continuation of the messages and warning to Sadie Jaramillo, a humble housewife from California.

The messages discuss how the Mother of all humanity wants her children to come back to the Lord. Messages disclose that if mankind does not return back to God there will be a worldwide economic collapse and natural disaster.

This is a book you must read if you want to learn how:

- The Time of all times is upon humanity
- How storms, volcanoes, earthquakes and wars are the means by which mankind will be brought to its knees
- Peace, security and wealth will be promised by the Antichrist to a world filled with disorder
- Signs from the heavens will cause bursts of fire to fall upon a humanity out of sync with its God
- A great new Era of Peace will descend upon a world that has been cleansed of sin.

"And unless those days had been shortened, no flesh should be saved; but for the sake of the elect those days shall be shortened." Matthew 24:22

This book also gives us hope about a glorious new ear of peace for God's remnant. 105 pages – soft cover

$9.95 plus $6.95 S&H

Day of Iniquity

By William A. Stanmeyer

A techno-thriller plot with profound spiritual insight, the story exposes such imminent developments as mandatory "smart cards," universal satellite surveillance, the microchip "Mark" and other events predicted by current visionaries and the Bible.

The section on The Warning is unforgettable. The author holds the reader spellbound with sudden reversal, personal redemption, and its amazing plot with an unforgettably powerful surprise ending. 261 pages – soft cover

"I pray that this riveting novel of total spiritual war in an apocalyptic age which all share, will move each of us out of our spiritual comfort zone of mere weekly worship and occasional prayer, to that of a personal commitment to engaging the spiritual combat through intense prayer and fasting!"

Fr. Jim Anderson, M.S.A., J.D., Ph.D.
Military Chaplain

$13.95 plus $6.95 S&H

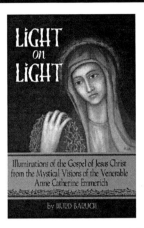